C000277631

The CITY of LONDON

A COMPANION GUIDE

EDITED BY NICHOLAS KENYON

The CITY of LONDON

A COMPANION GUIDE

Michael Hall / Kenneth Powell / Alan Powers / Aileen Reid

with 443 illustrations, 392 in colour

Prime Partner

A message from our Prime Partner: the City of London Corporation

The City of London Corporation is very pleased to support this authoritative guide to the architecture of the Square Mile. As Prime Partner, it welcomes this association with Thames & Hudson and with the eminent writers who have contributed to the content. The guide is an independent overview of the City's built environment and therefore the views expressed within it are not necessarily those of the City of London Corporation, its Members and officers.

About the City of London Corporation

The City of London Corporation has a wide and varied remit. It supports and promotes the City as the world leader in international finance and business services and provides local services and policing for those working in, living in and visiting the Square Mile. It also provides valued services to London and the nation. These include the Barbican Centre and the Guildhall School of Music & Drama; the Guildhall Library, Guildhall Art Gallery and London Metropolitan Archives; a range of education provision (including three City Academies); five Thames bridges (including Tower Bridge and the Millennium Bridge); the Central Criminal Court at Old Bailey; over 10,000 acres of open spaces (including Hampstead Heath and Epping Forest), and three wholesale food markets. It is also London's Port Health Authority and runs the Animal Reception Centre at Heathrow. It works in partnership with neighbouring boroughs on the regeneration of surrounding areas, and the City Bridge Trust, which it oversees, donates more than £15m to charity annually. www.cityoflondon.gov.uk

Additional Partner

The Worshipful Company
of Leathersellers

Contributors
Michael Hall: Chapters 1 and 4
Nicholas Kenyon: Additional Places to Visit
Kenneth Powell: Introduction; Chapters 6 and 8
Alan Powers: Chapters 2 and 7
Aileen Reid: Chapters 3 and 5

Frontispiece
The Heron Tower and no. 30 St Mary Axe (the 'Gherkin') exemplify the dynamism of the City today, but they look down on a street pattern largely surviving from the medieval period. The contrast between modernity and tradition is fundamental to the character of the City.

First published in the United Kingdom
in 2012 by Thames & Hudson Ltd,
181A High Holborn, London WC1V 7QX

Designed by Thomas Keenes

British Library Cataloguing-in-Publication Data

A catalogue record for this book is available from the British Library

ISBN 978-0-500-34279-4

First published in 2011 as *The City of London: Architectural Tradition & Innovation in the Square Mile*. This compact guidebook edition features additional places to visit.

Printed and bound in China
by C&C Offset Printing Co. Ltd

Contents

Preface

Nicholas Kenyon

Managing Director, Barbican Centre

The City of London is unique: in its governance, in its history, and also in its sense of place. At the heart of one of the world's great cities, the Square Mile of the City has a concentration and an intensity that give it a wholly distinctive character. The quick-fire counterpoint of ancient and modern, the rich texture of heritage and history jostling with the demands of business and tourism, create an atmosphere of focused activity and purposeful concentration, with an added air of veiled mystery.

As I set out from the Barbican, that extraordinary feat of postwar urban planning which the City Corporation made possible, within minutes in one direction I can encounter a bastion of the Roman wall, a skull-and-crossbones stone on the site of St Olave's church, near where Shakespeare lodged, an isolated Wren church tower, a neo-mannerist police station, and a cluster of contemporary buildings by Richard Rogers, Norman Foster and Terry Farrell. In another direction, cutting through the narrow Cloth Fair with its pair of 17th-century houses, is the glorious part-medieval church of St Bartholomew-the-Great, the baroque entrance to Barts hospital, a Michael Hopkins livery hall, the hectic buzz of the restored Smithfield Market, and an empty block from which is rising one of the new stations for Crossrail, which will transform access to the City.

This is no static theme park: the sense of busyness is overwhelming as you move through the narrow streets and surviving alleyways, from the Temple in the West to the Tower in the East. This book aims to guide both the newcomer and those familiar with the City through the riches of the built environment that it has to offer. There is something of fascination in almost every square inch of the Square Mile. This makes it all the more remarkable that although the City features as a chapter in most guides to London, its buildings have not been treated in a book such as this, save in Simon Bradley's indispensable revision of the City of London volume in Nikolaus Pevsner's *The Buildings of England* (London 1). I am most grateful to Thames & Hudson who saw at once the potential of this guide; and to the team of writers who, against unforgiving deadlines, assembled such a readable, scholarly and attractive survey of the City.

Responding both to the heritage of the Square Mile and to its ever-developing business activity is a daily task for the City of London Corporation, which provides world-class services for a world-class environment. Its support of enlightened architecture, like its patronage of finance and the arts, demonstrates why the City retains its leading edge as home for both financial services and cultural activity; the City Corporation's enlightened planning policy has played a critical role in shaping new buildings alongside the preservation of its unique heritage. Its Policy and Resources Committee generously agreed to support this volume, and we are very grateful to its Members, its Chairman Stuart Fraser and its Deputy Chairman Mark Boleat.

This Companion Guide divides the City into eight areas; the chapters move generally from west to east, as do the sites within each area. The City is so concentrated that a precise walking guide is scarcely necessary: however each pair of chapters is organized so that the first ends where the second begins, creating linked journeys around the City west (1 and 2), centre (3 and 4), north (5 and 6) and east (7 and 8), starting and finishing at or near stations.

1. **The Temple & Fleet Street**: Temple Bar to Blackfriars
2. **St Paul's**: Blackfriars to St Paul's

3. **Guildhall**: St Paul's to Bank
4. **The Bank of England & The Royal Exchange**: Bank to Bank (circular)

5. **Smithfield & The Barbican**: Holborn Viaduct to Moorgate
6. **Liverpool Street Station & The 'Gherkin'**: Moorgate to Aldgate

7. **The Mansion House**: St Paul's to Monument
8. **The Tower of London & The Monument**: Monument to Tower Hill

At the end of each chapter, 'Additional Places to Visit' highlight open spaces, sculpture, plaques and curiosities.

Many of the buildings described here are private, and while they are viewable from the outside, there is no public access inside. The visitor attractions and main buildings open to the public (apart from shops, public houses, bridges, stations and open spaces) are indicated at the top of their entry with the symbol ➲, and further details may be found under Practical Information on pp. 354–5 and at www.visitthecity.co.uk.

Following pages
This outline plan of the City of London extends here beyond its boundaries to include the Tower of London and Tower Bridge.

Baltic Street West
Golden Lane
Goswell Road
Beech Street
Charterhouse Street
Aldersgate Street
5
Holborn
Holborn Circus
Holborn Viaduct
Farringdon Street
Newgate Street
St Martin's le Grand
3
New Change
Cheapsi
1
Fleet Street
Ludgate Circus
Ludgate Hill
2
Strand
New Bridge Street
Cannon Street
Queen Victoria Street
Blackfriars Underpass
Upper Thames Street
Victoria Embankment
Blackfriars Bridge
Millennium Bridge
N
0
1/8 mile
0
0.25 km

swell Street
Worship Street
North Folgate
Sun Street
Appold Street
Wilson Street
South Place
Moorgate
Brushfield Street
Fort St
Sandy's Row
Bishopsgate
6
ndon Wall
Moorgate
London Wall
Wormwood Street
Middlesex Street
4
Bishopsgate
Prince's Street
Threadneedle Street
Aldgate High Street
Poultry
Cornhill
Leadenhall Street
Mansell Street
Queen Victoria Street
Lombard Street
Gracechurch Street
Aldgate
7
King William Street
Fenchurch Street
Minories
Eastcheap
8
Great Tower Street
Upper Thames Street
King William Street
Tower Hill
Byward Street
Lower Thames Street
Tower Bridge Approach
London Bridge
Tower Bridge

Introduction
Kenneth Powell

London Bridge, seen here around 1900, with streams of commuters crossing into the City.

The City of London wears its history lightly. It is the most ancient quarter of London, a global business centre and the focus for great state occasions, with a history extending back nearly 2000 years. Of Roman London, only fragments of the City walls remain above ground level, but physical evidence of medieval London is also relatively sparse, and of the City that rose after the catastrophic fire of 1666 only St Paul's Cathedral, fewer than half the Wren churches rebuilt after the fire and a few livery halls and public buildings (for example, the College of Arms) survive today. The transformation of the City in the 19th century swept away the picturesque, if often squalid, London of Charles Dickens. Broad new roads were carved through the medieval street pattern and banks, office buildings and warehouses replaced houses – the population of the City in 1901 was only a fifth of the number resident a century earlier and continued to dwindle through the 20th century. Already a great European city, London became a world city and the City of London the financial powerhouse of the British empire. The Victorian City – where the poet John Betjeman waited 'for the spirit of my grandfather/Toddling along from the Barbican' – suffered disastrously in the Second World War, with entire areas flattened by bombing in the Blitz. The postwar rebuilding, beginning in the mid-1950s, was thorough but not always architecturally distinguished (though many damaged churches and other historic buildings were conscientiously restored). The 1960s and 1970s saw further needless destruction of historic buildings – most notably the Victorian Coal Exchange – that had survived the war. During the last quarter of a century a further wave of reconstruction has transformed the City yet again: 'groundscraper' buildings with spacious dealing floors and a new generation of high-rises reflect the role of the Square Mile as a global business capital. The City of the 21st century is likely to be a more diverse place, with hotels, residential developments, shops and restaurants making it a place of activity day and night, seven days a week. The City, in short, has an enormous capacity to reinvent itself and is doing so yet again.

London was created by the Romans. The attractions of the site for the conquerors of Britain were obvious, not least its location on a tidal river that had already been a trade artery for centuries and which became the gateway to a great port. There is no evidence that any previous settlement of significance existed there. The Romans quickly created a thriving commercial and military base, but the new city was effectively razed to the ground in the revolt led by Boudicca in AD 60–61. Rebuilt from

Opposite
This section of the ancient wall of the City, in close proximity to the medieval church of St Giles Cripplegate and with the towers of the Barbican in the background, was exposed by wartime bombing and remains visible as a symbol of the continuity of human occupation in the City over two millennia.

A view of Roman London c. 120. In this reconstruction the major buildings of the Roman City, and the first London Bridge, are in place.

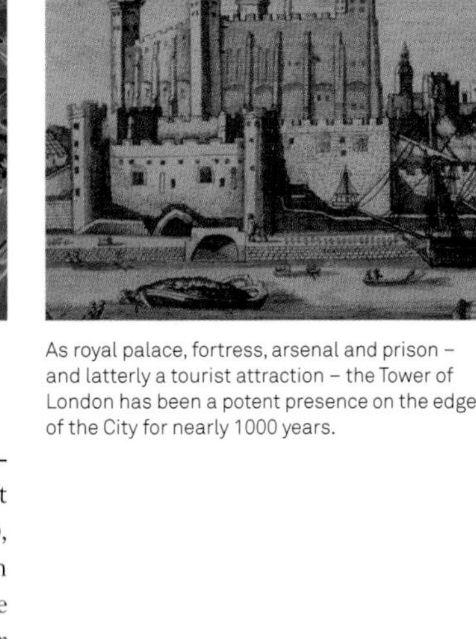

As royal palace, fortress, arsenal and prison – and latterly a tourist attraction – the Tower of London has been a potent presence on the edge of the City for nearly 1000 years.

AD 70 on, it boasted a spectacular forum (straddling the present-day Gracechurch Street) with a basilica longer than Wren's St Paul's. Remains of the amphitheatre, completed around AD 80, lie beneath Guildhall Yard. Postwar redevelopment has given archaeologists the opportunity to map significant areas of the Roman City of London and to uncover the remains of other major public buildings and temples – their findings are vividly documented in the Museum of London's displays. The Romans built the first London Bridge – of timber. Archaeology has also provided plenty of evidence of the downfall of Roman London. The construction of a permanent masonry wall around the City in the early 3rd century doubtless gave its inhabitants a new sense of security, but by the beginning of the next century London was in decline and the forum was largely demolished. By the middle of the 5th century the City was a near-ghost town, with streets of abandoned houses, in the aftermath of the Roman withdrawal from Britain. Anglo-Saxon London remains elusive. Although it is certain that parts of the Roman City were re-inhabited during the reign of King Alfred, London was developing to the west, along the Strand and towards what became the seat of royal power at Westminster, where Edward the Confessor built his palace and abbey.

If the Romans were the founders of London, the Norman Conquest of 1066 was an event of fundamental significance for the future of the City. William the Conqueror marked his hold on London with the construction of the Tower. Today the Tower of London is outside the City boundaries, in the Borough of Tower Hamlets, but its history is inextricably linked to that of the City. William's White Tower, a structure designed to overawe the native population and completed some years after his death in 1087, was on a scale previously unknown in Britain. It remains (later embellishments notwithstanding) a building of enormous power and a remarkable survival. The Normans also rebuilt St Paul's Cathedral – the first on the site dates from 604 – on a massive scale. Alongside the cathedral, the City housed a growing number of monastic houses, including Holy Trinity Priory at Aldgate, the nunnery of St Helen at Bishopsgate and, from the

A reconstruction of how the City might have looked from the air c. 1400. The medieval St Paul's Cathedral, destroyed in the Great Fire, towers over the streets of timber-framed houses. The growing suburb of Southwark is visible on the south bank of the Thames.

13th century on, the premises of the various orders of friars. A large collegiate church was founded at St Martin's le Grand in the 11th century. The order of Knights Templar had their base south of Fleet Street. Following the dissolution of the order in 1312, the Temple began to be colonized by lawyers; the remarkable Temple Church survives today. Other religious foundations provided alms and medical care for the poor. Of the latter, only the east end of the church of St Bartholomew's Hospital remains, a magnificent Romanesque fragment set in a picturesque churchyard extending over the site of the demolished nave. The church of St Helen's, which was always in part a parish church, also survives, though now recast as a rather bare preaching hall. The greater part of the church of the Austin (Augustinian) Friars survived until the Blitz of 1940, when a direct hit reduced it to rubble. The Second World War also saw the loss of the church of All Hallows by the Tower, one of the few medieval parish churches to survive the Great Fire. Other survivors of the 107 City churches standing before the Fire included a small number still standing today – for example, St Andrew Undershaft and St Ethelburga Bishopsgate, the former damaged and the latter all but destroyed by IRA bombs in the early 1990s. The greatest medieval survival in the City is, of course, the 15th-century Guildhall – damaged in the Great Fire and, more severely, in the wartime Blitz, but still recognizably a medieval building and an

CORNWELL
S. Denys
STILIARDS
S. Magnus
Lombarde strete
London Stone

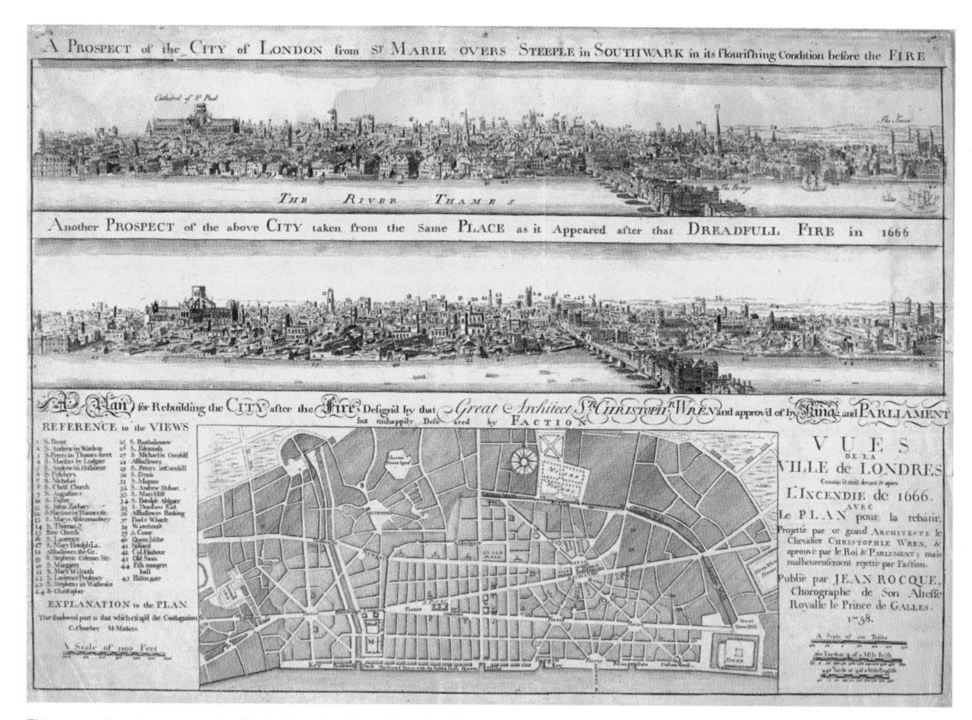

This engraving shows, top, the City before the Great Fire of 1666 and, centre, after the Fire. The lower panel shows Sir Christopher Wren's plan for rebuilding the City, with broad avenues extending from Aldgate to Fleet Street and from the Tower to St Paul's Cathedral. The plan was never seriously considered and the City was rebuilt along the old pattern.

expression of the importance of the City as a hub of trade and commerce. Of the medieval halls of the City's livery companies, equal expressions of the pride and independence of the City, only fragments remain from before the Fire. The most vivid record of lost medieval London is John Stow's *Survey of London*, first published in 1598 but started nearly forty years earlier when the Dissolution of the monasteries and the sack of churches begun under Henry VIII were still relatively recent memories.

In 1598 the population of London was in excess of 200,000, and it more than doubled in the next fifty years. By 1700 London was Europe's largest city, its phenomenal growth reflecting the expansion of England's trading empire in the Americas and India. Daniel Defoe, writing in the 1720s, was quite clear: while the court at Westminster was the centre of London's 'gallantry and splendour', 'the City is the centre of its commerce and wealth'. The Great Fire had been disastrous: 13,500 houses destroyed, along with churches and public buildings, and most of the inhabitants left homeless. Yet the City sprang back quickly – most of the housing was rebuilt by 1673. Although various plans (among them Christopher Wren's) for rebuilding the City on rational lines, inspired by European ideas of city planning, came to nothing – the City was rebuilt to the medieval street plan – one consequence of the Fire was the passage of

Opposite
The first known map of London – the Copperplate Map of the 1550s – was made in fifteen sections, of which only three survive, two of them in the Museum of London. This section shows the area of the City north of the old London Bridge. The names are in reverse because this is the plate from which the map was printed.

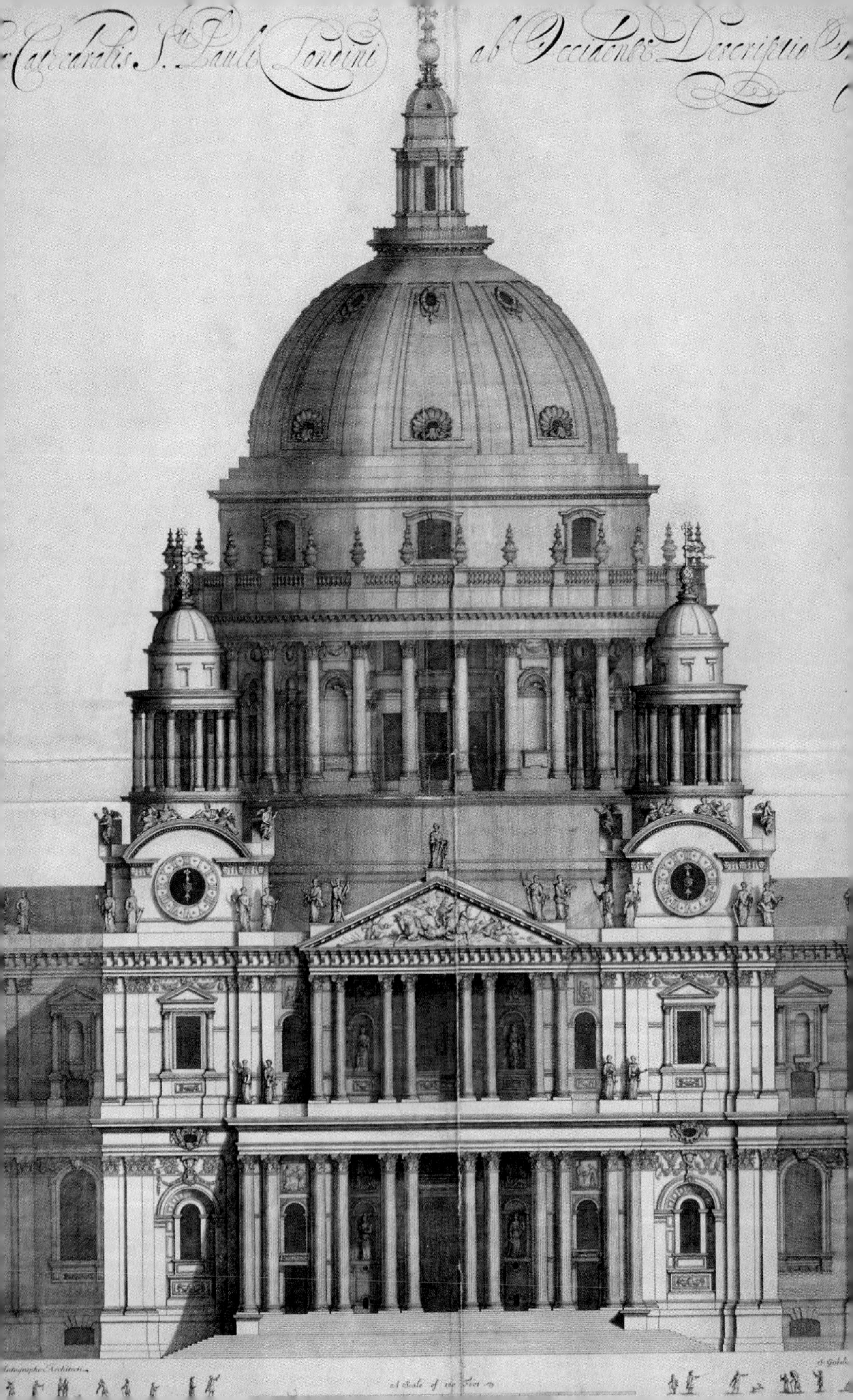
Cathedralis S.ti Pauli Londini ab Occidente Descriptio
A Scale of 100 Feet

legislation (effectively the first planning act) which governed the materials used for the new housing and codified a series of house types. With this the City became a place of brick rather than timber. Brick was the raw material for most of the new churches designed by Wren and his team of assistants, foremost among them the polymath scientist Robert Hooke, with costly Portland stone generally confined to steeples except for the grandest churches. The rebuilding of St Paul's – the form of the new building was decided only after a long period of debate – took more than a quarter of a century. Whatever the imperfections of Wren's built design, the cathedral has become one of the indelible symbols of the City, of London, and indeed of Britain – the image of Wren's dome seen through the smoke of the burning City in 1940 is particularly potent.

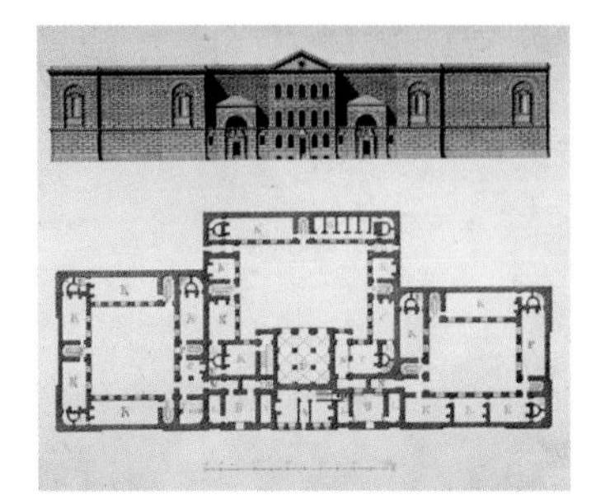

Elevation and plan of Newgate Prison, perhaps the finest of all the City's Georgian public buildings but demolished in 1902 to make way for the Central Criminal Court in Old Bailey.

As London continued to grow inexorably through the 18th century, the City offered little scope for the comprehensive programmes of urban planning that created the generous streets and squares of Mayfair, Marylebone and Bloomsbury. (Finsbury Circus was one of the few new City squares.) But it is easy to underestimate the scale of the campaign of 'improvements' that demolished most of the City's walls, paved the streets, gave London a new river crossing at Blackfriars and created two prominent City landmarks in the form of the new Mansion House and Newgate Prison, the latter demolished in 1902 but a powerful influence on the architecture of the Edwardian era. The greatest of public-building works was the new Bank of England, begun by Sir Robert Taylor but completed as the masterpiece of Sir John Soane, the greatest of English classical architects. Investment in public works continued after 1815, with Southwark Bridge and the new London Bridge finished, new streets opened and public buildings including the Custom House and General Post Office, the latter designed by Robert Smirke, inaugurated. The tide of redevelopment accelerated in the first half of the 19th century and saw many craft trades and industries, as well as residents, gradually displaced from the City and driven to its fringes, to areas such as Spitalfields and Shoreditch. Venerable City institutions also moved out, including Charterhouse School in 1874 and Christ's Hospital in 1902 – its magnificent neo-Tudor hall, designed by John Shaw and modelled on the chapel of King's College, Cambridge, and older work by Wren, ruthlessly demolished to make way for new buildings for the Post Office. Once these had been built, Smirke's splendid Greek Revival General Post Office, completed in 1829, was itself torn down. Nor were City churches immune from the hand of the developer: between 1860 and 1905 twenty were closed and demolished, their sites sold for commercial development. Indeed, in 1905 it was reckoned that around 80 per cent of the City's fabric had been rebuilt in the previous fifty years.

The Victorian rebuilding of the City, though including major public projects such as the new Leadenhall and Billingsgate markets, the new Royal Exchange and Tower Bridge, was essentially driven by commerce, with banks and insurance companies taking the lead and entire streets rebuilt to provide for

Opposite
A detail of Wren's definitive design for the west front of St Paul's, showing the cathedral much as built.

The City in the mid-18th century: this view shows the animated scene around the Mansion House and along Cheapside.

Robert Smirke's General Post Office was a building of enormous dignity but it lasted little more than a century, being demolished soon after this photograph was taken in 1911.

their needs. Both used architecture as a means of advertising their wealth and unshakeable security, appealing to a growing middle-class clientele. The most impressive of the City's Victorian banking buildings is John Gibson's former National Provincial Bank in Bishopsgate, a spectacular example of the classical style generally favoured by bankers. The banks and offices of the City were serviced by a constantly expanding army of clerical workers who resided in increasingly distant suburbs. Charles Pooter, central character of George and Weedon Grossmith's *The Diary of a Nobody* (1892), was a City clerk who commuted daily from Upper Holloway. Mass commuting became possible because of the advent of the railways. Fenchurch Street, opened in 1841, was the first of the City termini, but by the 1860s railways were invading the Square Mile from north and south, bringing in not only commuters but also freight, including huge quantities of coal, and livestock. With other City termini since destroyed or surviving only in part, the elegant western train shed at Liverpool Street, dating from the 1870s, with the adjacent Great Eastern (now Andaz) Hotel, are the prime monuments of the railway age. The greatest legacy of the Victorian period was the Underground, which reached the City in the form of the Metropolitan Railway in 1865. Twenty-five years later, the City and South London Railway (the world's first electric underground railway, later incorporated into the Northern line) provided a direct link to the suburbs of south London. The windowless, dimly lit carriages, popularly known as 'padded cells', were not for the claustrophobic, but the C&SLR charged a flat two-pence fare rather than the system of first-, second- and third-class tickets levied on the Metropolitan. The Waterloo and City ('the Drain') and Central lines followed within the next decade, both serving Bank Station, which became one of the key hubs of a new transit network that was to extend across most of London.

Sir John Soane's Bank of England was rebuilt by Herbert Baker in 1923–39. Most of Soane's interiors were lost.

The years between the death of Queen Victoria in 1901 and the outbreak of war in 1939 could be seen – the Great Depression of the 1930s notwithstanding – as a golden era for London. By the mid-1930s, the weekday working population of the City was around half a million, rather more than that of the present day. The continuing financial hegemony of the City was reflected in a further wave of rebuilding in the interwar years – most obviously in Herbert Baker's radical, and inevitably destructive, reconstruction of Soane's Bank of England, but equally in magnificent new commercial palazzi such as Adelaide House abutting London Bridge, Unilever House on the Embankment at Blackfriars, the Lloyd's Building on Leadenhall Street and, finest of all, Lutyens's Britannic House, part of a wholesale reconstruction of Finsbury Circus. Fleet Street boomed, with the new premises of the *Daily Telegraph* and *Daily Express* symbolizing the power of the press. (Before its dispersal in the 1980s, the newspaper district was the last large-scale manufacturing quarter of central London.)

The era of peace and, for the City at least, continuing prosperity came to an end in 1939. Wartime bombing destroyed

Part of a panorama of the City photographed by Arthur Cross and Fred Tibbs in 1942 to record the extent of bomb damage. This section shows an area extending from Coleman Street on the left to Old Bailey on the right, with London Wall in the foreground.

around a third of the City; whole areas, including those around St Paul's and the Barbican, were flattened. Half the City churches and two-thirds of the livery halls were either destroyed or badly damaged, and the Guildhall itself was gutted by incendiaries. Entire City trades (for example, the publishing industry based around Paternoster Row) were wiped out. As in the aftermath of the Great Fire, radical proposals for civic reconstruction emerged after 1945 but were only partially realized: the rebuilt Paternoster Square (an 'outstandingly well conceived precinct', commented Nikolaus Pevsner) and the Barbican, a vast project planned in the mid-1950s which began in 1963 and took nearly twenty years to complete, were rare examples of comprehensive redevelopment. Elsewhere the existing street pattern was largely retained, and from the mid-1950s on the private development industry took the lead in the rebuilding process, often with architecturally mediocre results. City institutions tended to be conservative patrons so that a cautious Modernism was the dominant style, though more traditionally minded architects such as Victor Heal, Terence Heysham and Albert Richardson were responsible for major City projects – Richardson for the *Financial Times*'s Bracken House, described by Ian Nairn as

'friendly, loveable, logical'. Sir Giles Gilbert Scott, a senior traditionalist, was given the job of reconstructing and extending the damaged Guildhall.

One of the innovations of the postwar planning regime was the introduction of plot ratios in place of the previous 24-m (80-ft) limit on cornice height. This opened the way for the City's first tall buildings, overtopping (to the dismay of some critics) the steeples of the Wren churches. By the mid-1960s the City skyline was being transformed by new office towers, including Britannic (formerly BP) Tower, the Commercial Union (later Aviva) Tower and Richard Seifert's Drapers' Gardens. Seifert's NatWest Tower (now Tower 42), in essence a 1960s building though completed only in 1981, was until recently the City's tallest building. The development boom of the 1960s led to the destruction of some well-loved landmarks, most notably the Coal Exchange, demolished in 1962 despite the best efforts of John Betjeman and the Victorian Society to save it. The Coal Exchange was a victim of a road-widening scheme and, as late as 1974, the east end of Wren's Christ Church Newgate Street was also demolished for road widening – an incomprehensible act of vandalism at a time when the City was beginning to take seriously the preservation of its historic buildings. The first conservation areas in the City were designated in 1971, and plans totally to demolish Liverpool Street Station and the Great

The Coal Exchange was demolished in 1962, despite a campaign, in which John Betjeman was active, to preserve it.

Eastern Hotel were quashed after a spirited campaign in which Betjeman again played a prominent role.

The last quarter century has seen a further dramatic reconstruction of the City. The catalyst was the programme of deregulation launched by the Thatcher administration elected in 1979. In 1986 the so-called 'Big Bang' opened up the market in stocks and shares, and foreign banks and other institutions found it imperative to have London bases. The City faced competition for new office developments to house them from Docklands, where a new office city was emerging at Canary Wharf. The Broadgate development, begun in 1985 and constructed to a 'fast-track' schedule, provided buildings with the large dealing floors demanded by the financial sector. Broadgate was notable less for its architecture than for its generous provision of public space, traditionally a rare commodity in the City. The scheme made use of derelict railway land and expanded to exploit 'air-rights' space over the eastern half of Liverpool Street Station. At the end of 1993 it was reckoned that half of all the City's office space had been built since 1985. The boom continued into the 1990s but, in contrast to the 1960s, redevelopment was not usually at the expense of the architectural heritage of the City. Unloved 1950s and 1960s buildings were demolished to provide sites for new projects, which included designs by major contemporary architects such as Richard Rogers and Norman Foster. The election of Ken Livingstone as Mayor of London in 2000 unexpectedly gave the development impetus a further boost: Livingstone championed the cause of high buildings, opening the way for recent and ongoing projects, including the Heron Tower, Leadenhall Building, no. 20 Fenchurch Street (on the site of the banal 1960s Kleinwort Benson tower) and the 'Pinnacle'. Ten years later, in a period of retrenchment, the Square Mile is becoming a more diverse place, with shops, hotels and residential developments leavening the commercial mix. In the second decade of the 21st century, the City's confidence and dynamism seem undimmed.

Opposite
The Monument, a symbol of the resurgence of the City after the Great Fire, seen against a background of 20th-century commercial buildings, with the tower of Wren's church of St Magnus the Martyr just visible.

TEMPLE BAR
STRAND WC2
THIS SIDE
OTHER SIDE
CITY OF WESTMINSTER

1 The Temple & Fleet Street

Entering the City at its western boundary, Temple Bar in Fleet Street, one crosses over from the world of those who spend it to the world of those who make it. That distinction is weaker now than at any time in the past four hundred years, thanks to the deregulation of the markets in 1986, which has scattered financial institutions all over London, and the City's recent renaissance as a retail centre. However, west and east will never completely elide while the ancient buffer zone between the two, the strip of land that runs north from the Thames to Holborn, preserves its traditional character.

This area takes its tone overwhelmingly from one profession, the law. In the wake of the lawyers came archives, including the Public Record Office, and newspapers. They are more interconnected than may be apparent: English common law is based on historical precedent, and history's first draft is written by journalists. The sense of historical continuity on which the law depends has also encouraged a long tradition of architectural conservation: it is lawyers who have preserved – and continue to use – the first Gothic church in the City of London and its finest Elizabethan building. This part of the City has escaped overpowering modern developments and has a notably high share of some of its most imaginative restorations and reuses of old buildings.

In Roman and early medieval times the western edge of the City was marked by a natural barrier, the Fleet river, which rises in Kenwood and flowed out to the Thames close to what is now the northern end of Blackfriars Bridge; in its lower reaches it was joined by a tributary, the Holebourne (hence Holborn). By the time the first Blackfriars Bridge was built, in 1769, the Fleet had been channelled underground, below Farringdon Street and New Bridge Street, where it still flows as part of London's sewers. Yet although the river has vanished from sight, the valley it created remains an important part of the City's topography, as is strikingly evident in the view from Holborn Viaduct down into Farringdon Road below. At the point where Ludgate Circus was laid out in 1864–9 there was once a bridge across the Fleet, linking Ludgate to Fleet Street and thence to the Strand and Westminster. Architecturally speaking, this is still the most enticing approach to the City, since Fleet Street curves gently as it unfolds, so that it is not until one comes level with Whitefriars Street that St Paul's begins slowly to reveal itself.

Without a cathedral as a climax, the northern approach along High Holborn and Holborn cannot hope to compare, although the Victorians did their best to improve it with the creation in 1863–9 of Holborn Circus and the Holborn Viaduct.

Opposite
Temple Bar, the point in Fleet Street where the City meets Westminster. It is marked by a monument, erected in 1880, which now is capped by a bronze dragon, symbol of the City. In the background are the Royal Courts of Justice, designed by G. E. Street and opened in 1882.

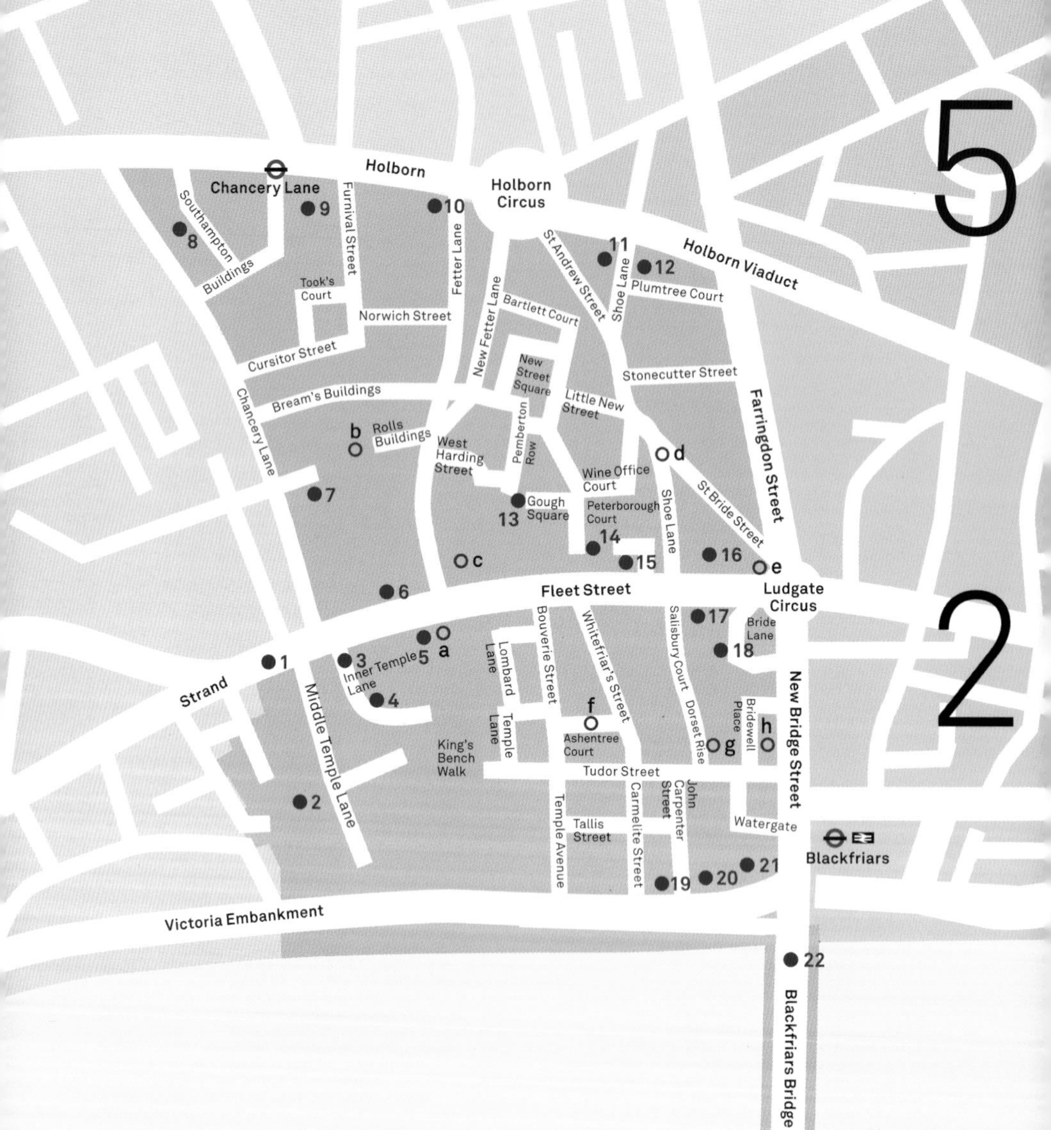
5
2
Holborn
Chancery Lane
Holborn Circus
Holborn Viaduct
Southampton Buildings
Furnival Street
Fetter Lane
St Andrew Street
Shoe Lane
Plumtree Court
Took's Court
Norwich Street
New Fetter Lane
Bartlett Court
Cursitor Street
Stonecutter Street
New Street Square
Bream's Buildings
Little New Street
Farringdon Street
Chancery Lane
Rolls Buildings
West Harding Street
Pemberton Row
Wine Office Court
St Bride Street
Gough Square
Peterborough Court
Shoe Lane
Fleet Street
Ludgate Circus
Strand
Bouverie Street
Whitefriar's Street
Salisbury Court
Bride Lane
Inner Temple Lane
Lombard Lane
Middle Temple Lane
Temple Lane
Ashentree Court
Dorset Rise
Bridewell Place
New Bridge Street
King's Bench Walk
Tudor Street
John Carpenter Street
Temple Avenue
Tallis Street
Carmelite Street
Watergate
Blackfriars
Victoria Embankment
Blackfriars Bridge
1
2
3
4
5
6
7
8
9
10
11
12
13
14
15
16
17
18
19
20
21
22
a
b
c
d
e
f
g
h

KEY TO AREA 1

● 1	Temple Bar
● 2	Middle Temple Hall
● 3	Inner Temple Gateway
● 4	Temple Church of St Mary
● 5	C. Hoare & Co.
● 6	St Dunstan-in-the-West
● 7	Public Record Office (former)
● 8	London Silver Vaults
● 9	Staple Inn
● 10	Gresham College
● 11	St Andrew Holborn
● 12	City Temple
● 13	Dr Johnson's House
● 14	Ye Olde Cheshire Cheese
● 15	*Daily Telegraph* Building (former)
● 16	*Daily Express* Building (former)
● 17	Reuters Building (former)
● 18	St Bride
● 19	Sion College
● 20	City of London School for Boys (former)
● 21	Unilever House
● 22	Blackfriars Bridge
○ a	Site of the Mitre Tavern, 37 Fleet Street
○ b	Walter Crane plasterwork; St Dunstan-in-the-West Garden; John Wilkes
○ c	Fleet Street alleys
○ d	Resolution
○ e	Edgar Wallace
○ f	Magpie Alley
○ g	St George and the Dragon
○ h	Bridewell Palace

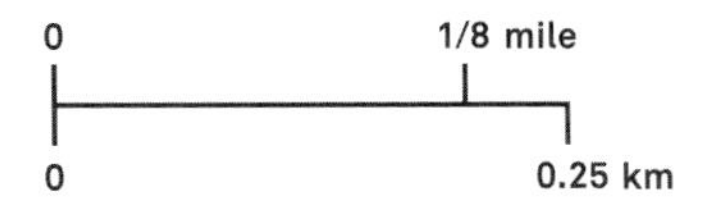

However, any sense of a ceremonial route is rather spoiled by the positioning of Charles Bacon's 1874 bronze equestrian statue of Prince Albert in Holborn Circus. Bacon thought the Prince 'ought not to turn his back on those who erected the statue', with the result that this major road into the City is dominated by a horse's hindquarters to a degree that *The Builder* in 1874 thought 'neither edifying nor agreeable'.

By the early 12th century the City had expanded to its present western limit, along the line of what is now Chancery Lane. The street name (like Fetter Lane, which winds from Holborn to Fleet Street) reveals the presence of the legal profession: Chancery is a variant of 'Chancellor' and Fetter may be a corruption of *faitor*, Old French for lawyer. By the 14th century lawyers had colonized the Temple, the expropriated estate of the Knights Templar, and established there the two Inns of Court that lie within the City: Inner Temple and Middle Temple. In this case 'Inn' simply means a residential complex, with lodgings and a hall: a traditional medieval domestic arrangement from which the Inns of Court have developed, like the colleges at Oxford and Cambridge. They did not at first train barristers, a role performed largely by the Inns of Chancery scattered over the area, but by the 18th century these were little more than social clubs, and the reform of the legal profession in the 19th century deprived them of their vestigial educational role. Most survive only as names of modern buildings or courtyards – Clement's Inn, Clifford's Inn, Furnival's Inn, and so on – but two have left significant buildings, Barnard's Inn and Staple Inn, both off Holborn.

As a stroll up Chancery Lane reveals, legal London flourishes and is expanding, although some of the buildings attracted here by the lawyers' presence, such as the Public Record Office and the Patent Office (in Southampton Buildings), no longer serve their original function. Thirty years ago it might have seemed that the other great profession associated with this area was just as much a fixture, but Rupert Murdoch's decision in 1986 to break the power of the print unions by moving News International, publishers of the *Times* newspapers, to Wapping began an exodus that was concluded by the departure of Reuters in 2005.

Fleet Street was a natural location for newspapers, as the area's association with printing and publishing went back to the early 16th century – Caxton's collaborator Wynkyn de Worde set up his press here in 1500 – and was closely linked with St Paul's Churchyard, the centre of London's book trade from the 15th to the 18th century. That history is commemorated in the St Bride Library, the national museum of printing and typography, in St Bride's Institute, a handsome neo-Wren building in Bride Lane, designed by Robert C. Murray in 1893. Although thirsty journalists have largely departed, Fleet Street's bars have multiplied, thanks to the fashion for converting former bank buildings. Although the price is usually the loss of original fittings, the result can be surprisingly sympathetic to the building, as demonstrated by the transformation into a pub of Arthur Blomfield's

Looking west along Fleet Street towards the original Temple Bar. It was moved in 1878 and re-erected at Paternoster Square in 2004. This aquatint of about 1812 by an unknown artist shows, on the right, St Dunstan-in-the-West, a medieval building that was replaced in 1830–33 by the present church as part of a road-widening scheme at this notoriously congested junction.

Holborn Viaduct seen from Farringdon Street in a watercolour of about 1867 by Arthur Croft. Farringdon Street runs along the valley of the Fleet river, which was spanned by the 430-m (1,400-ft) viaduct in a road improvement scheme of 1863–9.

Opposite
Looking east along Fleet Street and Ludgate Hill in a wood engraving of around 1890. For over a century this picturesque approach to St Paul's Cathedral was marred by the cast-iron bridge to the former Holborn Viaduct Station, built in 1866 and removed in 1990.

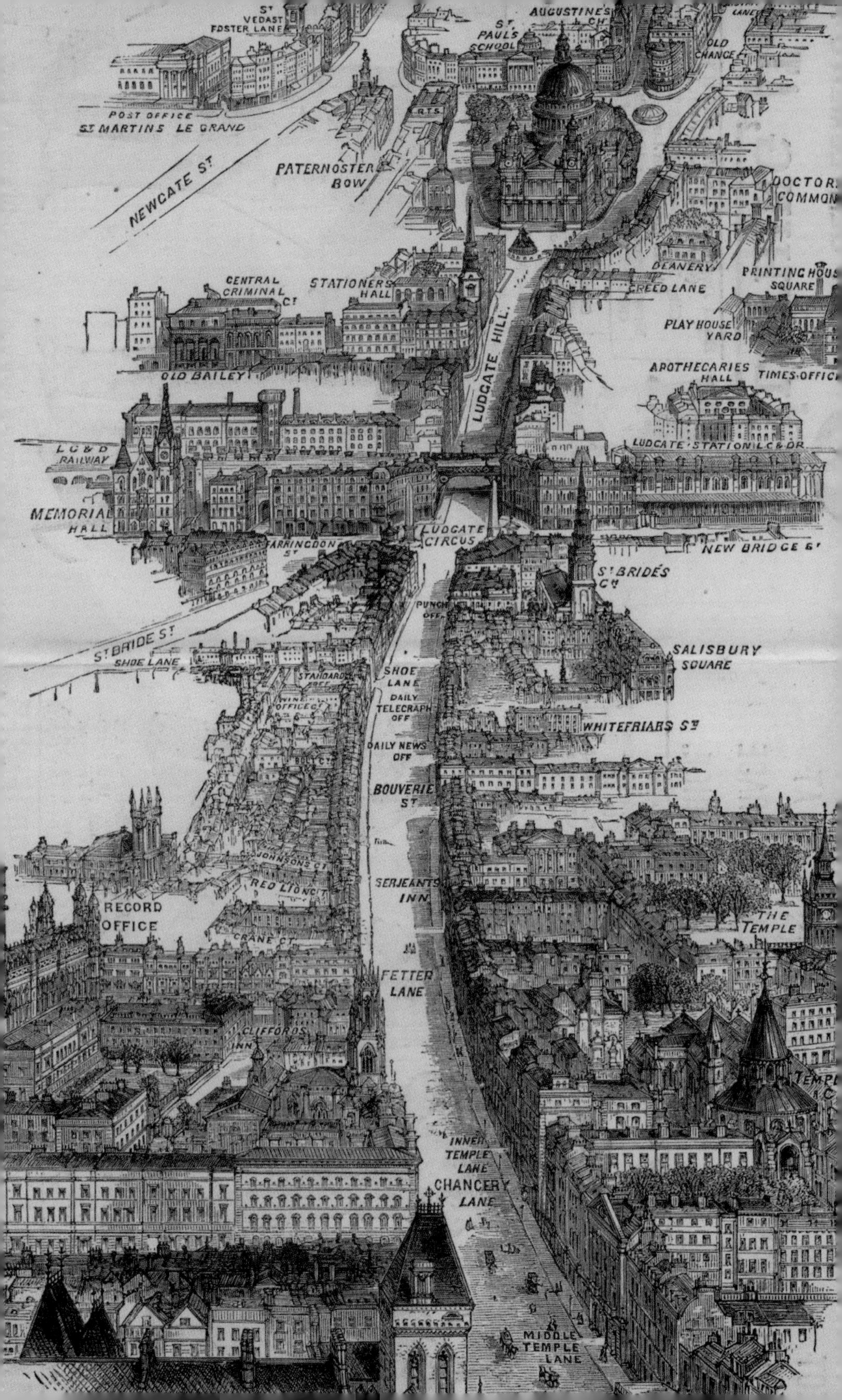

ST VEDAST
FOSTER LANE
AUGUSTINES CH
ST PAULS SCHOOL
OLD CHANGE
POST OFFICE
ST MARTINS LE GRAND
NEWGATE ST
R.T.S.
PATERNOSTER ROW
DOCTOR
COMMON
DEANERY
PRINTING HOUS
SQUARE
CREED LANE
CENTRAL CRIMINAL CT
STATIONERS HALL
LUDGATE HILL
PLAY HOUSE YARD
APOTHECARIES HALL
TIMES OFFIC
OLD BAILEY
LUDGATE STATION L.C.&D.R.
L.C.&D. RAILWAY
MEMORIAL HALL
FARRINGDON ST
LUDGATE CIRCUS
NEW BRIDGE ST
ST BRIDES CH
PUNCH OFF
ST BRIDE ST
SHOE LANE
SALISBURY SQUARE
STANDARD OFF
SHOE LANE
DAILY TELEGRAPH OFF
WINE OFFICE CT
WHITEFRIARS ST
DAILY NEWS OFF
BOLT CT
BOUVERIE ST
JOHNSONS CT
RED LION CT
SERJEANTS INN
RECORD OFFICE
CRANE CT
THE TEMPLE
FETTER LANE
CLIFFORDS INN
TEMPLE
INNER TEMPLE LANE
CHANCERY LANE
MIDDLE TEMPLE LANE

opulently High Victorian Renaissance 1886–8 branch of the Bank of England next to the Royal Courts of Justice.

The Great Fire of 1666 reached as far west as Inner Temple with the result that little in the area dates from before 1700, although it does contain two of the best pre-Fire domestic buildings in the City, Inner Temple Gateway and the Holborn frontage of Staple Inn, both half-timbered. Domestic architecture of the 18th century survives only in tiny enclaves: famously in Gough Square and more atmospherically in Took's Court. The Blitz caused major damage to the Temple, but otherwise its effects were felt mostly round Fetter Lane, which as a result has little of historic interest – one major exception being the 1902 building designed by Treadwell & Martin for Buchanan's Distillery at no. 80, where the carving (by Daymond & Son) takes Renaissance ornament about as far into Art Nouveau as the British were prepared to go. Fetter Lane has been greatly improved by recent developments. Following the departure of the Mirror Group of newspapers, its site at the junction of Fetter Lane and Holborn, facing into Holborn Circus, was redeveloped to form a new headquarters for Sainsbury's with a curved low-rise building of sheer, gleaming surfaces by Foster & Partners, completed in 2001. Better still is the development of New Street Square between New Fetter Lane and St Andrew Street. Designed by Bennetts Associates and built in 2003–8, this is a serious and convincing attempt to combine large-scale redevelopment of over a hundred thousand square metres (over a million square feet) of office space with a plan that respects its dense urban context – it is immediately north of Gough Square – by being broken up into four well-composed blocks of varied silhouettes (the highest 18 storeys) grouped tightly around a small square of shops and restaurants.

The sole surviving fragment of the former Buchanan's Distillery in Fetter Lane. Designed by Henry J. Treadwell and Leonard Martin in the delightful blend of Tudor, Baroque and Art Nouveau that they also used for many pubs, it was built in 1902.

This has enhanced the major contrast in the area's urban fabric, between the dense warren of alleys and courtyards north of Fleet Street and the broad, regular grid of the roads laid out to its south following the embankment of the Thames in 1868–74. The former is well known, although an enticing archway can lead just as often to an air-conditioning unit or a barman snatching a quick cigarette as to a Georgian house or Victorian tavern. The much less visited roads south of Fleet Street equally reward exploration: see, for example, St Bride's pretty redbrick 'Queen Anne' rectory, designed by Basil Champneys in 1885, which so beautifully closes the view north up Bridewell Place, or, in New Bridge Street, the remaining fragment of Bridewell Prison (successor to Henry VIII's Bridewell Palace), James Lewis's handsome 1802–8 classical gatehouse. From here it is only a short walk to the Victoria Embankment, but the architectural pleasures it offers cannot easily be enjoyed thanks to the traffic – it is best to walk over Blackfriars Bridge and look backwards, from where one can also see the most unusual of the City livery halls, HQS *Wellington*, built in 1934 and moored since 1948 at Temple Stairs as the home of the Honourable Company of Master Mariners.

Opposite
New Street Square, just off Fetter Lane. Completed in 2008, this dense office development designed by Bennetts Associates ingeniously extends the network of alleys and small enclosed squares that runs between Fleet Street and Holborn.

1 TEMPLE BAR

Fleet Street EC4 • Sir Horace Jones 1880

Although the magnificently spiky bronze dragon clutching the City arms that crowns the monument marking the site of Temple Bar is eye-catching (see p. 24), the traffic that swirls past its high polychromatic granite plinth does not encourage closer examination. Yet it surmounts a fine sculptural ensemble, designed by the City Architect and Surveyor, Horace Jones, which includes full-length statues of Queen Victoria and the Prince of Wales – carved, at the Queen's suggestion, by Sir J. Edgar Boehm.

This royal involvement was prompted by the fact that as the main gate leading from the City to Westminster it is traditionally the place where the monarch is met by the Lord Mayor when visiting the City. Two such visits by Queen Victoria are depicted on the monument, in bronze reliefs by Charles H. Mabey and Charles Kelsey. The dragon is by Charles Birch and the relief on the front of the monument is also by Mabey; it depicts Time and Fortune drawing a curtain over the old Temple Bar. This previous structure was the last of the City's gates to be removed: royal associations helped to preserve it, as did the belief that it had been designed by Christopher Wren, but by the 1860s it was clear that it would have to be moved, as it had become a serious traffic obstacle. In 1878 the City Corporation dismantled it, numbering its stones for later re-erection. It was reconstructed by Sir Henry Bruce Meux at his country estate, and neglected until the Temple Bar Trust acquired it; the City Corporation restored it and returned it in 2004 to a new site in the City at Paternoster Square.

The newly unveiled Temple Bar, depicted in a woodcut of 1880, with the Royal Courts of Justice behind.

2 MIDDLE TEMPLE HALL

Middle Temple Lane EC4 • John Lewis 1562–c. 1565

Simply the fact that Shakespeare's *Twelfth Night* is documented as having been performed here on 2 February 1601 would make Middle Temple Hall a place of pilgrimage, but it is remarkable in its own right as the finest Elizabethan building in the City. Its mighty double-hammerbeam roof was probably designed by the carpenter John Lewis, who was working at Longleat in Wiltshire when he was summoned to Middle Temple in 1562. Although such a roof is a medieval invention, the detail here is all classical. Even this splendid structure is overshadowed by the hall's magnificent galleried screen, which was probably built in two stages. It was begun soon after 1574, when contributions for its erection were solicited from members of Middle Temple. The lower stage is framed by handsome attached Doric columns, in complete contrast to the lively and lavish design of the upper part. Dominated by full-height female figures alternating with pensive satyrs, it deploys a repertoire of ornament derived from Flemish Mannerism, suggesting that it was added in the 1590s. Still an occasional setting for plays, concerts and other entertainments, the hall is used for dining throughout the legal term.

Middle Temple Hall, the City's finest Elizabethan interior, is a triumph of the carpenter's work, notably the early 1560s double-hammerbeam roof by John Lewis and the screen, which was begun about a decade later. Students studying to become barristers are required to dine in hall a specified number of times before they can qualify.

Opposite
The original Temple Bar as rebuilt in 2004 at the entrance to the Paternoster Square development to the north of St Paul's Cathedral. The gateway was bought from Sir Henry Bruce Meux's family by the Temple Bar Trust, and re-erected with funds from the City Corporation.

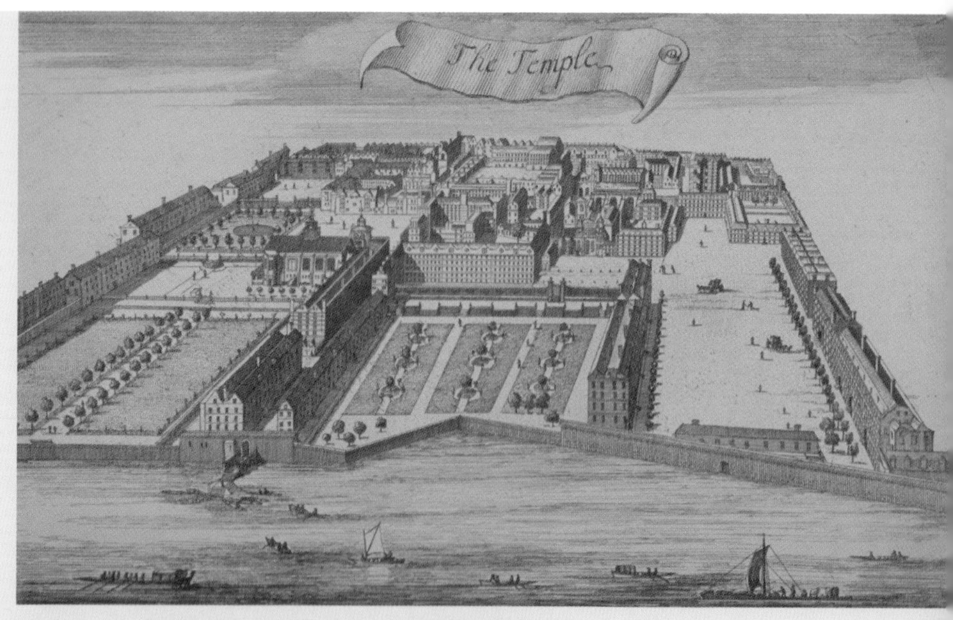

A bird's-eye view of the Temple, engraved by Johannes Kip in about 1700. Before the Thames was embanked in the mid-19th century, Middle Temple Lane, which runs from top to bottom of the site, terminated at a water gate. Among the features that have survived to the present day are Middle Temple Hall and Fountain Court, in the top left.

Inner Temple gardens, looking towards Paper Buildings, which contains barristers' chambers. This end of the building stands on approximately the line of the river as shown in Kip's engraving, before the Embankment was built and the gardens were extended southwards. This part of Paper Buildings was designed in Tudor style by Sidney Smirke and built in 1847–8.

THE TEMPLE

Around 1160 the Knights Templar moved from their first London home in Holborn, where they had been based for about twenty years, to a larger and more prominent site close to the Thames. Here they built a new church and laid out a precinct of essentially monastic character around Middle Temple Lane, which runs from Fleet Street down to the river. After the religious order was suppressed in 1312 the property was given to the Knights Hospitaller, who already had large premises of their own in Clerkenwell. As a result most of the Temple was let to students of law, who by the mid-15th century were organized into two Inns, the Inner Temple to the east and Middle Temple to the west (the Outer Temple, which was never occupied by lawyers, has disappeared). Today Middle Temple Lane forms only an approximate boundary between the two Inns, whose buildings can, however, be distinguished by their badges – the winged horse of Inner Temple and the lamb and flag of Middle Temple (they share the use of Temple Church).

The four Inns of Court (the others, Gray's Inn and Lincoln's Inn, are outside the City) are the home of barristers, one of the two divisions of the English legal profession, who act as advocates. Most of the Inns are given over to their chambers (offices for groups of barristers), although some residential accommodation in the form of flats still exists in the Temple, usually for senior members of the profession. Chambers are organized around staircases, with their members' names painted next to the entrance door – one of the features of the Temple that recall Oxford or Cambridge colleges. Narrow, gas-lit Middle Temple Lane, entered from Fleet Street by a classical gateway of 1683–4 designed by Roger North, has an old-fashioned urban rather than collegiate feel – which makes the spacious Inner Temple gardens, extended as a result of the Thames Embankment, all the more of a pleasurable surprise.

Apart from its major historic monuments, Temple Church and Middle Temple Hall, the Temple's chief architectural attraction is the survival of domestic buildings of a wide range of dates, notably the late 17th-century timber-framed houses at nos 2–3 Middle Temple Lane and the handsome redbrick terrace of King's Bench Walk, begun in 1670. The 19th century introduced a more institutional flavour, with such additions as the enjoyably pompous French Renaissance gateway at the south end of Middle Temple Lane, designed by E. M. Barry in 1878. However, rebuilding after serious damage in the Blitz means that the predominant tone of much of the Temple is polite neo-Georgian, with many buildings by Sir Edward Maufe and Hubert Worthington, notably the latter's Inner Temple Hall.

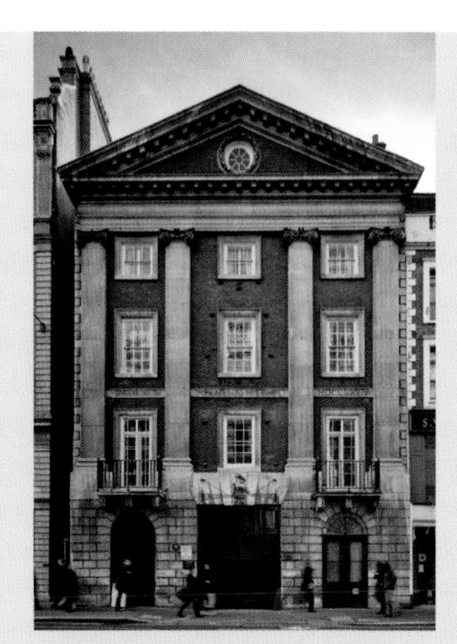

Middle Temple gateway on Fleet Street, designed by an amateur architect, Roger North, and built in 1683–4, the year North was treasurer of Middle Temple. Christopher Wren suggested that, to save money, the pediment be built of plaster, but North refused, in his own words, 'out of a proud high spirit', and insisted on stone.

King's Bench Walk, looking south. This terrace of late 17th-century houses provides a vivid impression of the City's main streets as they would have appeared when rebuilt after the Great Fire.

3 INNER TEMPLE GATEWAY AND PRINCE HENRY'S ROOM

17 Fleet Street EC4 • 1610–11; London County Council Architects 1900–06

Virtually all the shops, pubs and offices that separate Fleet Street from the Temple were redeveloped in the 19th and 20th centuries, but no. 17 escaped, perhaps because its lowest storey, built of stone, incorporates the entrance into Inner Temple Lane. Above it are two half-timbered jettied storeys, each with a pair of oriel windows, the upper ones capped by a pretty balustrade, behind which the building's twin gables are recessed. This very rare survivor of pre-Fire London was built in 1610 for John Bennett as an inn, the Prince's Arms. On the first floor, overlooking Fleet Street, is 'Prince Henry's Room'. It has a plaster ceiling richly decorated with strapwork, at the centre of which are the Prince of Wales's feathers and the initials PH, commemorating the short-lived Prince Henry, who became Prince of Wales in the year the inn was opened. In 1900 the building – which in the 18th century had become famous as the home of Mrs Salmon's tableaux of clockwork-powered waxworks – was acquired by the London County Council, which restored it. The rear of the building, facing onto Inner Temple Lane, has Arts and Crafts detailing characteristic of the LCC's turn-of-the-century buildings. It was transferred to the City of London Corporation in 1969.

Prince Henry's Room, photographed in 1908, shortly after the completion of restoration work by the London County Council. The armorial glass, by Burlison & Grylls, was added as part of this restoration. The fire surround and panelling on the east wall date from the 18th century.

The Prince of Wales's feathers and the initials in the plasterwork ceiling of the first-floor room in Inner Temple Gateway commemorate James I and VI's eldest son, Prince Henry (1594–1612), who was created Prince of Wales in 1610.

4 TEMPLE CHURCH OF ST MARY

The Temple EC4

Built for the Knights Templar, the Temple Church is extraordinary in many ways: in design, for its circular nave, modelled on the church of the Holy Sepulchre in Jerusalem, as was customary for this crusading order; in status, as a 'royal peculiar' outside diocesan control, like Westminster Abbey; and historically, since its nave is one of the very earliest Gothic buildings in England. It scarcely matters that barely a single medieval stone is visible today, thanks to a succession of restorations from 1825 onwards, most significantly after a bomb in 1941; it is a hauntingly beautiful building. The nave, built in about 1160 and probably designed by an architect trained in the far north of France, originally had a small, unaisled apsed chancel. This was replaced by the present spacious chancel, of hall-church form (that is, with aisles as high as the central vessel), which was consecrated in 1240 in the presence of Henry III. The king intended that it should be his burial place, a role that was eventually usurped by Westminster Abbey.

Although nave and chancel make such an enjoyable spatial contrast, they share an austere elegance, simple in outline but rich in detail and materials, notably the lavish use of Purbeck 'marble' (in fact, a polished limestone, but expensive nonetheless). These qualities reflect something of the character of the Templars: military, monastic, but formidably wealthy and powerful as well. They are recalled in the church today by a celebrated

Opposite
Inner Temple Gateway. Originally built as an inn, this remarkable survivor of the pre-Fire City incorporates the arched entrance to Inner Temple Lane, framed by boldly rusticated stone pilasters.

17
INNER TEMPLE
HAIR AND BEAUTY
CITY OF LONDON
FLEET
STREET EC4

series of 13th-century Purbeck marble effigies of knights in the nave, all but one of which were badly damaged in 1941. Although the identity of most is uncertain, they appear to represent the order's patrons rather than the Templars themselves.

In 1608 James I presented the church to the lawyers who by then occupied the Temple, and ever since it has been maintained by two Inns of Court, the Inner Temple and the Middle Temple. The restoration after the Second World War (by Walter H. Godfrey) removed most of the last remains of a rich Victorian decorative scheme and brought back to the church the handsome oak reredos made in 1682 by William Rounthwaite under Wren's supervision, which had been removed in 1840. It is set under windows by Carl Edwards, installed in 1957–8; their small figures and jewel-like colours imaginatively evoke 13th-century glass.

The chancel of the Temple Church from the north-east. The circular nave is just visible on the far left. This view emphasizes the 'hall-church' design of the chancel, with a central vessel and aisles of equal height.

The interior of the Temple Church, looking from the nave, built in about 1160, into the chancel, consecrated in 1240. Set into the floor is part of the celebrated group of 13th-century Purbeck marble effigies of knights.

5 C. HOARE & CO.

37 Fleet Street EC4 • Charles Parker 1829–30

In architectural terms, Hoare's Bank may not seem unusual as a survivor of the modest premises of London's private banks – Child's Bank can be seen a few doors away at no. 1 Fleet Street, for example – but it is unique as the only privately owned retail bank in the country and is still owned and run by the Hoare family, who founded it in 1672. Its original premises were in Cheapside, but only eighteen years after its creation it moved to the present site. Its Bath stone building, completed in 1830, was designed by Charles Parker in a restrained classical manner (with advice on the planning from Sir Jeffry Wyatville, of whom he had been a pupil). As was customary, a ground-floor banking hall, separated by a screen wall from the counting-house, is combined with first-floor family accommodation. Does any interior in London have such an atmosphere of hushed professional discretion as Hoare's banking hall? At its centre is a bronze columnar stove, designed in Grecian style by Parker's brother Samuel, 'Bronzist to His Late Majesty'. The bank's old-fashioned air might be misleading: in 2010 its balance sheet was almost £2 billion.

Hoare's Bank, the City's finest early 19th-century bank building, is still owned by the Hoare family. The doorway on the left leads both to the banking hall on the ground floor and to the Hoares' private apartment above.

6 ST DUNSTAN-IN-THE-WEST

Fleet Street EC4 • John Shaw 1830–33

Rearing over the narrow pavement on the north side of Fleet Street, St Dunstan's high tower is the first prominent architectural accent on this approach to the City from the west. Built of buff Ketton limestone, it is capped by an octagonal openwork lantern, modelled on that of All Saints Pavement in York, which dates from about 1400. To its right is a large clock, made in 1671, thrust out on a bracket below two Hercules figures who strike the hours with their clubs. Below it, a bronze bust by Kathleen Scott on an obelisk designed by Sir Edwin Lutyens commemorates the newspaper proprietor Alfred Harmsworth, 1st Viscount Northcliffe (1865–1922). Over the vestry door is a full-length sculpture, perhaps late 17th century in date, of Queen Elizabeth I. It once stood on Ludgate, the ancient City gate on Ludgate Hill, demolished in 1760.

So correct is the church's Perpendicular detail – the architect, John Shaw, had demonstrated his confident handling of medieval styles in his alterations to Newstead Abbey, Lord Byron's family home – that the interior comes as a complete surprise. The original St Dunstan, in existence by 1170, stood on a larger site, reduced by the street widening that caused it to be demolished. To make the best use of the remaining space, Shaw designed a centralized church on an essentially classical octagonal plan, with shallow vaulted niches in each wall. A tall clerestory that rises to a star rib vault (in essence an iron

St Dunstan-in-the-West, which replaced a medieval church demolished for road widening in 1830. The church does not occupy the whole of the site made available for it, and in 1834 John Shaw Jr, whose father had designed the church, was able to add, to the church's left, the bow-windowed Law Life Assurance Building. This very early example of a purpose-built office is a pioneer of the Jacobean revival.

structure) bathes the church in cool, aqueous light – a relief after the glare and bustle outside. Shaw's well-preserved interior (probably completed after his death in 1832 by his son John) has been embellished by fittings added as a result of the wish of Geoffrey Fisher, Archbishop of Canterbury from 1945 to 1961, that St Dunstan should become a centre of prayer for Christian unity: most prominent is the wooden iconostasis from Romania that fills the north-east niche.

7 PUBLIC RECORD OFFICE *(former)*

Chancery Lane WC2 • Sir James Pennethorne and Sir John Taylor 1851–96; Gaunt Francis 1998–2001

Nobody has ever much warmed to the elephant-grey, grimly Gothic former Public Record Office, which lowers over the east side of Chancery Lane. 'The general effect combines the workhouse, the jail, and the Manchester mill', wrote the *Saturday Review* when the first stage of the building was opened in 1855. Like those buildings it was intended to be as secure and fireproof as possible. One result of the burning of the old Palace of Westminster in 1834 was a new sense of urgency about the vulnerability of the national archives, which were divided between several highly unsuitable buildings, including the chapter house of Westminster Abbey. In 1837 an Act of Parliament acquired the estate of the Master of the Rolls – head of the Chancery division of the High Court – for a new Public Record Office. Among the buildings on the site was the Rolls Chapel, founded in 1232 by Henry III for converted Jews.

The commission was given to Sir James Pennethorne, Architect and Surveyor for Metropolitan Improvements to the Crown Estate. He had to lay out the enormous structure on the module of a small iron and brick compartment – essentially a cell – designed by the Fire Brigade as ideal fireproof storage. Pennethorne's efforts to compose the resulting grille-like façades into monumental forms were hampered by his orientation of the building to look north so that it could be seen from a new 'Great Central Thoroughfare', which he had designed to link Piccadilly to the City. The road was never constructed and so the building faces into a narrow lane, Rolls Place. However, it is given presence by its massive tower, added in 1865–7, which is embellished with statues of four queens by Joseph Durham. Pennethorne wished to incorporate the Rolls Chapel into the building, but it was demolished and its 13th-century chancel arch was re-erected in the grounds. Its monuments – which include an exquisite Renaissance sculpture commemorating Dr Yonge (d. 1516), attributed to Pietro Torrigiani – were moved inside the Public Record Office's west entrance. In 1997 the records were transferred to the National Archives in Kew, and the following year the building was sold to King's College, London, which has cheered it up greatly by converting it into the Maughan Library, designed by Gaunt Francis.

The former Public Record Office, home of the national archives from the 1850s to 1997, when they were transferred to Kew. This was the first major Gothic Revival public building after the new Palace of Westminster, and was built by the same contractors, J. & H. Lee.

The monument to John Yonge, Master of the Rolls, who died in 1516. The first wholly Renaissance tomb in England, it is attributed to the Florentine sculptor Pietro Torrigiani, who designed and made the tomb of Henry VII and Elizabeth of York in Westminster Abbey. Dr Yonge's monument was made for the demolished medieval Rolls Chapel, on the site of the Public Record Office.

Opposite
The interior of St Dunstan-in-the-West, looking north-east to the iconostasis made in about 1860 for a monastery in Bucharest and installed here in 1966. The church is used for both Anglican and Romanian Orthodox services.

8 LONDON SILVER VAULTS ➲

Chancery House, 53–64 Chancery Lane WC2 • Richardson & Houfe 1947–53

At first glance there is nothing remarkable about Chancery House, at the northern end of Chancery Lane. Although its architect, Sir Albert Richardson, was one of the best classical designers of the postwar years, this is not one of his memorable buildings. What makes it worth visiting is invisible from outside – the Silver Vaults. These perpetuate the safe-deposit vaults in the previous building on the site, completed in 1890, which were designed to serve the goldsmiths and jewellers of nearby Hatton Garden. A few of the dealers began to open them to customers. This tradition still flourishes: deep in the basement of Chancery House, more than thirty strongrooms (each with an enormous iron door) are opened as shops by specialist silver dealers serving a clientele that ranges from serious collectors to people buying a christening mug. Shopping here is rather like being allowed to rummage through the safe-deposit boxes of a big bank.

The stern, rather blank 1950s façade of the London Silver Vaults gives no clue to the glittering treasure on sale within.

9 STAPLE INN

Holborn EC1 • 16th century; Alfred Waterhouse 1887

Most people who pass the long, high range of black-and-white half-timbered shops that overhang Holborn opposite Chancery Lane Tube station probably assume that they are a Victorian confection. In fact they are, despite substantial restoration in the 19th and 20th centuries, essentially Elizabethan, the only authentic large-scale survivor of the City's 16th-century street architecture. The main five-gabled range, on the left, was commissioned in 1586 by Staple Inn, now the last intact Inn of Chancery. Its central archway leads into the Inn's small paved courtyard, enclosed by largely 18th-century brick ranges, sensitively restored by Sir Edward Maufe in the 1950s after severe

The half-timbered frontage of Staple Inn, on the south side of Holborn, photographed in about 1900. It is in two parts. The five-gabled range on the left, with two overhanging storeys, was built in 1586. The two-gabled range on the right, originally a separate house, was added a little later. The building's Elizabethan appearance was enhanced in the 1880s, when the closely placed timber studs were added, following the removal of 18th-century plaster.

The gas-lit courtyard of Staple Inn, which was largely rebuilt in the 18th century and reconstructed in the 1950s, looking towards the tall bay window of the hall, built in 1581.

damage from a flying bomb. On the far side is the four-bay hall, built in 1581, which has Gothic doors added in 1753. There are few more magical spots in the City, especially at dusk in autumn, when the gas lights filter through the branches of the plane trees. Yet Staple Inn has a further surprise to spring: the archway beside the hall leads into a pretty, secluded garden, centred on a fountain and overlooked to the south by the former Patent Office.

Staple Inn probably derives its name from its hall – *stapel* is the Old English name for a post of the sort used to build an aisle – as there is no evidence that it was ever used by the wool merchants of the Staple. It was occupied by lawyers from the early 15th century onwards, and in 1529 its freehold was bought by Gray's Inn. Like the other Inns of Chancery, it was dissolved in the 19th century and the buildings were sold, partly to the Patent Office and partly to the Prudential Assurance Company, whose enormous redbrick and terracotta headquarters are on the opposite side of Holborn. The Prudential's architect was Alfred Waterhouse, who restored Staple Inn in 1887. It is now occupied largely by the Institute of Actuaries.

The exterior of the hall of Barnard's Inn, a forme[r] Inn of Chancery, and now the home of Gresham College. It retains its original octagonal louvre in the roof, designed to take smoke from a cent[ral] hearth. The coved cornice was added in about 1660. The hall faces onto a tiny courtyard.

10 GRESHAM COLLEGE

Barnard's Inn, Holborn EC1

The interior of the 15th-century hall of Barnard['s] Inn, depicted in a watercolour of 1885 by John Crowther.

Sir Thomas Gresham, founder in 1566 of the Royal Exchange, was deeply conscious of his status as head of England's most famous merchant dynasty, but the death in 1564 of his only son, Richard, meant that he had no legitimate heir to perpetuate his name. This was an important motive in his foundation and endowment of Gresham College, which came into existence in 1596, following the death of his widow. The college consists of seven professors, appointed jointly by the City Corporation and the Mercers' Company, who were to lecture on successive days of the week on seven sciences: astronomy, divinity, geometry, law, music, physic (medicine) and rhetoric. Originally housed in Gresham's old home in Bishopsgate, the college had a distinguished intellectual history in the 17th century, not least as a point of contact for several of the founders of the Royal Society.

Gresham College still fulfils its founder's intentions, with regular (although no longer daily) lectures. Since 1991 it has been based in one of the City's most unexpected medieval survivals, the hammerbeamed hall of Barnard's Inn, one of the former Inns of Chancery, founded by Lionel Barnard in 1435. The hall was described as 'new built' in 1439, but its panelling, which incorporates Renaissance motifs, dates from the early 16th century. Only 11.3 m (37 ft) long, it has a charming doll's-house feel, emphasized by the way it is tightly hemmed in by small 18th- and 19th-century buildings, mostly redeveloped as offices by Green Lloyd Architects in 1991–2 for the Mercers' Company, which has owned the Inn since 1892.

St Andrew Holborn in 1804, as depicted in an aquatint of 1804 by J. C. Buckler. When Wren encased the medieval tower that is all that survives of the previous church on this site he added the pinnacles capped with weathervanes.

11 ST ANDREW HOLBORN

5 St Andrew Street EC4 • Christopher Wren 1684–6; Seely & Paget 1961

Unlike most City churches, St Andrew sits on an ample island site, although the unimpeded views that now greet visitors heading east into the City along Holborn were created as recently as 1970, when the buildings that screened the church from Holborn Circus were replaced by a garden. The largest of Wren's City churches, its rebuilding was necessitated not by the Great Fire but by the decay of its 15th-century predecessor. Wren preserved the medieval west tower, although in 1703–4 he (or perhaps Hawksmoor working under him) encased it in Portland stone and heightened it. Gutted in 1941, the church was reconstructed to Wren's design – which is very similar to his St James Piccadilly – by Seely & Paget, and reopened in 1961. A late 17th-century carved relief of the resurrection at the end of the world is set over a door on the north side of the church. Made for the gateway of the paupers' cemetery once in Shoe Lane, it was moved here in the 1860s, when the cemetery was cleared. It is of high quality – who could have carved it? St Andrew's barrel-vaulted and galleried interior is a gleamingly unatmospheric setting for fittings from elsewhere: the font, pulpit and organ case were made for the chapel of the Foundling Hospital in Coram's Fields, Bloomsbury, demolished in 1926. The simple organ case was given to the Hospital by Handel in 1750. In the chapel in the tower's ground floor are mid-1730s altar rails and part of a reredos from St Luke Old Street, which is now a concert hall. Nothing now survives of the church's redecoration in 1869–72 by the architect S. S. Teulon, but his stock-brick Gothic rectory, court house and vestry clerk's office still form a picturesque tightly knit group to the south of the church.

A detail of a 17th-century relief set into the church's external north wall. Depicting the resurrection preceding the Last Judgment, presided over by Christ, it looked over the church's walled cemetery, which is shown in its original state in Buckler's view.

12 CITY TEMPLE

Holborn Viaduct EC1 • Lockwood & Mawson 1873–4; Seely & Paget 1955–8

By far the most imposing building in the City of London for non-conformist worship, the City Temple occupies an eye-catching position on Holborn Viaduct. Opulently classical in style, its two-storeyed portico confidently evokes St Paul's Cathedral, but the architects – H. F. Lockwood and William Mawson of Bradford (where they designed the town hall) – introduced a very un-Wren-like note of asymmetry in the tall west tower that rises in three stages to a cupola. The pediment contains imposing figures of Faith, Hope and Charity; their sculptor is unknown. The basement (entered from Shoe Lane) contained the

The City Temple as reconstructed. The opulent façade and the back wall were retained, sandwiching a new concrete-framed building by Seely & Paget.

minister's house, together with offices and schoolrooms. This multifunctionality has been enhanced in the almost complete internal reconstruction by Seely & Paget that followed bomb damage in 1941. The clerestory of the original vast auditorium was replaced by a floor of offices, and further subdivision, by the same architects, followed in 1971. The history of the church's Congregational ministry can be traced back as far as 1640, when it occupied a chapel in Poultry.

Dr Johnson's House presides over Gough Square, which still retains its atmospheric gas lighting. Much of the square, such as the building on the right, was rebuilt after the Second World War in a style that respects the Georgian survivors.

13 DR JOHNSON'S HOUSE

17 Gough Square EC4 • c. 1700; Alfred Burr 1911

Only one house in London has authentic links to Samuel Johnson. In 1748 he moved into no. 17 Gough Square, part of a development built for the Gough family in about 1700, in order to be close to the printer William Strahan, who would be producing the *Dictionary of the English Language* that Johnson had undertaken to complete in three years. It was to take him three times as long. The attic was fitted out 'like a counting-house', in Boswell's words, to accommodate six clerks who transcribed the entries drafted by Johnson. In 1911 the house was rescued from dilapidation by Cecil Harmsworth, chairman of Associated Newspapers, and restored by Alfred Burr. Since 1914 it has been open to the public as a museum; it houses an important research library and a collection of paintings and objects associated with the writer. Burr added the curator's cottage in the garden, reputedly the smallest house in the City of London. At the far end of the 'square', in truth a pleasantly peaceful if rather over-restored L-shaped courtyard, is a 1997 bronze statue by Jon Bickley of Johnson's cat Hodge, who has just consumed two of the oysters with which his master fed him.

Wine Office Court, looking towards Fleet Street. The entrance to Ye Olde Cheshire Cheese, on the left, incorporates an 18th-century shop front.

14 YE OLDE CHESHIRE CHEESE

Wine Office Court, off Fleet Street EC4

So tenacious is the association of this penumbrally atmospheric pub with Samuel Johnson that it seems rather mean to mention the lack of documentary evidence that he ever drank here. However, since Wine Office Court forms an approach to Gough Square, where Johnson had a house in the 1750s, and since the Cheshire Cheese was certainly in existence by then, it seems inconceivable that he did not visit it – in 1858 the Victorian journalist Cyrus Redding claimed to have interviewed a very old man who had seen Johnson here. The Cheshire Cheese is in essence two small late 17th-century houses thrown together and heightened in 1755. In the 18th century, part was used as a shop, the front of which survives in Wine Office Court. The pub's fittings date largely from the early to mid-19th century and have been little altered since – if Johnson can for a moment be forgotten, the Cheshire Cheese is in essence a well-preserved chop house of Dickens's time (and he certainly did drink here).

In the 1890s it was the chief meeting place of the Rhymers Club, who included W. B. Yeats, Arthur Symons and Ernest Dowson. Many of the walls are hung with photographs and press cuttings that absorbingly chart the history of a Fleet Street pub in the 20th century, with a special display given over to the obituaries of the parrot Polly, who died in 1926 aged forty, famous for her perfect imitation of the pop of a champagne cork – a feat that she performed four hundred times on Armistice night.

A panelled interior in Fleet Street's best-known pub, Ye Olde Cheshire Cheese, an essentially lat 17th-century building that preserves many of it early to mid-19th century fittings.

⓯ *DAILY TELEGRAPH* BUILDING (*former*)

135–141 Fleet Street EC4 • Elcock & Sutcliffe with Thomas Tait 1928–31; Kohn Pedersen Fox Associates 1988–91

In 1927 the *Daily Telegraph* was bought by Sir James Berry (from 1929 Lord Camrose), who in 1930 halved its price to a penny, doubling its circulation as a result. This revitalization was reflected in an impressive new building. Although at first glance its six mighty attached columns springing from first-floor level seem conventionally classical, the detailing draws on fashionable Art Deco motifs, including Egyptian architecture. Great care

The *Daily Telegraph* building, photographed by Bedford Lemere in 1931, the year it was completed. It now forms part of a large development for Goldman Sachs that also incorporates Mersey House to its right. The architect of this inventive and attractive 1904–6 building is unknown.

Opposite
The City's most celebrated 1930s building: the former headquarters of the *Daily Express* in Flee Street. It is clad in black Vitrolite, an opaque pigmented glass, made in the UK by Pilkington, which is set in strips of chromium – a stylish us of up-to-the-minute materials.

130

went into the building's embellishment: the giant projecting clock is by the Birmingham Guild of Handicraft, and the stone panel over the main door, depicting racing figures of Mercury, is attributed to A. J. Oakley, who also came from an Arts and Crafts background but here, like the Birmingham Guild, worked in an Art Deco style. More individual are two heads high up at attic level on the two side bays, carved in a deliberately primitive idiom by Samuel Rabinovitch. Representing the Past and the Future, they demonstrate an unexpected investment in Modernism by a traditionally conservative newspaper. The *Daily Telegraph* moved out in 1987 and its restored building now forms part of a large development by the American architects Kohn Pedersen Fox for Goldman Sachs, most of which consists of a vast new building on the site of the paper's former printing works in Peterborough Court, behind Fleet Street. It takes its name from the London home of the bishops of Peterborough, first recorded here in the 15th century.

16 *DAILY EXPRESS* BUILDING (*former*)

120–129 Fleet Street EC4 • Sir Owen Williams with Ellis & Clarke and Robert Atkinson 1930–33; Hurley, Robertson & Associates 2000

London can offer only one Art Deco building worthy to be set beside the skyscraper lobbies of mid-town Manhattan. When its new headquarters were built the *Daily Express* was Britain's best-selling newspaper, thanks to the partnership of a dynamic proprietor, Lord Beaverbrook, and an inspired editor, Arthur Christiansen. Beaverbrook had an astute grasp of the value of what would now be called PR, one reason why the newspaper

The foyer of the *Daily Express* building, photographed in about 1971. Its designer was Robert Atkinson, an architect who had made his name with luxury cinemas, where he developed the flair for inventive Art Deco glamour so well demonstrated here.

was given such an eye-catching architectural setting. Yet the design by Owen Williams, who was both its architect and structural engineer, has a practical purpose, as its concrete frame allowed for a large uninterrupted basement for the paper's printing presses. Its most memorable feature is the smoothly curving exterior, of black Vitrolite glass set in chrome strips. This is London's earliest curtain-walled building – that is, with walls that bear no structural load. Beaverbrook commissioned two similar *Daily Express* buildings from Williams, in Manchester and Glasgow. Both happily still survive, but neither can match the Fleet Street building's sensational entrance hall. Designed by Robert Atkinson with an oval staircase, reliefs by Eric Aumonier and a massive silvered pendant lamp hanging from a recessed aluminium-clad ceiling, it was well restored in 2001. Although now offices for Goldman Sachs, the building still evokes the 'Byzantine vestibule and Sassanian lounge' of *The Daily Beast* in Evelyn Waugh's 1933 novel *Scoop*.

The former Reuters building demonstrates Edwin Lutyens's unrivalled ability to shape an office building into subtle and powerful architecture, using only a minimum of ornament. The concave set-back upper storeys originally contained executive suites for Reuters; they are now offices for bankers and lawyers.

17 REUTERS AND PRESS ASSOCIATION BUILDING (*former*)

85 Fleet Street EC4 • Sir Edwin Lutyens with Smee & Houchin 1934–8; Crouch Butler Savage 2005–7

In November 1851 the first underwater telegraph cable linking the UK with Europe was inaugurated. The opportunity this presented for the rapid dissemination of news was exploited by the German-born Paul Julius Reuter, who had settled in London earlier that year. His first great coup was negotiating a contract with the Stock Exchange that allowed him to send London prices to stockbrokers in Paris in return for supplying information about prices on exchanges on the Continent. In 1934 Reuters collaborated with the Press Association, the leading national news agency, in commissioning new headquarters. This was the last of the large City office buildings designed by Lutyens, a sequence that had begun in 1921 with Britannic House in Finsbury Circus. It has a greater suggestion of the Modern movement than his earlier commercial buildings, which were more formally classical (note, for example, the way the windows are recessed only very slightly in the wall, and the absence of a cornice), but Reuters demonstrates his extraordinary ability to use a classical vocabulary with abstract freedom. On one corner, where there was once a bank, Doric pilasters dissolve into the rusticated ground floor, and the gently battered walls of the upper floors culminate in a recessed concave attic storey supporting a flat-roofed drum. In the oculus over the main entrance is a winged bronze figure of a herald blowing a trumpet by William Reid Dick, originally gilt (and originally high up on the parapet). Reuters departed for Canary Wharf in 2005. Its former headquarters, converted by Crouch Butler Savage, houses not only financial and legal offices but also Lutyens – a restaurant, bar and private members' club owned by Terence Conran and Peter Prescott – which opened in 2009.

THE NEWSPAPER INDUSTRY

A plaque erected in St Bride's church in 2002 commemorates the 300th anniversary of the issue of Britain's first daily newspaper on 11 March 1702. The *Daily Courant* was published from the White Hart, an inn at the eastern end of Fleet Street, so beginning an association with the newspaper trade that survived the Second World War – it was the only one of the City's major manufacturing industries that did not move out in the postwar period – and did not end, with the departure of Reuters, until 2005.

Architecturally, the major monuments to journalism – the headquarters of the *Daily Telegraph*, *Daily Express* and Reuters, all rebuilt in the interwar period – are in Fleet Street itself, but the industry was spread from the Mirror Group at the north end of Fetter Lane to Associated Newspapers (the *Daily Mail* and other titles) in Bouverie Street to the south. *The Times* was in an enclave of its own, in Printing House Square, to the east of New Bridge Street. All these sites have been redeveloped for offices, but the major Fleet Street buildings have been restored for their new uses – indeed, they look better than they did in the hands of their original owners. Nothing now, however, quite conjures up the Fleet Street described by Michael Frayn in his 1967 novel *Towards the End of the Morning*: 'Great cylinders of newsprint went swinging above your head from the articulated lorries blocking every side-street. Through grimy pavement-level skylights here and there you could glimpse the web racing on the huge machines thundering in the basement...And wafting from every bay and ventilator and seedy lobby, that intoxicating smell...ink, hot metal, sweat.'

The bars and pubs that were as much a feature of journalists' lives as the newspaper offices survive, although now with a very different clientele – old hands still recall, for example, the *Express* writers at 'Poppins' (the Red Lion in Poppins Court), or the *Mirror* staff in the 'Mucky Duck' (the White Swan in Fetter Lane). Another major monument to the trade is St Bride's church, which was restored after the war largely with money from newspaper publishers. Despite their departure from Fleet Street, their old relationship with the area is perpetuated by the tradition that memorial services for journalists and other members of the trade are still held here.

A London newspaper boy in about 1910. He is clutching a poster for the *Star*, an evening newspaper founded in 1888 that was notorious for its sensational reporting.

Fleet Street, looking east, photographed in about 1902. Note the sign for the *Liverpool Post*: many leading provincial newspapers as well as the national titles had offices here.

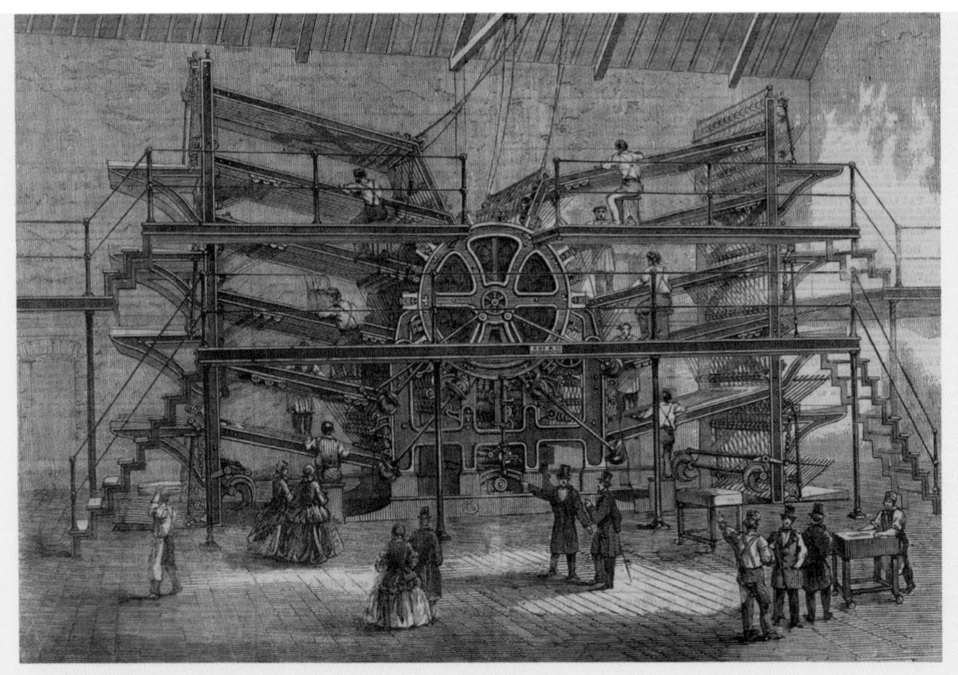

A woodcut of 1860 depicting a gigantic 10-feeder steam-powered press in the *Daily Telegraph*'s printing works.

The *Daily Telegraph*'s printing works in Peterborough Court, behind its Fleet Street headquarters, as depicted in the *Illustrated London News* in 1882.

St Bride from the north-west, with St Paul's in the distance, in an engraving of 1753 by John Donowell. The open setting depicted here is misleading: St Bride has always been tightly hemmed in by buildings.

18 ST BRIDE

Fleet Street EC4 • Christopher Wren 1671–8; Godfrey Allen 1955–7

We have Lutyens to thank for the best approach to St Bride. Walking east along Fleet Street, turn into Salisbury Court, but before reaching Salisbury Square turn left into an arched tunnel that extends through Lutyens's building for Reuters to the west porch of St Bride. As one advances, the most famous spire in London appears, extending upwards in four octagonal stages to its diminutive steeple. It is a design that makes writers strain for similes; a comparison with tiered cakes, linked to the church's dedication (a corruption of St Bridget), gave rise to the story that it inspired the classic wedding cake, but few have bettered David Piper's evocation of the way the spire soars out of its hemmed-in site, 'like a hollyhock that escapes from the pressure of undergrowth'.

The spire, Wren's tallest at 69 m (226 ft) – Hawksmoor may have had a hand in the design – was added in 1701–3 to the church that replaced a medieval predecessor destroyed in the Great Fire. This was gutted in the Blitz, and today only its tower, spire and outer walls remain. Inside, Wren's arcades of coupled columns were rebuilt by Godfrey Allen. The new fittings evoke their 17th-century predecessors in style but are arranged quite differently: Allen positioned the stalls in collegiate fashion, facing north and south, and gave them high backs screening out the aisles, to create what feels like a church within a church.

Before St Bride was restored there was a major archaeological excavation below its foundations, and the results are on display in an absorbingly interesting exhibition in the crypt. Surviving remains allow the history of the church to be followed back with

Opposite
One of the City's most celebrated landmarks, the telescopic spire of St Bride, the tallest of Wren's steeples, rises to 69 m (226 ft). It was originally 3 m (10 ft) taller but was cut down in 1764 after being damaged in a storm – an event that played a major part in encouraging the addition of lightning conductors to towers and steeples, following Benjamin Franklin's discovery in 1752 that lightning is an electrical discharge.

The interior of St Bride, looking east. The fittings were designed by Godfrey Allen in the 1950s, as part of his reconstruction of the church, which was gutted in the Blitz. Wren's church had galleries, which Allen did not replace. The reredos is a free copy of one designed by Wren for the Chapel Royal at Hampton Court. The 'apse' behind it is in fact an illusionistic painting by Glyn Jones, commissioned as part of Allen's scheme.

certainty to the 11th century, and possibly the 6th century, but even more thrilling are the fragments of the tessellated floors of two rooms of a late Roman villa. It is not utterly fanciful to imagine its inhabitants enjoying the views over the Thames and Fleet rivers with a cup of wine, just a few feet from the bars that cluster today below St Bride's shady little churchyard.

19 SION COLLEGE

Victoria Embankment EC4 • Sir Arthur Blomfield 1884–7

To the west of Blackfriars Bridge, the Victoria Embankment turns into an illustration from an architectural history book, thanks to a sequence of façades overlooking the Thames in a variety of styles – classical (Unilever House), Renaissance (former City of London School for Boys) and Gothic (Sion College and

A man leans over the parapet of the terrace of Somerset House to enjoy the view of the Victoria Embankment, completed in 1870, three years before this engraving was made by John O'Connor. Temple gardens and Middle Temple Hall are to the left of St Paul's; Blackfriars' bridges are on the far right.

the Thames Conservancy Offices). Despite its name, the origin of which is unknown, Sion College is not an educational institution: it is a society for Anglican clergymen in London, founded in 1630 by a bequest from Thomas White, rector of St Dunstan-in-the-West. Part of the money was used to establish a library for the use of the members, housed in a building on London Wall. In 1887 it moved to purpose-built premises by Arthur Blomfield (who had good clerical connections – his father had been Bishop of London). The redbrick and Bath stone Perpendicular Gothic design is dominated by the library's enormous five-light south window. The building operated as a club as well as a library until it was sold in 1996 and converted into offices. Its pre-1850 manuscripts and books are now in Lambeth Palace Library and the later material was given to King's College Library, but the College still functions as a social club, organizing events for its clerical membership from premises in Fleet Street.

Sion College. It was altered at street level when its original porch was demolished during the construction of a road underpass in the 1960s. The low flat-roofed extension in front of the building was added in 1965–6 to link it to its neighbour on the left, no. 9 Carmelite Street, the former Thames Conservancy Offices, designed by Hunt & Steward in 1893 in a style to match Sion College.

20 CITY OF LONDON SCHOOL FOR BOYS (*former*)

Victoria Embankment EC4 • Davis & Emmanuel 1880–82; BDP 1987–91

Even Eton does not have such a fine site as the City of London School for Boys, which moved into these purpose-built premises overlooking the Thames in 1883. The school originated in a bequest in 1442 by John Carpenter, Town Clerk of London, who left property to be used in perpetuity to educate four boys who would assist in the services at the chapel in the Guildhall. By the early 19th century the bequest had grown so enormously in value that the City Corporation decided to use it to found its

The former City of London School for Boys. Unilever House curves away to the right; to the left, running down John Carpenter Street behind the building, is the extension built for J. P. Morgan, which has occupied the building since 1991.

own school, originally in Milk Street, just off Cheapside. Its new building on the Embankment, in free French Renaissance style (although the architects called it Italian), is dominated by the five big arched windows of its first-floor hall under a steep hipped roof of green Westmorland slate with a tall, thin bell turret. The building's sculpture is of high quality: the decorative carving is by G. W. Seale and the figures are by John Daymond & Son. The inclusion of such writers as Shakespeare, Bacon and Milton may seem unexceptional, but they were selected by the headmaster, Edwin A. Abbott, a pioneer in the teaching of English literature.

In 1986 the school moved to new riverside premises on St Paul's Walk and the building was incorporated by BDP into premises for J. P. Morgan, completed in 1991. The old buildings are linked by a lower glazed entrance to a grey granite-clad block extending far along John Carpenter Street, which has a two-storey rusticated base below simple piers and a deep cornice. Despite the presence of Soanian details of the type fashionable in the 1980s, the overall effect recalls such American classicists as McKim, Meade & White and even, in its insistent horizontality, Frank Lloyd Wright.

21 UNILEVER HOUSE

New Bridge Street EC4 • J. Lomax Simpson with Burnet, Tait & Partners 1930–32; Kohn Pedersen Fox Associates 2004–7

The mighty quadrant of Unilever House, the City's most monumental interwar office building.

In 1930 the British soap manufacturer Lever Brothers, founded in Lancashire in 1885 by William Hesketh Lever, merged with the Dutch margarine manufacturers Margarine Unie, largely to create savings in the purchase of palm oil, used in the manufacture of both soap and margarine. The resulting company, Unilever, was housed in a new building commissioned by Lever Brothers and completed in 1932. It is the most impressive company headquarters built in the City between the wars, thanks in part to its magnificent position overlooking the Thames at the north end of Blackfriars Bridge. James Lomax Simpson, head of the Lever Brothers architecture department, claimed sole responsibility for the design, although all the drawings are signed by Burnet & Tait alone, but whoever was responsible exploited the site with great flair. The building is a quadrant with a giant Ionic order rising from the fourth to the sixth floor that leads the eye in a sweep from the Thames into New Bridge Street and the City beyond.

The lower stages of the building are austere – the rusticated ground floor has no windows, to screen out the traffic on the Victoria Embankment – relieved largely by sculptural accents. Most prominent are W. Reid Dick's dramatically massive pair of horses, one on each end block, which are shown being restrained by muscular figures, female on the Thames front, male over the north entrance. Over the main doors are keystones carved with voluptuous mermaids by Gilbert Ledward. In 1977–83 a refurbishment of the building (by Unilever Engineering Division, advised by Theo Crosby) included piercing the attic floor with windows to create a new storey. In a further major refurbishment, by Kohn Pedersen Fox in 2004–7, the original front entrance on Victoria Embankment was reopened and a striking new central atrium created.

22 BLACKFRIARS BRIDGE

EC4 • Joseph Cubitt and H. Carr 1860–69

As early as the 1830s the structure of the first Blackfriars Bridge, designed by Robert Mylne and opened in 1769, was showing signs of decay. In 1860 the City Corporation decided to replace it with a wrought-iron structure of five spans resting on caissons. It was designed by Joseph Cubitt, the principal engineer of the London, Chatham and Dover Railway, who worked simultaneously on the company's Blackfriars Railway Bridge, opened in 1864. The most striking features of the new bridge are the monumental polished red granite columns attached to the piers. Their Portland stone capitals were carved by John Birnie Philip: those facing west depict plants and birds found on the Thames's upper reaches, and those facing downstream have marine species. The capitals support half-octagonal platforms; the ones at each end of the bridge were intended for equestrian statues but they still remain empty.

Following pages
Looking to the City of London over Blackfriars' Victorian bridges: in the foreground is the road bridge, separated from the railway bridge by the piers that are all that remain of another bridge, which served a long-vanished rail terminus on Ludgate Hill. The photograph was taken before the construction of the new Blackfriars Station on the railway bridge – the first station to span the Thames. In the background the many cranes give a vivid picture of the amount of new building currently underway in the City.

Additional Places to Visit

O a Site of the Mitre Tavern, 37 Fleet Street

A City blue plaque next to Hoare's Bank (p. 38) marks the site of the famous tavern where dramatists and actors, including Shakespeare (1564–1616), Ben Jonson (1572–1637) and many others, drank in the late 16th century; later the great dictionary-maker Dr Johnson (1709–84) and James Boswell (1740–95) established their collaboration there in 1763. The Society of Antiquaries met there regularly from January 1718: the subjects of their discussions included the dilapidation of historic buildings. Opposite, at no. 186 Fleet Street, next to St Dunstan-in-the-West (pp. 38–41), is the reputed site of Sweeney Todd's infamous barber's shop.

O b Walter Crane plasterwork; St Dunstan-in-the-West Garden; John Wilkes

By the back of the bicycle stand outside the former Public Record Office (p. 41), now King's College Library, is a remarkable sequence of panels of the continents of the world (their contents an early attempt at multiculturalism?) in faded yellow and red ochre plaster relief, by Walter Crane (1845–1915). They were taken from the publishers' premises at St Dunstan's House in Fetter Lane, 1886–7, demolished 1976. Nearby, is a small new City garden north of St Dunstan-in-the-West (pp. 38–41) by Bream's Buildings, with the gravestones tastefully rearranged. At the junction of Fetter Lane and New Fetter Lane, there is a commanding statue (1988) of the great radical journalist and political reformer John Wilkes (1725–97) by James Butler (b. 1931), a tribute to 'A Champion of English Freedom'.

O c Fleet Street alleys

There is a series of atmospheric alleys running north of Fleet Street between Fetter Lane and Shoe Lane. A tablet in the floor of Crane Court, the most westerly of them, says that the first daily newspaper, the *Daily Courant*, was produced here on Wednesday, 11 March 1702. The Royal Society met here for over seventy years in the 18th century until 1780, though the Fellows' house by Wren was 'neither large nor handsome'. Nos 5 and 6, reconstructed in 1975, date from *c.* 1670. In no. 9, the early editions of *Punch* were devised, and in no. 10 the *Illustrated London News* began its life. Dr Johnson lived at no. 8 Bolt Court, now burned down, as well as nearby in Johnson's Court (coincidentally named) and Gough Square (p. 47).

O d Resolution

Walking from the west, through contemporary New Street Square, old Gough Square and then Wine Office Court, is a good traffic-free route to this 2007 sculpture by Antony Gormley

(b. 1950) at the corner of Shoe Lane and St Bride Street. It is an almost life-size cast-iron figure, of which Gormley says: 'seen from afar it looks like a man, from close up it looks like a city.'

O e **Edgar Wallace**

Down Shoe Lane to Ludgate Circus, a bronze relief (1934) on the north-west corner of the Circus by F. W. Doyle-Jones (1873–1938) commemorates Edgar Wallace (1875–1932), the journalist and author, best known for his vast output of thrillers, including *The Four Just Men* (1905), and his involvement in the screenplay of *King Kong* (1933), but who is connected with Fleet Street because early in his career he was a newspaper vendor.

O f **Magpie Alley**

On the south side of Fleet Street, in this narrow cut-through off Whitefriars Street, past a tiled display of newspaper history, down a staircase into a basement, is a small glimpse of the old Whitefriars Monastery, the Carmelite Friary founded in the mid-13th century. Like Greyfriars (p. 75), after the monastery was dissolved the buildings were used as a playhouse (1576), outside the City's jurisdiction. What remains is a crypt that was unearthed in 1895, restored in 1920, and moved here in the 1980s when the present building went up to house the late and unlamented *News of the World*. Another leading newspaper, the *Sunday Times*, was first published at nearby no. 4 Salisbury Court on 20 October 1822.

O g **St George and the Dragon**

This large-scale equestrian sculpture and fountain (1988) by Michael Sandle (b. 1936) is in Dorset Rise behind St Bride's Passage, to the west of New Bridge Street. St George's horse is at a steeply raked angle, allowing the saint to thrust his spear into the dragon on the structure below. The sculptor said the pose was not meant to be heroic: 'he's actually working very hard and is a nasty piece of work – a man who could kill a dragon.'

O h **Bridewell Palace**

Near the south end of New Bridge Street, no. 14, the elegant former Bridewell Gatehouse by James Lewis, 1802–8 (see introduction, p. 31), marks the historic site of Henry VIII's Bridewell Palace of 1515–23, later (1553) set up as a combination of hospital, workhouse and prison. A head of King Edward VI is the keystone.

2 St Paul's

Ludgate is the symbolic entrance to the city of King Lud, if he existed – the name probably means 'black gate'. This southerly of the two main westward entrances to the City wall was set about halfway up the hill to St Paul's and survived until 1760. Historically this area was given to religious houses, printing, the trial and imprisonment of criminals and the cathedral of St Paul which, at the time of its foundation in the 660s, looked over largely empty land towards the Anglo-Saxon settlement Lundonwic in the Covent Garden area. The cathedral became part of the trading city: scriveners wrote bills there and people used its transepts as a shortcut, even playing ball inside and shooting birds in the churchyard. Book publishing was concentrated around the churchyard until the Second World War, when the warehouses in Paternoster Row were destroyed in the Blitz.

Bounded by the Thames and Fleet rivers, within the wall, stood the first Baynard's Castle and Montfichet's Tower, the two non-royal Norman castles in the City, both taken down under King Edward I and the land given in 1274 to the Dominicans (Black Friars), who offered their space for meetings of the King's Council. Their church stood on the high ground with a large adjoining cloister. Other monastic buildings terraced down the slope to the Fleet river, where the line of the wall was pushed out. The Wardrobe, commemorated in the name of St Andrew's church, was a royal storehouse for arms and clothing between 1361 and the Great Fire of 1666.

The Dissolution of the monasteries in the 1540s destroyed the friary's physical form but strange traces remain, such as Church Entry, an alleyway that marks the line of the cross passage between the nave and choir. Parts of the friary guesthouse are incorporated in the Apothecaries' Hall, while the marginal character of this corner of London encouraged artisans and, briefly, a theatre in Playhouse Yard – an indoor space where, after 1608, the King's Men (Shakespeare's associates) performed with great success in the winter when the Globe was out of use. This was the only theatre in the City before the actor Bernard Miles opened the Mermaid Theatre nearby at Puddle Dock in 1959. Built in the walls of an old warehouse, its internal form, beneath a single vaulted roof with a simple single rake of seating and a 'thrust' stage projecting into the seating, was novel. It became famous, above all for the annual Christmas production of *Treasure Island*, until rebuilding in the 1990s led to its present conference use.

In 1865 the former monastic territory was cut through by the London, Chatham and Dover Railway, which as Walter Thornbury wrote in 1878 was 'bent on wedding the Metropolitan

Opposite
St Paul's Cathedral, built in 1669–1711, is an enduring symbol of the City of London.

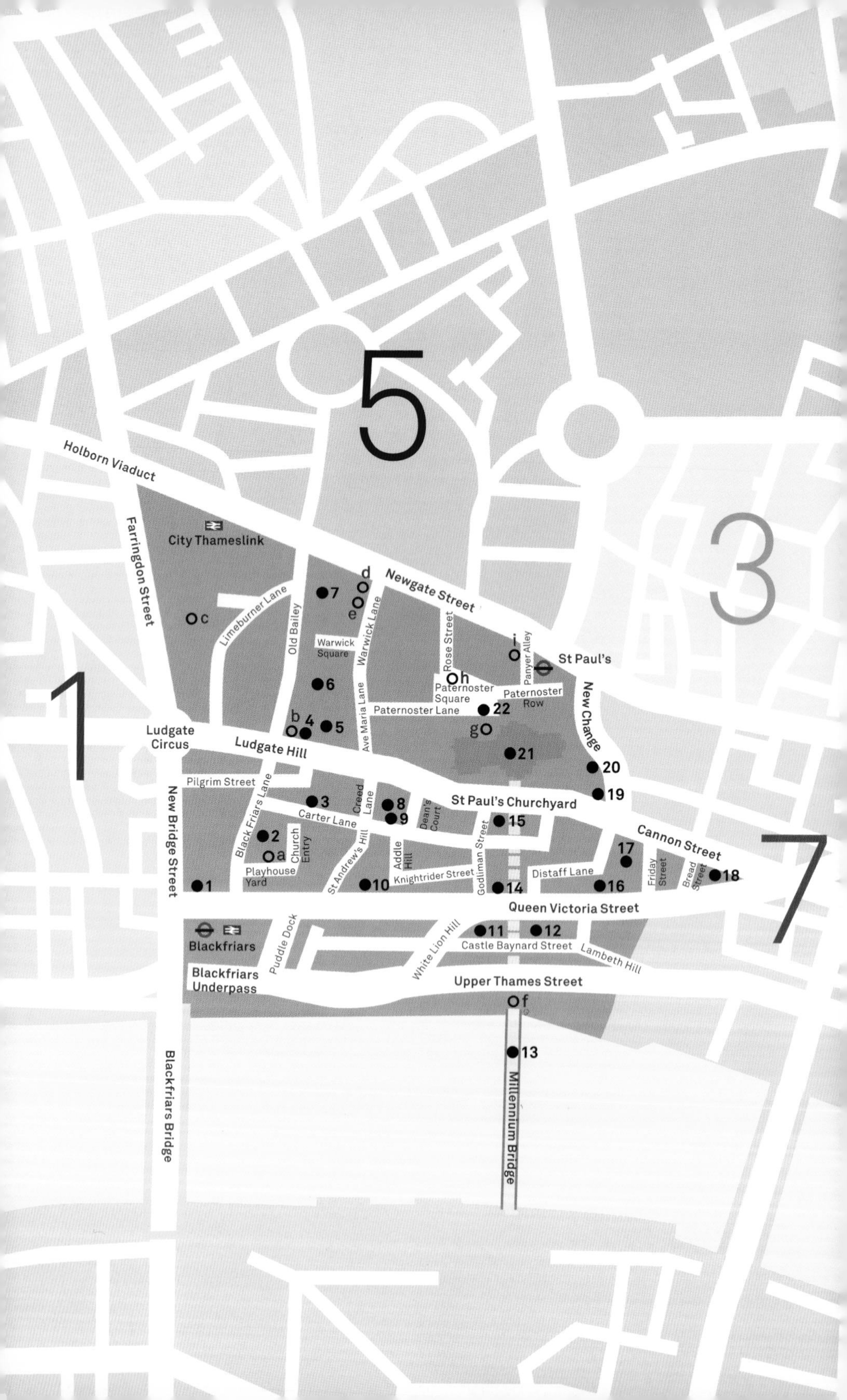

5

3

1

7

Holborn Viaduct

Farringdon Street

City Thameslink

Newgate Street

Limeburner Lane

Old Bailey

Warwick Square

Warwick Lane

Rose Street

Panyer Alley

St Paul's

New Change

Paternoster Square

Paternoster Row

Paternoster Lane

Ave Maria Lane

Ludgate Circus

Ludgate Hill

Pilgrim Street

New Bridge Street

Black Friars Lane

Creed Lane

Carter Lane

Dean's Court

St Paul's Churchyard

Cannon Street

Church Entry

Playhouse Yard

St Andrew's Hill

Addle Hill

Knightrider Street

Godliman Street

Distaff Lane

Friday Street

Bread Street

Queen Victoria Street

Blackfriars

Puddle Dock

White Lion Hill

Castle Baynard Street

Lambeth Hill

Blackfriars Underpass

Upper Thames Street

Blackfriars Bridge

Millennium Bridge

1, 2, 3, 4, 5, 6, 7, 8, 9, 10, 11, 12, 13, 14, 15, 16, 17, 18, 19, 20, 21, 22

a, b, c, d, e, f, g, h, i

KEY TO AREA 2

- ● 1 Black Friar
- ● 2 Apothecaries' Hall
- ● 3 Carter Lane
- ● 4 St Martin Ludgate
- ● 5 Stationers' Hall
- ● 6 Amen Court
- ● 7 Central Criminal Court
- ● 8 St Paul's Deanery (former)
- ● 9 St Paul's Choir School (former)
- ● 10 St Andrew-by-the-Wardrobe
- ● 11 St Benet Paul's Wharf
- ● 12 Salvation Army Headquarters
- ● 13 Millennium Bridge
- ● 14 College of Arms
- ● 15 City of London Information Centre
- ● 16 St Nicholas Cole Abbey
- ● 17 Bracken House
- ● 18 30 Cannon Street/84–94 Queen Victoria Street
- ● 19 Festival Gardens
- ● 20 St Paul's Cathedral School
- ● 21 St Paul's Cathedral
- ● 22 Paternoster Square

- ○ a Playhouse Yard; Wardrobe Place
- ○ b Ludgate
- ○ c Fleet Place
- ○ d Warwick Plaque
- ○ e Cutlers' Hall
- ○ f HSBC Gates; St Lawrence Jewry Fountain
- ○ g St Paul's Churchyard
- ○ h Paternoster
- ○ i Bread Basket Boy

N

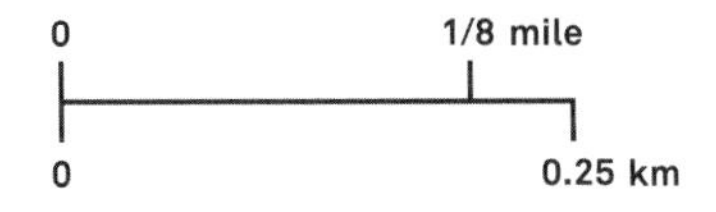

Railway near Smithfield'. The immediate result was the railway viaduct over Ludgate Hill, a structure universally hated. The line was used only for freight between 1916 and 1970, when it closed completely. This was the only railway line connecting north and south and passing through the City, and its potential was finally recognized by the reopening of the Snow Hill tunnel with the creation of Thameslink, including the new City Thameslink station opened in 1990. As part of this work, the despised viaduct went unlamented, and the view up to St Paul's was restored. The decommissioning of Holborn Viaduct Station at the same time opened up development land between Newgate Street and Ludgate Hill.

In 1867–71 Queen Victoria Street was created, slicing through many of the small streets and alleys that went back to the time of King Alfred the Great. It was more than just a road, for beneath it ran the sewerage and other mains services required by a modern city. In the process, the intersection between this diagonal and the mainly north-south existing streets produced many sharp-cornered triangular sites: a challenge to architects then, and again some hundred years later when many came up for redevelopment. Among the successful modern solutions, no. 30 Cannon Street by the architects Whinney, Son & Austen Hall (for Crédit Lyonnais) stands out for creating an elevation system that looks good on both the curve and the straight.

This corner of the City is more tangibly bisected by Upper Thames Street, a historic route that was widened in the 1960s, as the wharves and warehouses began to be replaced by offices, in order to bring four-lane traffic from London Bridge towards Whitehall, with a new approach from Queen Victoria Street making this part of the City the least friendly to the pedestrian or cyclist. Several fine Victorian buildings were lost, while the survivors, including four Wren churches in a line from London Bridge, seem to cling on to the cliff's edge.

In the history of London planning, few sites have been more controversial than the setting of St Paul's. Access to the medieval cathedral was by narrow streets coming into the kite-shaped churchyard, whose effects of surprise we might now admire. After the Great Fire, Wren's plan would have approached the cathedral via a wedge of open space that continued eastwards into Cheapside and Cannon Street. In reality, the cathedral was quite closely surrounded by buildings of no particular note, although none rose higher than its lower cornice.

Whether by accident or as a result of Wren's understanding of picturesque principles, the approach to St Paul's did not lack admirers. The profile of the spire of St Martin Ludgate seems designed to complement St Paul's, although it would be hard to explain why. Arguments over this site revolve around a fundamental divergence in taste. For some, the right answer is always a formal one, with a recognizable pattern of simple geometry, while for others, the accidental charm of a jumble of buildings is preferable. The first has often been conceived as a continental European outlook and the latter typically British: inherently politically and intellectually liberal and closer to nature.

Lud Gate, in its final form, refronted in 1586, wit a triumphal arch inscribed on its upper surface sheltering a statue of Queen Elizabeth I.

Generations of children flocked to Puddle Dock to Bernard Miles's musical adaptation of R. L. Stevenson's *Treasure Island* in the postwar decades.

Opposite
A lithograph by Thomas Shotter Boys, 1842, shows Ludgate Hill in its prime as a street specializing in drapers' shops, hence attracting a female crowd.

WIGS

The plain brick tower of St Andrew-by-the- Wardrobe overlooks the creation of Queen Victoria Street in the 1870s.

The cathedral survived the Blitz substantially intact, due to a mixture of luck and the vigilance of the St Paul's Watch in putting out incendiary bombs, while the surroundings were devastated. Architects from the Royal Academy developed a plan for reshaping London in a series of grand boulevards and traffic roundabouts, seeing this as the opportunity to achieve what Wren could not do after the Great Fire and bring order into chaos. It was not so much that the proposed buildings were substandard classical designs as the lack of understanding of London's hidden and secret nature that repelled the majority of the architectural establishment. Close to St Paul's there was a stronger case for a formal solution, and Sir Albert Richardson tried to persuade the relevant minister, Duncan Sandys, by calling late at his office and demonstrating his ideas with a set of wooden blocks around a cathedral model. William Holford, co-author of the City of London Plan, was of the informal persuasion and doubted whether a Mediterranean-style piazza would work in London. Perhaps he was wrong, although ironically it was the raised piazza he ultimately created in the old Paternoster scheme that seemed to have failed. The realization of Holford's scheme had some fatal flaws typical of its time, with too many dull repetitive buildings that failed to animate the spaces between them, and so it disappeared unlamented in the 1990s, but not without a great deal of controversy over the next move. This time the tables were turned: the moderns were the formalists

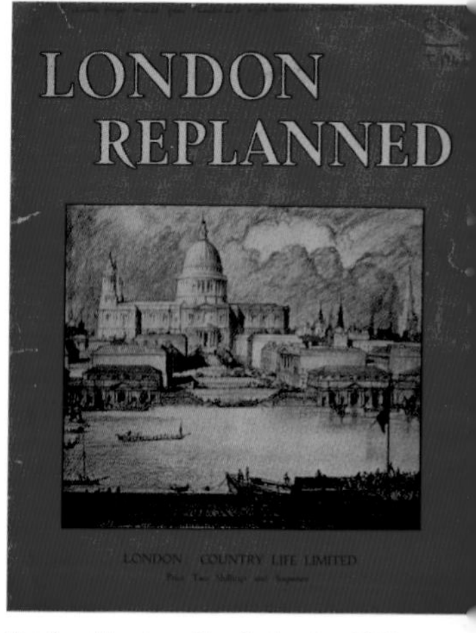

The Royal Academy Plan for London, 1942, offered grandiose visions for the postwar future around St Paul's.

Inspired by Wren, Gibbs and Dance, Mountford's Central Criminal Court is a magnificent piece of architecture as theatre.

(the selected scheme by Arup Associates was a grand crescent) while the opposition, cheered on by the Prince of Wales, offered an informal 'background' solution, as eventually implemented.

St Paul's exercises a wider control over London through the St Paul's Cathedral Preservation Act of 1935 (usually known as 'St Paul's Heights'). The legislation was prompted by Faraday House, an international telephone exchange in Queen Victoria Street, and Unilever House by Blackfriars Bridge, two buildings that breached the previous height limit of 24.4 m (80 ft), as permitted by legislation in 1930. The restrictions still in place are resented by developers but test their ingenuity. The most recent development to submit to their discipline is One New Change by Jean Nouvel which, in its guise as a 'stealth bomber', has tried to make a virtue of the problem.

Trial and punishment belong chiefly in the Old Bailey, built on the site of Newgate Prison, itself the subject of several rebuildings in the quest for security on both sides of its walls. Public executions took place outside the prison between 1783 and 1868. The original Central Criminal Court stood nearby and continues on the Newgate site; the running of the building is financed by the City of London Corporation. Not far away, the Fleet Prison stood on Farringdon Street between 1197 and 1846 in a succession of buildings, one of London's several debtors' prisons so prominent in the fiction of the time. Ludgate was also used as a prison – bringing us back to where we began.

1 BLACK FRIAR

174 Queen Victoria Street EC4 • H. Fuller Clark 1905, 1917–21

This ordinary 1870s Victorian pub was 'themed' into a fantasy of masculine bonhomie in 1905, prompted by the monastery of the Black Friars (Dominicans) that covered much of this area. The landlord, Alfred Pettitt, was responsible for this unaccustomed outburst of aestheticism, aided by the architect H. Fuller Clark, using all the tricks of the Art Nouveau style during its brief heyday. The saloon bar with its domestic inglenook, complete with devils on the andirons and copper bas-reliefs by Frederick Callcott, was extended in 1917–21 with the snack bar section, in the same style, making a cosy room behind the saloon bar, formed beneath the railway arch. Here the sculptor was Henry Poole RA, and the quality of wit rather higher. This is one of the City's stranger experiences, and drinkers may choose between different assessments: 'musty imagination…like a pint of bad bitter' (Ian Nairn) or 'harmless but concentrated profanity' (Andrew Saint).

Details of the Black Friar drawn by Geoffrey Fletcher, a prolific artist who revived interest in the buildings of London.

Conventional above, but Art Nouveau fantasy below, the 'themed' Black Friar is a unique experience among London pubs and a lucky survival.

The Apothecaries' Hall, with carving from 1673, will seat 130 for dinner below the fine collection of portraits.

2 APOTHECARIES' HALL

Black Friars Lane EC4 • Thomas Lock 1668–73

The Worshipful Society of Apothecaries was incorporated in 1617, and in 1632 they bought the former Cobham House here. Built after the Dissolution on the site of the Dominican monastery, the mansion incorporated some of the fabric of the friary guesthouse – this was retained in the Hall, which grew around a courtyard and included the function of a warehouse for medical supplies to the Royal Navy. After the Great Fire, the Hall was rebuilt with a sumptuous staircase and panelling. No famous architects were involved in its construction and alteration over time, but its informality adds to the 'secret world' character of this section of the City between St Paul's and Queen Victoria Street.

The view through the heraldic entrance archway into the light-reflecting courtyard, where the 1780s neo-classical make-over of the Hall elevation fills the far side, is a reminder of the pre-Fire character of London as a city of courtyard complexes, even though almost everything visible is of a later date. To the rear in Playhouse Yard a pleasant open space reveals the functional back wall.

The secret quality of City backstreets is epitomized by the narrow entrance to the Apothecaries' Hall.

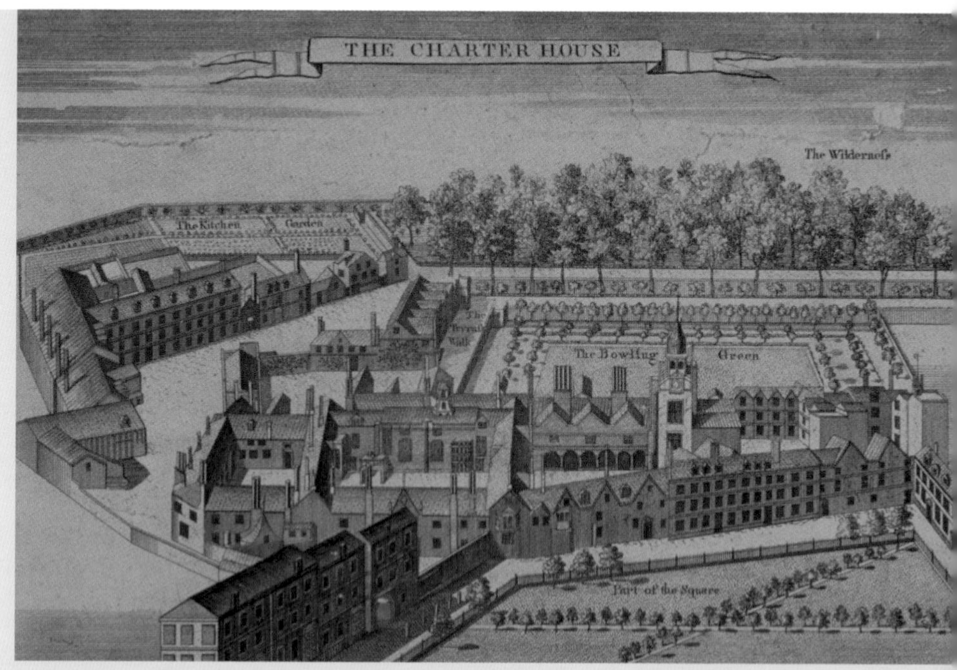

The Charterhouse at Smithfield, just outside the City, still conveys the impression of the many monastic houses lost in the Reformation, whose imprint is still traceable.

RELIGIOUS ORDERS

With Roman social stability a dwindling memory in Western Europe, the rule of St Benedict, composed at Monte Cassino *c.* 530, called religious men and women to an organized life of piety and seclusion rather than attempting to 'go it alone' as hermits. The consequences shaped the re-emergence of civilization under the Church of Rome. Monks commanded literacy and the collection and development of knowledge and often played significant political roles.

In medieval London, the churches and ancillary buildings of monks, nuns and friars would have been highly conspicuous, interrupting the street plan with their precincts in the same way that we can now sense at Westminster Abbey or around the Charterhouse, just across the City boundary in Islington. The common European pattern was for these to be established beyond the walled enclosure of a city, but in London the intramural ones were largely the earlier foundations. As well as being communities of prayer and learning, some provided practical services in specialized hospitals, notably at St Bartholomew-the-Great and the priory of St Mary of Bethlehem (later known as 'Bedlam', specializing in the care of the insane from 1403 onwards) on the site of Liverpool Street Station.

A romantic reimagining of the Charterhouse before the Reformation.

Friars were inspired by the call of St Francis of Assisi and St Dominic to religious men to go out into the world and save souls

A surviving fragment of the Blackfriars monastic complex in Water Lane, in use in 1830 as a coffin-making workshop.

while also living in a community. They looked for sites close to markets, where there would have been opportunities for street preaching. The Franciscans were at Greyfriars, where the chancel of their church lies under the ruins of Christ Church Newgate Street – the remainder of the site became Christ's Hospital School. When this moved to Horsham in Sussex, the site was divided between St Bartholomew's Hospital and the General Post Office, which also occupied the site of the religious house of St Martin's le Grand, still identifiable by its street name. The Black Friars (Dominicans) are more easily located in terms of modern place names, although there is hardly a visible trace of their presence after 1270 on the plateau above the Fleet river and the Thames, apart from the oddity of the street planning around St Andrew-by-the-Wardrobe and the Apothecaries' Hall.

From the substantial physical presence of religious houses, the Temple Church is the most complete and beautiful survival, while the Austin (Augustinian) Friars' church survives as part of the Dutch church in a street pattern that still feels like a precinct. Great St Helen Bishopsgate is a more substantial survival of a Benedictine nunnery, established in conjunction with an existing parish church. St Bartholomew-the-Great is the other site where, albeit through a substantial amount of late Victorian guesswork, we can still feel what a monastic community on the edge of the City might have been like. With the annual Bartholomew Fair, at the cost of unholy chaos at the door of his church, the prior was able to increase his income.

In the City of London, as elsewhere in Britain, Henry VIII's Dissolution of the monasteries in the 1540s opened up many new property opportunities for wealthy men at court, such as Lord Cobham at Black Friars, who made a house out of the friary guest-house. While a few of the churches survived, most were raided for building stone and their sites built over, or put to a mix of religious and secular uses, as at St Bartholomew's where, alongside its use as a parish church, there was a blacksmith's forge in the north aisle and a carpenter's shop in the sacristy basement, beneath a non-conformist chapel.

3 CARTER LANE
EC4

Carter Lane is a quiet backwater, containing buildings numerous and old enough to evoke the pre-Victorian scale of the City. It owes its survival to a long-standing threat to run a main road along this route, which prevented redevelopment. Carter Lane starts abruptly from a T-junction with Ludgate Broadway and Black Friars Lane that represents its collision with the former precinct of the friary. It bends and narrows as it approaches Creed Lane, and then passes by the former St Paul's Choir School before opening out at the back of the City of London Information Centre, an area recently landscaped.

With the adjacent alleyways, such as the misleadingly named Ludgate Square, it is a favourite for film locations at weekends. The latter recently did duty for a small street in France, complete with French street signs and window displays in the shops, while the remains of set-dressing in prewar style, encountered in the small hours, caused the psychogeographer Iain Sinclair to suspect hallucinations.

Carter Lane in the 1930s, a period that is still evoked by the surviving shopfronts.

Buildings of many periods coming up to the narrow pavement edge in Carter Lane make a perfect scale for a modern pedestrianized city.

4 ST MARTIN LUDGATE

Ludgate Hill EC4 • Sir Christopher Wren and Robert Hooke
1677–86

A 'Wren' church in which Robert Hooke may have played a major role, St Martin's lead spire, with its counter curves and miniature tempietto beneath a tall spike, provides a foil to the west front of St Paul's, as seen in many paintings and photographs. The interior is a Greek cross, with four Corinthian columns supporting a shallow groin vault, approached in an unusual way from the entrance door in the symmetrical south façade, through a narthex in the south aisle. St Martin's escaped air-raid bombing and has a particularly fine panelled gallery across the south side, with carved Ionic doorcases. A large painting of the Ascension by Robert Brown (1720) came from the church of St Mary Magdalen in Old Fish Street, along with other fittings such as the unusual 'bread shelves' for donations from rich parishioners to their poorer neighbours. The church is open during the week and on Sunday is used by a Chinese congregation.

St Martin Ludgate's spire has the upward thrust of a space rocket, appropriate for a building whose design was shared between two architect-astronomers.

Robert Mylne's elegant entrance retains its fine lamps, although the building to the right was replaced in 1885.

5 STATIONERS' HALL

Stationers' Hall Court EC4 • Robert Wapshott 1670–74; Robert Mylne 1800–01

Through the opening beneath the modern building in Ave Maria Lane, the 1799 white stone façade of Robert Mylne's livery hall has a rare elegance that, in the words of the critic Sir John Summerson, shows this Scottish architect, designer of the first Blackfriars Bridge, 'at his neo-classical best'. The balance between ornament and plain surface is beautifully calculated, as in the best silverware of the period.

The remainder of the building complex dates from before and after this date, ranging from the 17th-century storehouse, a detached building backing onto St Martin Ludgate, to post-bombing repairs. The interior of the livery hall is of 1670–74, with an ebullient carved screen belying the exterior sobriety. The Court Room was faithfully reconstructed in 1957 on the lines of the original of two hundred years before, with an unusual outburst of rococo ornament, carved and gilded.

Woodwork in the livery hall of the Stationers predates the external architecture by 130 years.

A glimpse of green peace behind the gateway to Amen Court, for many years the London home of the Oxford University Press.

6 AMEN COURT

EC4

Amen Court, off Warwick Lane, mixes periods and styles in a quiet enclave that forms an outlying property of St Paul's. First in date, reached through a pair of brick gate piers with stone balls, are nos 1–3, built in 1671–3 for canons of the cathedral in the simple redbrick style of the time. The roadway returns in a U-shape past another south-facing row of houses in the 19th-century 'Queen Anne' style (much more elaborate than the original) by Ewan Christian, with shell-headed doorcases and a gatehouse and the present Deanery (no. 9) facing outwards to the world.

Fronting Warwick Lane between the two entrances is Amen Lodge, a block of 1960s flats by Norman Bailey & Partners that seems intrusive but has an elegance not unworthy of the setting – a reproof to many more recent buildings in the City.

A scene fit for a rural cathedral close: Canons' houses in Amen Court.

7 CENTRAL CRIMINAL COURT ➲

Old Bailey EC4 • E. W. Mountford 1900–07; McMorran & Whitby 1966–72

The prolific architect E. W. Mountford designed an ebullient building to cap the corner where Newgate Prison (the master-piece of George Dance the Younger) formerly stood with carved

THE LAW OF THE WISE IS A FOUNTAIN OF LIFE

manacles and chains, and grim, windowless rustication. The serpentine curve of the north elevation contributes a Baroque sense of movement, with a granite podium reminiscent of Dance's much-lamented design. The use of the grand order and the domed tower are a respectful tribute to Wren and Hawksmoor's Royal Naval Hospital at Greenwich, then considered the epitome of Englishness. The Great Hall inside, rarely seen by the public, is one of the great Edwardian spaces, decorated with murals and decorative sculpture, while the figure of Justice on the dome (sculptor F. W. Pomeroy) is a landmark on the City skyline.

In 1966 the architects McMorran & Whitby began the southward extension of Mountford's building. Although out of step with the fashions of its time, it can now be seen as a forerunner of the more subtle kind of Postmodernism that derived from attempts by the American Louis Kahn to give back to architecture a sense of physical and moral weight by using massive materials – in this case Portland stone to the front with brick behind.

The Central Criminal Court Extension by McMorran & Whitby, completed in 1972, is one of the great modern buildings of the City, continuing classicism in a new way.

8 ST PAUL'S DEANERY (*former*)

Dean's Court EC4 • Sir Christopher Wren 1672

Glimpsed through the twin openings in a tall brick wall, where stone pineapples top the gate piers, the former St Paul's Deanery presents an image of Church of England moderation to the world. Designed by Wren's masons, if not by Wren himself, it is a medium-sized house of 1672 with a carved doorcase and two-tone red brickwork, beneath a timber cornice and slate roof with dormers – a perfect example of its type. The large sash windows are dominant in the north-facing entrance front. Inside, the plan is informal and the detailing sober. The most famous Dean of St Paul's was the 17th-century poet John Donne ('send not to know for whom the bell tolls'), who lived in the former house on the site. Having ceased to be the Dean's residence in 1981, it subsequently became the palace of the Bishop of London in 1996, when the current Bishop, Richard Chartres, moved in.

The delightful cobbled and paved Deanery courtyard is overhung by plane trees.

Opposite
The 'salle des pas perdus' of the Central Criminal Court displays Edwardian mural painting and sculpture as an architectural unity.

9 ST PAUL'S CHOIR SCHOOL (*former*)
Carter Lane EC4 • F. C. Penrose 1874–5

If F. C. Penrose failed to create great architecture, he succeeded in making excellent street decoration.

This is a demonstration by F. C. Penrose, a passionate advocate of classicism in a cold climate, that the Victorians could do 'delight' as well as 'commodity and firmness'. Beside the Old Deanery, the two-tone brick and stone elevations are enlivened by decorative panels on the ground floor and a frieze of Latin lettering created using Italian Renaissance sgraffito. This was a favourite technique of Prince Albert's architects who created the cultural quarter of South Kensington, evoking some princely palace in Ferrara.

It is hard now to believe that this building was threatened by a road-widening scheme, which resulted in the construction of the new choir school in the 1960s. Used as a youth hostel since 1975, it provides a focus for one of the City's most delightful hidden networks of streets, shops and restaurants.

10 ST ANDREW-BY-THE-WARDROBE
Queen Victoria Street EC4 • Sir Christopher Wren 1685–94; Marshall Sisson 1959–61

The approach to St Andrew's along Knightrider Street provides a wonderful moment of transparency, with east and west windows in alignment. The church offers a convenient daytime shortcut beneath its tower between a 17th-century sense of enclosure to the north and bleak 20th-century open spaces to the south, where it hangs on a cliff edge over Queen Victoria Street, with its churchyard acting as a terrace.

The exterior is a plain brick box, with a barrel-vaulted nave supported on square piers – suggestive of neo-classicism

In a context changed by new roads, St Andrew-by-the-Wardrobe is one of Wren's plainer churches but enjoys a fine elevated site.

a hundred years later. It was bombed then coolly but sensitively restored by Marshall Sisson in fudge-coloured oak, with a practical subdivision of the space. The west window is a Baroque depiction of the conversion of St Paul by Joshua Price, *c.* 1712–16 after Sebastiano Ricci, of the kind that should have been installed in all Wren's churches but was not, owing to suspicion of papism. It came from Bulstrode Park, Buckinghamshire.

11 ST BENET PAUL'S WHARF

Queen Victoria Street EC4 • Sir Christopher Wren and Robert Hooke 1678–84

Robert Hooke's unostentatious brick church (generically Wren, but the work of his lesser-known scientific associate) stands exposed like a chess piece on a sloping board between Queen Victoria Street and the Thames, longing for some sympathetic company. It is worth catching its Sunday service opening times to enjoy one of the few post-Fire interiors that was neither heavily Victorianized nor bombed and that retains all the dignified trappings of a Restoration City church, with a richly carved communion table instead of an altar, a reredos inscribed with the Ten Commandments, Creed and Lord's Prayer, the vigorous painted royal arms over the inner door, and the delicate marble font.

The College of Arms has been associated with St Benet since 1555. In 1879 the church was redundant and adopted by Welsh Anglicans. Services are in the Welsh language, as noted in a rusty enamel sign with a pointing finger on the outside.

St Benet has one of the handful of Wren interiors that escaped both intrusive Victorian restoration and the Blitz.

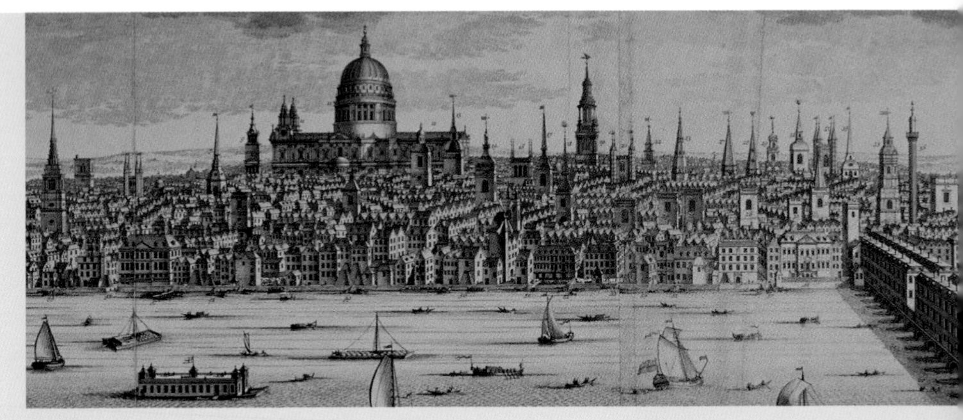

By 1710, London displayed the invention of Wren and his colleagues, rising in white Portland stone above the tiled house roofs.

THE CITY CHURCHES

In the Great Fire of 1666, 85 of the 107 parish churches crowded into the City were burned. These churches were not simply places of worship but also formed part of the City's system of governance. Physically, they mostly dated from the period after 1100 when London expanded and was largely rebuilt, but their foundation dates, where known, are largely pre-Conquest. The crypts of St Bride Fleet Street (consisting of the original 11th-century church at a lower level rising from the pavement of a Roman riverside villa) and St Mary-le-Bow (dating from the first wave of Norman reconstruction in the 1070s) still give a sense of this deeper past. Some of the pre-Fire survivors (St Bartholomew-the-Great, St Helen Bishopsgate) belonged to religious houses rather than parishes, but survivors in the latter category include an early example, St Ethelburga, and St Giles Cripplegate, right at the end of the Gothic period. Both have been battered by later events and reconstructed. St Katharine Cree is a fascinating piece in the jigsaw from the reign of Charles I, when classical and Gothic came together as a symbol of continuity.

Burnt in the Blitz, the church of St Vedast by Wren was rebuilt by Stephen Dykes Bower in 1953–63 and features practical, non-tarnishing aluminium leaf on the ceiling.

Above ground level, the 24 remaining churches from the 51 rebuilt after the Fire dominate our impression today, and one is seldom more than a few minutes' walk from several of them. These are generically the work of Sir Christopher Wren, who oversaw the work of a team of designers, masons and other craftsmen but may have had less direct contact in some cases than has generally been supposed. The funds came through a coal tax distributed by the Crown, which thus controlled the architectural activities of the parishes.

Three aspects of Wren's churches, each independent of the others, should be highlighted. First, the church plans differ according to the nature of the site and, it seems, the architect's desire to create variations on a theme. Two themes dominate, as in the whole history of Christian architecture: namely the polarity between central planning and longitudinal planning, a drama equally played out in the design of the new St Paul's. Longitudinal was the dominant inheritance, commonly handled by Wren with a series of columns carrying a central barrel vault leading to a short chancel, with galleries over the aisles for the large congregations expected after former parishes were amalgamated. Central plans are most commonly square or nearly so. Altars were never centrally placed (St Stephen Walbrook is a controversial 'retrofit'), but this shape was economical and suited to what Wren called an 'auditory', a Protestant church in which the spoken word was the main medium of worship. It is particularly intriguing when these two genres cross over, as at St Mary-le-Bow, or when the square box becomes a polygon, as in the lost St Benet Fink and St Antholin. At St Mary Abchurch Wren inscribed a circular ceiling within the square, while at Walbrook he 'squared the circle' by managing the transition from a grid of columns to a dome, via a ring of equal arches.

The second aspect is the design of towers and spires. Spires are a Gothic form, unknown in the ancient world and barely attempted in the Renaissance. Early in the rebuilding campaign Wren established a new form of classical spire at St Mary-le-Bow, assembling a hierarchy of forms that play with their own visual logic. Other outstandingly original variants are St Bride and St Vedast, the latter revealing Wren's discovery of the works of Francesco Borromini with the play of concavity. Spires were often added after the completion of the church, as funds became available. Some are of stone and others timber, covered in lead, such as the bell-shaped St Martin Ludgate. Wren seems to have considered how the whole set would look in conjunction, rising above the housetops. Finally, the churches contain wood panelling, carving and ironwork, some of it surviving the Blitz, others part-reconstructed, with the addition of modern stained glass.

The story continues with Hawksmoor's St Mary Woolnoth and George Dance's All Hallows London Wall, both outstanding works spaced fifty years apart in the 18th century, but in Victorian times it becomes a tale of restoration (sometimes tactful, often destructive) and demolition from street-widening, railway works or redundancy combined with financial greed. Before the Blitz, the Wren count had dropped from 51 to 31. Further losses are explained by St Mary Aldermanbury, shipped to Fulton, Missouri, and other churches retained after bombing only in fragmentary or ruined form.

With barely any congregation in the usual sense, the City churches have found roles as weekday places of worship and instruction, including concert programmes. Several have regular Sunday services held by non-English Anglican groups (Welsh at St Benet Paul's Wharf, Chinese at St Martin Ludgate, Indian at St Mary Aldermary). Many have been the starting point for wider missions, notably the Samaritans, founded at St Stephen Walbrook by the Rev. Chad Varah in 1953.

St Stephen Walbrook, designed by Wren in 1672, is modest in scale, despite the grandeur of its interior. It is now dwarfed by surrounding buildings.

As Wren's works returned to favour among the Victorians, they delighted in making encyclopedic drawings of them grouped as if in a museum display.

The Salvation Army building, while lacking nothing in its modernity, shows a rare understanding of contextual design in the way it occupies an important site that sits on the route from the Millennium Bridge to St Paul's.

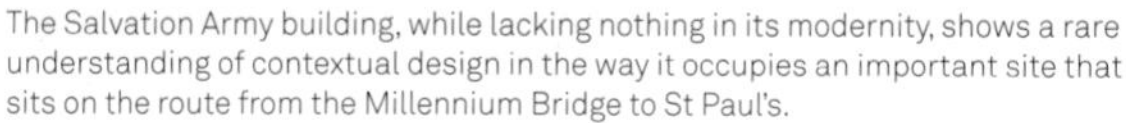

12 SALVATION ARMY HEADQUARTERS

99–101 Queen Victoria Street EC4 • Sheppard Robson 1999–2005

The Salvation Army was founded in the East End of London in 1865 by William and Catherine Booth to help the poor by saving them from drink and the devil. It rapidly grew to become an international organization. In 1881, the 'Sally Army' opened a headquarters in Queen Victoria Street, and the building by Sheppard Robson is their third on the site.

With the initial opening of the Millennium Bridge in 2000, the site gained value and is now shared between the parent organization and other tenants. With its west-facing elevation screened from the sun by sheets of fritted glass, the building is exemplary in many ways. It provides visual interest without losing the legibility of its structure, a white-painted steel frame seen through clear glass on the lower floors. The gospel texts on the window glass remind us of the alignment between the daily life of the City and Christian morality and the commandment to help the less fortunate.

The Millennium Bridge offers views of changing light effects, with river and sky uninterrupted by traffic.

13 MILLENNIUM BRIDGE

EC4 • Foster & Partners with Ove Arup & Partners and Sir Anthony Caro 1996–2001

Walking on air is more easily said than done. The Millennium Bridge, won in competition in 1996 by Foster & Partners, with the sculptor Anthony Caro and the engineers Arup, put the proposition to the test by attempting to create a 'blade of light' at a crossing point long considered an obvious position for an extra bridge aligned to the south transept of St Paul's. The conversion of Bankside Power Station to Tate Modern provided the prompt to create the sole pedestrian-only bridge over the Thames.

Initially, the bridge revealed a tendency to sway under the rhythmic pressure of many feet and had to be closed for re-adjustment, when extra weights were inserted. It has since proved a huge success with Londoners and visitors, and has

provided a vital new route between the South Bank and the City. In engineering terms, it is a flattened suspension bridge, with cables barely higher than the timber deck, held by Y-shaped supports rising from the water.

The Court Room in the College of Arms, with the Earl Marshall's throne and balustrades to keep the crowds at bay.

14 COLLEGE OF ARMS

Queen Victoria Street EC4 • Maurice Emmett Jr 1671–88

'Arms' means 'coats of arms' in a world of specialized language dating from the Middle Ages, now institutionalized in a 'College' that is not, in a conventional sense, a college but is still a place of learning. The quaintly dressed and poetically named heralds ('Rouge Dragon Pursuivant', for example), who appear at royal functions and create 'grants of arms' for a fee, were based in the Blackfriars area even before 1555, when they were given the town mansion of the Earls of Derby. It stood on the site of the present building, which was a reconstruction after the Great Fire with various smaller changes. The fine Baroque iron gates (probably a clever Victorian imitation of the 18th-century style) only arrived in 1956 from Goodrich Court in Herefordshire to create a fitting frontispiece a century after Queen Victoria Street had sliced the fourth side off the original quadrangle.

The College of Arms is a treasured national institution, carrying on a long tradition in the City.

On a typical weekend, the City is thronged with visitors around St Paul's. The City Information Centre is instantly recognizable and welcoming.

15 CITY OF LONDON INFORMATION CENTRE

St Paul's Churchyard EC4 • Make 2004–7

In 2004 the architect Ken Shuttleworth made a noisy departure from Norman Foster & Partners to found a new practice, Make. One of their first projects was small but eye-catching, replacing Sir Albert Richardson's 1951 Information Kiosk on a triangle of land opposite St Paul's, adding to the efforts to make the City a visitor destination.

The tent-like structure seems to grow out of the ground, shaped by the geometry of its site, to create an inviting yellow-lined interior space, offsetting the pointed aggression of the steel-panelled exterior, gently acclimatizing the non-orthogonal style of Daniel Libeskind and Zaha Hadid in heritage land. Rainwater is collected by the roof and used to flush toilets and irrigate the nearby planting. All the furniture was constructed from recycled timber.

The parapet heights of Wren's churches tallied with those of the surrounding non-religious buildings, as this print of 1812 demonstrates.

St Nicholas stands as a shell after bombing. People at the time felt that many churches should remain as ruins, witnesses of the destruction.

16 ST NICHOLAS COLE ABBEY

Queen Victoria Street EC4 • Sir Christopher Wren 1672–8; Arthur Bailey 1961–2

The architect's son, Christopher Wren Jr, wrote of St Nicholas that 'the structure is elegant without great expense and may serve the architect as a model of that kind of building'. The church is named after the Bishop of Myra and the medieval 'Cold Harbour' for travellers, mistranslated into a non-existent abbey. Originally placed in a maze of streets, it now stands exposed to the four-lane traffic of Queen Victoria Street. The church was burnt out in 1941, and the conical lead-covered spire rebuilt taller, but similar to the original design.

One of the main features of the rebuilding is the richly coloured stained-glass window by Keith New (1962), who became famous in the same year for his work at the new Coventry Cathedral. St Nicholas is the subject of radical remodelling proposals by the Culham Institute, promoting religious education in schools.

Michael Hopkins's skilful infill to Bracken House, seen here without its robust postwar classical bookends by Sir Albert Richardson.

17 BRACKEN HOUSE

Cannon Street EC4 • Richardson & Houfe 1955–9; Michael Hopkins & Partners 1988–91

Bracken House, formerly the home of the *Financial Times*, was the first postwar building in the City to be listed. It was subsequently successfully transformed into modern offices.

The *Financial Times* chose the arch-conservative Sir Albert Richardson as their architect on this bombed site. Active in the City before 1914, Richardson here produced the crowning glory of his long career, with elevations combining classical dignity, Baroque swagger, exquisite detail and a few touches of modernity in the glass bricks of the attic storey. The pinkish-red brick and stone were a tribute to the pink paper on which the *FT* is still printed. In the 'astrological clock' over the original main door, modelled by Philip Bentham, the sun has the face of Winston Churchill, who made the political career of the paper's postwar publisher, Brendan Bracken.

In 1987 Bracken House was due for demolition but was saved by becoming the first postwar listed building. A scheme by Michael Hopkins for a Japanese client was revised to become an insertion in place of the original printing works and won universal praise for its combination of bravura, integrity and contextual sensitivity.

18 30 CANNON STREET/84–94 QUEEN VICTORIA STREET

EC4 • Whinney, Son & Austen Hall 1973–7

The former Crédit Lyonnais building shows how a simple architectural idea can be animated by light, shadow and reflections in glass.

This slice of outward-leaning layer cake with crisp white icing is one of the most distinguished office buildings of the 1970s, created for the Crédit Lyonnais, whose influence may have added a touch of French élan. The arches over each bay were carefully modelled with sculptural curves in a new material, cast glass-fibre reinforced concrete that gave extra strength for their fine profiles. Black bands at each floor level add to the effect of weightlessness.

The new roads such as Queen Victoria Street that were pushed through the City in the 1860s produced many such 'flatiron' sites when they met the earlier street grid, in this case Cannon Street. Each generation brought its own solution (or non-solution) to the design problem. This is a clever one, because the close rhythm of the bays and their inherent curves allows them to bend, apparently without effort, round the corner. Even with today's computer modelling this would be a struggle to get right.

19 FESTIVAL GARDENS

Cannon Street EC4 • Sir Albert Richardson 1951

The aerial view of Festival Gardens from the adjacent church tower, taken in the 1960s, reminds us how much public space in the City has been reclaimed from roads since the war.

In 1951, Blitz-weary London was benignly reignited by the Festival of Britain, whose main focus was the South Bank exhibition. The City's contribution was modest, including this small sunken garden in a former bombsite to the south-east of St Paul's that gives daily pleasure to many workers and passers-by. It was designed by Sir Albert Richardson, a defender of traditional architecture, within sight of his late masterpiece, Bracken House. His Information Kiosk, a temporary circular building only recently replaced, stood nearby before being moved in 1956.

To compete with Wren's cathedral would have been absurd, and Richardson provided a tactfully understated frame for plants and people, with a sunken lawn and a raised paved terrace around it. The water jets falling into a rectangular basin, with ramped Portland stone parapets, provide sparkle and movement against a wall of frosted rustication. Above this a semi-circular stone bench forms a background for *The Young Lovers*, a bronze (1973) by Georg Ehrlich. With the removal of the adjacent coach park from the south of St Paul's Cathedral, and subsequent landscaping, this area will receive another new lease of life.

20 ST PAUL'S CATHEDRAL SCHOOL

2 New Change EC4 • Architects' Co-Partnership 1962–7

Who dares to build in the shadow of St Paul's? The enigmatic volumes of the 1960s choir school, forming a set of courtyards attached to the former tower of St Augustine Watling Street

The Festival Gardens are ideally placed for catching the afternoon sun, refracted in the moving water of the French-style fountain wall.

by Wren, were a controversial enterprise that signalled a new stage of acceptance for modern architecture in ancient institutions. A neo-Georgian scheme by the cathedral architects Seely & Paget was rejected after public controversy with a call for something new. A competition in 1962 was won by Architects' Co-Partnership, a left-leaning firm that combined a specialism in schools with a growing expertise in working within historical settings. The roach bed Portland stone with its prominent fossils was combined with a lead top storey to echo the materials of its towering neighbour.

Ian Nairn described the blocky pavilions as 'a tough-minded set of square mushrooms determined not to be diverted by the cathedral's rollicking ornament suspended so far above them' and 'over-serious in the way that a really responsible civil-servant can be.'

Cavalier and Puritan juxtaposed at the east end of St Paul's in a perennial cultural conflict.

21 ST PAUL'S CATHEDRAL

St Paul's Churchyard EC4 • Sir Christopher Wren 1669–1711

The architectural problem of fitting a drum sha on a rectangular base was solved by Wren both inside and outside St Paul's.

Nothing substantial remains now of old St Paul's Cathedral, but it survived into the age of accurate drawing and recording. It was of prodigious size, with a Gothic nave 30.5 m (100 ft) wide and longer than any other English cathedral. The spire, built in 1315, was of commensurate height but vulnerable to lightning strikes, so that from 1561 it remained incomplete. The decline of the building during the Reformation was reversed in part during Charles I's reign with a grand Corinthian portico added to the west end by Inigo Jones. From 1660, with a new Stuart king, the state of St Paul's was again an anxiety. Christopher Wren, having visited Paris where domed churches were a new experimental form of architecture, proposed the addition of a dome on top of the old piers at the crossing, surprisingly similar to the one he eventually built, after the Great Fire overtook this makeover project.

Many lucky coincidences helped to make St Paul's the great building of its age. Most of these lay in the personality of the architect, Sir Christopher Wren. He was the right age and stood high in royal and ecclesiastical favour. As a designer, he was scarcely less a professional than anyone else in the country, given the fluid definition of architect, and he was able to build up his skills before the design was finalized and constructed. He lived long enough, and was sufficiently resistant to the appalling treatment he received from his client body in later years, to enable his project to be seen to completion. He was also able to bring together a reliable team of highly skilled craftsmen.

Wren never saw the choir of St Paul's open as it is today, with the controversial 1890s mosaics b Sir William Blake Richmond in the vaults above.

Wren's training in mathematics showed in his logical and geometrical approach, and a sequence of drawings, plus the wonderful timber 'Great Model', allow us to follow the stages through which he took the project. The 'Great Model' represented an extreme solution, virtually a circular building with only a short gesture towards a separate nave. The shape provided a suitable base for raising a dome, in which the intention was always to rival St Peter's in Rome, a building that Wren never saw.

When the conservatism of the clergy made this solution impossible, Wren began to confront the problem of putting a tall enough dome on to the crossing of the nave and transepts formed in what was essentially a Gothic cruciform plan. The solution involved a number of deceits, including the triple-layered structure with its brick cone bearing the main weight and stability of the stone lantern at the top, an outer dome for external show, raised on a ring of columns, and, inside the cone, two smaller domes, one glimpsed through the oculus of the other, that appear to be optically the right size from the floor. All this can be discovered in the unforgettable experience of climbing up to the 'Golden Gallery' of the lantern. Stability was managed with timber bracing combined with iron chains holding in the structure's tendency to spread.

Flying buttresses, the Gothic solution to counteracting the thrust of a vault, were not in the classical vocabulary, but Wren

Sir James Thornhill's painted dome soars into poetry as it rises into a second dome with more fictive architectural ornament.

used them and raised the side walls of the cathedral to become a screen that looks like an upper storey, a deceit which for some architects and critics is unforgivable. It gave the advantage, however, of projecting the body of the cathedral above the surrounding buildings, which came, as it were, only to waist height. There is consequently a discrepancy between the inside and outside. The design is not only about engineering, however, and Wren had sound judgment about how things would look in the foreshortened view from the ground as well as from a distance.

The west front follows the two-storey pattern, flanked by the towers with their joyful belfry stages and domes. The interior marches regularly to the epiphany of the crossing and dome with its paintings by Sir James Thornhill, and then into the choir, with its late 19th-century mosaics and baldacchino over the high altar, designed with skill and appropriateness by Stephen Dykes Bower, completed in 1958 to replace a Victorian reredos after some bomb damage. To either side are the iron screens by Jean Tijou, contemporary with the building, and the exquisite carving of Grinling Gibbons on the choir stalls.

The hands of many ages have left their traces, but in the early 21st century St Paul's is looking exceptionally well kept, with some decluttering and cleaning of all the surfaces for the 300th anniversary of the completion in 2010. It deserves a visit of several hours to appreciate the monuments and other works of art.

Opposite
The new buildings of Paternoster Square have restored the amenity of this area with a car-fr set of squares and alleyways. The reinstated o Temple Bar can just be seen in the bottom left hand corner (see also pp. 32–3).

22 PATERNOSTER SQUARE

EC4 • Sir William Whitfield (masterplan) 1996–2000

The buildings surrounding the central square and alleyways leading in and out to the north of St Paul's are serenely somnolent, like the piazza of one of Mussolini's new towns, but metaphorically pockmarked from guerrilla skirmishes of two 'style wars'. The original Paternoster area was home to publishers' warehouses, all of which were destroyed in the Blitz, but it was after 1945 that the 'style wars' began.

In the first, between 1945 and 1965, the victory was to the Moderns. William Holford planned a quasi-picturesque jumble of smaller buildings, raised on a car park to provide a paved area for office workers to eat their lunches. Grubby and unfashionable, it went with few regrets, but the selected replacement in 1987 by Arup Associates was noisily displaced by a classical scheme. Recession and ownership changes prolonged the completion to around 2000 of William Whitfield's masterplan, including his own Mannerist classical Juxon House part-framing the cathedral. Individual buildings completed by 2003 include St Martin's Court (Allies & Morrison), King Edward Court (Eric Parry), Building Six, Juxon House, One Paternoster Row (Whitfield & Partners with Sidell Gibson) and the Column monument (Whitfield & Partners).

Left
Approximately the same vie as the one opposite, looking towards the Central Crimina Court in Old Bailey from the top of St Paul's Cathedral, photographed in 1942 after buildings damaged in the Blitz had been cleared. The circular shapes are water dams for firefighting. The shell of Christ Church Newgate Street can be seen on the right.

Additional Places to Visit

O a Playhouse Yard; Wardrobe Place

Apart from the name, there is not much sign that this was the site of a theatre established by Richard Burbage (1568–1619), which was built in the remains of the former Blackfriars Monastery (because it was thus outside the City's jurisdiction). The nave area of the old church of St Anne Blackfriars is a small square accessed by the aptly named Church Entry. Shakespeare bought a house in Ireland Yard in 1612 (the signed deed is in Guildhall Library) but he rarely lived there. Across St Andrews Hill, below Carter Lane (p. 76), is the secluded Wardrobe Place, named after the King's Wardrobe, which was kept here until 1666: a blue plaque on no. 5 marks the site.

O b Ludgate

A plaque on St Martin Ludgate (p. 77) marks the site of the Roman or pre-Roman entrance to the City (see introduction, p. 65). It was demolished in 1760 but statues from it are preserved at St Dunstan-in-the-West (pp. 38–41): Queen Elizabeth I is well kept but King Lud and his two sons in the vestry porch look less loved.

O c Fleet Place

Further north, the large 1990s office development behind the unappealing City Thameslink station in Newgate Street has created a fine open space, which houses works of art including Stephen Cox's (b. 1946) pair of grey abstract torsos, *Echo* (1993). This can be reached from Bishop's Court off Old Bailey, next to a good fountain. No. 5 Fleet Place (access also from Farringdon Street) marks the Congregational Memorial Hall where the Labour Party was founded in 1900.

O d Warwick Plaque

A curiosity from 1668: a stone tablet of a knight in armour with his shield, restored in 1817 and currently mounted on the corner of Warwick Lane and Newgate Street. Turn into Warwick Square below Cutlers' Hall, and in the corner (by the back entrance to the Central Criminal Court) there is a peculiar fragmentary colonnade in an attractively quiet garden.

O e Cutlers' Hall

The brick exterior of this livery hall in Warwick Lane, by Tayler Smith, 1886–7, has a fascinating and detailed terracotta frieze by Benjamin Creswick (1853–1946), a protégé of John Ruskin, showing the manufacture of cutlery. It is echoed in the present-day decoration of no. 1 Poultry (p. 292).

O f **HSBC Gates; St Lawrence Jewry Fountain**

Approaching St Paul's from Millennium Bridge (pp. 87–8), there are two pairs of stainless steel portals by Anthony Caro (b. 1924), assisted by Gavin Morris, from 1999–2000; they lead directly to the south of the Cathedral and the City of London Information Centre (p. 89). The St Lawrence Jewry Memorial Fountain, once in Guildhall Yard, has now been restored to hygienic working order and placed at the top of Old Change Place: the site of Old Change, 'a City street dating from 1293', is marked on the side of the Festival Gardens' fountain (p. 92).

O g **St Paul's Churchyard**

In the garden area north of the Cathedral, stands a statue of John Wesley (1703–91), from 1988, re-cast from the original of 1825 by the Mannings, father and son. Close to Wesley's statue is a simple low circular *Memorial to the Londoners killed in World War II Bombardments* (1999), by Richard Kindersley, inscribed 'Remember before God the people of London'. To the east, the large St Paul's Cross of 1910, a commemoration of the old cross, as an inscription records, 'whereat amid such scenes of good and evil as make up human affairs, the conscience of church and nation through five centuries found public utterance'. On the south-east side is a powerful statue from 1971 of Thomas Becket (*c.* 1118–70) at the moment of his death in Canterbury Cathedral, by Bainbridge Copnall (1903–72), perhaps inspired by the dramatization of the event in T. S. Eliot's *Murder in the Cathedral* (1935). On the south-west, the foundations of the old Cathedral Chapter House have been recreated and set into the pavement.

O h **Paternoster**

This sculpture in Paternoster Square (p. 96) by Elisabeth Frink (1930–93) of Christ as a shepherd guarding his flock was made in 1975 and unveiled by the distinguished violinist Yehudi Menuhin. While Paternoster Square was redeveloped it was moved to near the Museum of London, and restored to the newly rebuilt square in 2003.

O i **Bread Basket Boy**

Just by St Paul's Tube station on the wall of Panyer Alley, is a stone tablet of a little naked boy with the inscription 'When ye have sought the Citty round/Yet still this is the highest ground' and the date 27 August 1688. Though the statue was originally in Paternoster Row, in fact the highest City spot is apparently in Cornhill.

3

Guildhall

This block of streets, marked out firmly in the north by the modern London Wall and in the south by ancient Cheapside, is the heart of the Square Mile. While the financial core, with its bristle of tall buildings, has drifted south-east from here over the centuries, the medieval Guildhall and its yard remain the seat of government in the City. With the Great Fire having destroyed all but a couple of tiny corners to the north-east and north-west of this area, Guildhall itself is one of the few tangible reminders of the medieval City here, beyond street names and plan. The pattern of the Blitz, fierce in the north-west towards the Barbican and mild in the south-east towards the Bank, has also left its mark in the varied street scene that shifts markedly from one to the other, as shiny 21st-century offices by the likes of Lords Foster and Rogers give way to a smaller-scaled Victorian City of brick and stone, with here and there a hardy little survivor of the 17th or 18th century.

Guildhall Yard is also the ancient centre of this area. It was always thought that Roman London must have had an amphitheatre, the 'circuses' to go with the 'bread' of the forum that lies beneath Gracechurch Street. Walls of the forum were found in the mid-19th century, but it was barely twenty years ago that the 1st-century AD amphitheatre (rebuilt in the 2nd) finally turned up – right under Guildhall Yard, as foundations were being dug for the new Guildhall Art Gallery. This only confirmed the vibrancy of this area in Roman times, already suggested by the quantity of 2nd-century remains thrown up every time new foundations are sunk.

After the Romans left in the 5th century it has been mooted that the Anglo-Saxon King Offa had a palace and chapel here in the late 8th century, its chapel marked now by the tower of St Alban Wood Street, but the most significant event in the early Middle Ages was the establishment of Guildhall in the 12th century as the home of the City's government, the City of London Corporation. A yard began to grow south of the hall in the 13th century, with chapel and gatehouse. The fact that the latter was built on the foundation of the Roman amphitheatre's south entrance, and the offsetting of the site of St Lawrence Jewry beside it, may suggest that the yard's position is owed to the amphitheatre – the Romans cast a long shadow. The key period for Guildhall was the 15th century, when the present hall was built along with the lost library, gatehouse and Mayor's Court. The presence here of the City's government influenced the livery companies in their choice of sites for their halls nearby. The Goldsmiths were here by 1339, Armourers and Brasiers by 1346, Saddlers by 1395, Brewers by 1403, Grocers by 1426,

Opposite
George Dance the Younger's four-storey porch of 1788–9 dominates the façade of the medieval Guildhall.

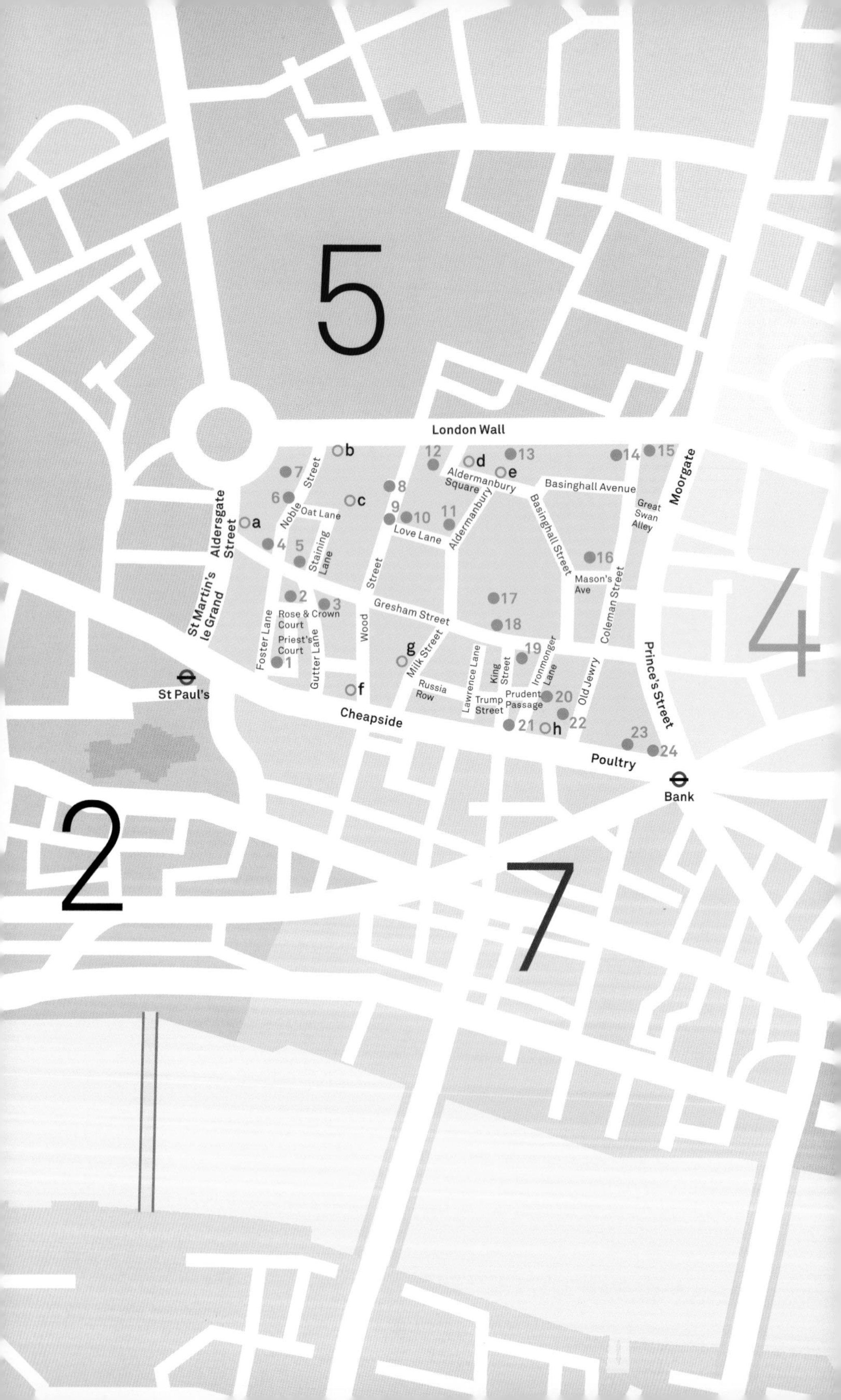

5

4

2

7

London Wall
Aldersgate Street
St Martin's le Grand
Noble Street
Oat Lane
Staining Lane
Wood Street
Love Lane
Aldermanbury Square
Aldermanbury
Basinghall Avenue
Basinghall Street
Great Swan Alley
Moorgate
Mason's Ave
Coleman Street
Gresham Street
Rose & Crown Court
Priest's Court
Foster Lane
Gutter Lane
Milk Street
Russia Row
Lawrence Lane
King Street
Trump Street
Prudent Passage
Ironmonger Lane
Old Jewry
Prince's Street
Cheapside
Poultry
St Paul's
Bank

a b c d e f g h

1 2 3 4 5 6 7 8 9 10 11 12 13 14 15 16 17 18 19 20 21 22 23 24

KEY TO AREA 3

- 1 St Vedast
- 2 Goldsmiths' Hall
- 3 Wax Chandlers' Hall
- 4 St Anne and St Agnes
- 5 No. 25 Gresham Street
- 6 Roman wall
- 7 One London Wall & Plaisterers' Hall
- 8 No. 88 Wood Street
- 9 St Alban Wood Street
- 10 Wood Street Police Station
- 11 St Mary Aldermanbury
- 12 No. 5 Aldermanbury Square
- 13 City Place House
- 14 One Coleman Street
- 15 Armourers' Hall
- 16 Woolgate Exchange
- 17 Guildhall Complex
- 18 St Lawrence Jewry
- 19 Nos 42–44 Gresham Street
- 20 St Olave Jewry
- 21 No. 3 King Street/92 Cheapside
- 22 Frederick's Place
- 23 Midland Bank Headquarters (former)
- 24 National Westminster Bank

- a Aldersgate
- b St Olave Silver Street
- c St Mary Staining Garden
- d Aldermanbury Square
- e Aldermanbury Garden
- f Wood Street
- g Milk Street; St Olave's Court; Old Jewry
- h Thomas Becket

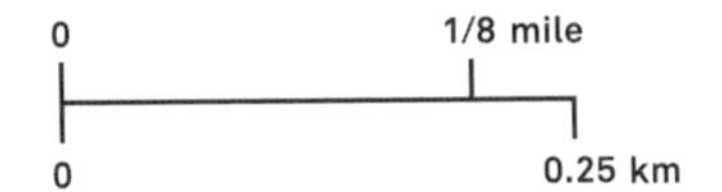

Girdlers by 1431, Mercers by 1524 and Wax Chandlers by 1525. Many more were here, but these are the halls that are still on their original sites in this area, even though the Great Fire or Blitz or both have deprived them all of their medieval buildings.

This was also the area for shopping in the Middle Ages. Great, wide Cheapside ('cheap' or 'chepe' means market) was by the 12th century, as it remains, the main retail street in the City, with the specialized stalls recalled in the names of the streets off it – Milk, Poultry (plus Honey Lane to the north, Bread Street and Friday Street – referring to the Fish market – to the south). Other names reflect local industries and associations: Ironmonger Lane, Coleman Street for the charcoal burners, Wood Street. Old Jewry was home to the synagogue until the expulsion of the Jews in 1290.

By the time of the Great Fire, the Guildhall area was a tinderbox of narrow streets and closes lined with timber-framed houses, and the fire thundered through it, reducing even the stone buildings – with the exception of Guildhall (although it lost its roof) – to rubble. Wren's grand plan for wide, continental boulevards to replace the maze was too radical, too complicated and too expensive for all the landowners to agree. King Street, part of a grand processional route from the river to Guildhall, was the only major new road. This conservatism means that today even a street such as Milk Street, entirely lined with shiny offices barely a decade old, keeps to a street line laid down at

King Street, seen here around 1840 in a watercolour by T. H. Shepherd, built as part of a processional approach to Guildhall. It was one of the few grand new streets created in the City after the Great Fire.

Cheapside, seen here from the west end near St Paul's in 1890, is still the City's main shopping street, as it has been since the 12th century.

least 850 years ago. Elsewhere though, surviving alleyways and courts also preserve some of the atmosphere and scale of the pre-Fire City. Between Foster Lane and Gutter Lane run narrow Priest's Court and Rose and Crown Court, their modest doorway entrances easily missed. On the east side of the area the paved alley of Mason's Avenue runs all the way between Moorgate and Basinghall Street. Although it ends there in preposterous 1920s Hollywood-Tudor, the street itself goes back at least to the 1540s.

Wren may not have got his way here over planning the post-Fire City, but ten churches were rebuilt to his or his office's designs. None survives unscathed, though three were restored after the Blitz (St Lawrence Jewry, St Anne and St Agnes, and St Vedast) and two survive as towers (St Alban and St Olave Jewry) while one has emigrated to the United States (St Mary Aldermanbury). Many other churches were not rebuilt, such as St Peter Cheap at the bottom of Wood Street, now marked by a sheltered garden with impressive railings of 1712 and a huge, ancient plane tree. This is separated from Cheapside by the tiny (refronted) shops at nos 123–126 Cheapside, just one room with another above, a rare late 17th-century survivor.

Although Guildhall itself acquired its 'Hindoo-Gothic' porch in 1788–9, 18th-century survivals in this area are rare – houses at nos 58 and 80 Coleman Street, Thomas Fletcher's 1768 home and counting-house at no. 11 Ironmonger Lane and,

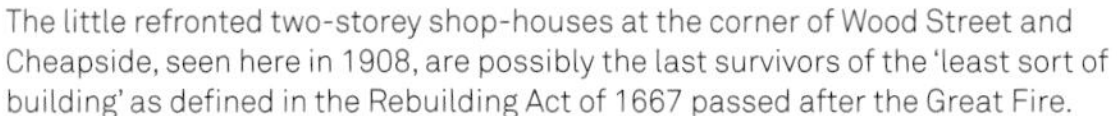
The little refronted two-storey shop-houses at the corner of Wood Street and Cheapside, seen here in 1908, are possibly the last survivors of the 'least sort of building' as defined in the Rebuilding Act of 1667 passed after the Great Fire.

Goldsmiths' Hall, seen in 1942, sits among the ruins of Gresham Street after the firestorm of December 1940. In front is what became Goldsmiths' Garden, and next to it the surviving ground floor of Wax Chandlers' Hall.

outstandingly, the Adam brothers' development in Frederick's Place. Major development had to wait until the 19th century when the southern half of present-day Moorgate was created in the 1830s. Originally lined with continuous stuccoed terraces, the only survivors now are the block at the west side adjoining London Wall. But soon a grander scale of office building became the norm as the commercial City grew. Gresham Street was a new street of the 1840s made up from existing narrower streets. The eastern half, spared by the Blitz, retains buildings and character from the mid- to late 19th century (e.g. nos 42–48), as does the far west end next to St Anne and St Agnes (nos 1–7). Typically, office buildings of this period are of brick and stone, sometimes stuccoed, four or five storeys, with plenty of variety and decoration, but all notable for continuous bands of windows where the divisions become narrower so the effect is of a glassy grid. Of livery halls, the Grocers' off Prince's Street retains a Dutch-style brick and stone frontage from the 1890s.

Little from the interwar period has survived the Blitz or fashion's short attention span. The major survivors are the big Midland and NatWest banks, but also notable is Sylvester Sullivan's former Courtauld warehouse at no. 16 St Martin's le Grand, in the super-sharp neo-Greek of the 1920s, almost Art Deco. The devastation of the north-west half of this area in the

The 15th-century Guildhall with its late 18th-century 'Hindoo-Gothic' porch and 1960s glazed cloister.

Blitz of 1940 and 1941 means that most of what we see today is less than half a century old, some of it much newer as rebuilding took place in two waves. The many livery halls burnt out were mostly rebuilt in an underfed neo-Georgian style: Brewers', Wax Chandlers', Girdlers', Saddlers' and Mercers', the last a feeble imitation of Lutyens's almost-adjoining Midland Bank. While many burnt-out buildings – Guildhall itself and several Wren churches – were restored, others became welcome garden spaces, including St John Zachary in front of Goldsmiths' Hall, whose ruin was first made into a garden by firewatchers in 1941. In the 1950s came the wholesale rebuilding scheme of London Wall with its slab blocks and towers, and a series of rather similar office blocks, meekly modern grid-like frontages faced with Portland stone, along the worst-hit streets such as Noble Street, Foster Lane, Gresham Street and Wood Street. There were occasional flashes of brilliance, including (unexpectedly) a police station in Wood Street. Further east, where the damage was much lighter, modernization of 19th-century offices has tended to take the form of 'façadism', where the old building is scraped off the back of its frontage and a new office built behind, for example the two turn-of-the-century blocks at the south end of Moorgate.

Remarkably few of the 1950s office blocks survive today. From the 1980s offices needed much greater floor heights to accommodate computer cabling, so wholesale rebuilding started on London Wall with some Postmodern monsters such as Alban Gate and City Place House. More subtle is no. 1 Love Lane. Since then the Blitzed half of this area has become a showcase for a more refined approach to office design. The proximity of Guildhall means heights are restricted, and many are faced in 'contextual' stone, such as Sidell Gibson's respectful, curvaceous no. 30 Gresham Street opposite St Lawrence Jewry. Many of the big architectural names of the day have been busy here: the work of Norman Foster at no. 100 Wood Street, with its diamond-patterned roof and its curving rear scooping out round the remains of St Mary Staining, One London Wall and the black-and-white no. 10 Gresham Street, with chamfered top and corners, contrasts with Kohn Pedersen Fox's curvier no. 20 Gresham Street. The most interesting buildings are perhaps those less constrained by planning, such as no. 88 Wood Street and no. 5 Aldermanbury Square. There will always be a tension between the City's global importance as both a financial centre and a heritage site, and responses to that tension contribute to the dynamism of its architecture.

Opposite
The tower of St Alban Wood Street, all that was salvaged of the church burnt out in the Blitz, is now a private house. It is seen against the striking patterns of Norman Foster's no. 100 Wood Street office building of 2000.

Jolly ventilation shafts next to Richard Rogers's no. 88 Wood Street, finished in 2001, look back to his Pompidou Centre in Paris of the early 1970s, which introduced the high-tech style in architecture.

1 ST VEDAST

Foster Lane EC2 • Sir Christopher Wren 1695–1701; Nicholas Hawksmoor 1709–12; Stephen Dykes Bower 1953–63

This is a rare dedication – there have only ever been three churches named St Vedast in Britain – and recalls a 6th-century bishop of Arras. The medieval church here had been largely rebuilt in the 16th century by the time it was reduced to a burnt-out shell in the Great Fire, and Wren's rebuilding came only after it had been rebuilt once afterwards, badly, by someone else. Remnants of the medieval church are clear outside on the rough, ragstone south wall. Wren turned what had been a conventional church plan into a boxy auditorium with one aisle, like St Clement Eastcheap and St Margaret Lothbury, and a tower at the south-west corner towards Cheapside. The asymmetrical arrangement makes for a slightly awkward west front, an infelicity soon forgiven because of the tour de force above – the steeple of grouped pilasters, scrolls and an obelisk, not added until 1709. It is all alluring curves, playing the kind of spatial games enjoyed by the Roman Baroque architects (Borromini's name is always mentioned). It might well be by Wren's pupil Nicholas Hawksmoor, but this cannot be proved. Burnt once again in the Blitz, the church was rebuilt in 1953–63 by Stephen Dykes Bower for the artistically inclined Canon Mortlock, inducted as Rector in the roofless wreck in 1947. It is very peaceful and low-key, with dark-stained pews arranged collegiate style, and practical, non-tarnishing aluminium leaf on the ceiling (see p. 84). Many furnishings were acquired from the salvage at St Paul's after the war – the 17th-century sword rest and fine font are from St Anne and St Agnes. Up in the tower the walls are scored with 18th-century graffiti, the work of bored bell-ringers. Outside again, on the north side, is the quiet Fountain Court with a pretty, two-storey loggia linking a 17th-century brick schoolroom, now used as the church hall, and Dykes Bowers's plain neo-classical rectory. Displayed here is a not very interesting section of Roman pavement and a vigorous portrait of Canon Mortlock in profile by Jacob Epstein.

The swaggering display of curves with pilaster, scrolls and obelisk that is the tower of St Vedast was added in 1709 to Wren's church, plausibly by Nicholas Hawksmoor.

2 GOLDSMITHS' HALL

Foster Lane EC2 • Philip Hardwick 1829–35

It would be appropriate if the livery company representing the most luxurious of trades had the grandest hall, and it does – with the possible exception of the Fishmongers. It is not the largest hall (bizarrely, that honour belongs to a 1970s building, the Great Hall of the Plaisterers' Company, now accessed via One London Wall) nor the oldest surviving building (Merchant Taylors'). But the Goldsmiths have been on the one site the longest (since 1339) and from the first their hall was one of the largest with an array of parlours, an armoury and a chapel. This was rebuilt in the 1630s by Nicholas Stone, Inigo Jones's master mason at the Banqueting House. But the Goldsmiths neglected the upkeep of their hall in the early 19th century – they blamed

The columned entrance front of Goldsmiths' Hall in Foster Lane is grand in a restrained way that only hints at the sumptuousness of the interiors.

Opposite
Rising through two storeys, the staircase hall in Goldsmiths' livery hall was lined in marble in the 1870s, perhaps because Hardwick's wooden panelling was found insufficiently opulent.

having to pay for the Napoleonic Wars – and by the 1820s the building was shored up and the dancing gallery 'only safe under its present quiescent uses'.

But they did not stint when they rebuilt. The architect for the rebuilding was Philip Hardwick, the company's surveyor, best known as architect of the Euston Arch. He was able to occupy the entire block, so the hall is totally detached, and the grandeur is heightened by his deployment on the main Foster Lane front of six giant Corinthian columns in Portland stone over a granite plinth, the frontage rich and Italianate. When it opened in 1835 the press noted approvingly the 'palatial grandeur' of the interiors which is still the case today. The first eye-catching space is the domed double-height staircase hall, made yet grander in the 1870s by the application of marble to every surface but the ceiling. More splendid still is the livery hall itself, lit by six vast windows on the Gutter Lane side, with appropriate quantities of gold decoration applied to the capitals of the great Corinthian scagliola columns and the deep red and greens of the coffered ceiling retained from redecoration by George Aitchison in the 1890s. The company's plate sits in a top-lit apse at one end, an altar to Mammon.

With decoration adapted from a scheme of the 1890s, the Goldsmiths' hall features lavish use of colour and, of course, gold. The niche at the end displays the company's fine plate.

Ranged across the main Foster Lane frontage are three principal reception rooms of extraordinary diversity. The Court Room is the most sumptuous, reusing for effect and economy fittings from the 1660s hall including the panelling, the 1735 fireplace by Henry Cheere, and the gold and silver plaster cornice – a riot of swags, scrolls, figures and unicorns – designed by Edward Jerman when he repaired Nicholas Stone's 1630s hall after the Great Fire.

The other two rooms – the drawing room and exhibition room – are 1950s reconstructions after localized war damage. The drawing room is white and gold, while the exhibition room feels like a rather upmarket funeral parlour. Everywhere in Goldsmiths' Hall are signs of the company's continuing engagement with the trade – assaying still goes on here, and contemporary silverware is on display.

The 1950s Wax Chandlers' Hall sits on the rusticated ground floor salvaged from the 1850 building, lending it a certain gravitas.

3 WAX CHANDLERS' HALL

Gresham Street EC2 • Charles Fowler 1852–4; Seely & Paget 1954–8; FLACQ 2004–7

Sitting quietly alongside the commanding bulk of Goldsmiths' Hall is the home of the Wax Chandlers, traditionally defenders of the purity of beeswax as opposed to tallow candles and now more widely associated with bee-keeping, honey and wax as an industrial commodity. The building looks at first like one of several nearby livery halls (e.g. Girdlers', Brewers', Mercers') rebuilt after wartime destruction in a starved neo-Georgian manner, made all the more meagre by the paucity of materials available during the time of rationing.

But the Wax Chandlers' history is more complicated than it looks. It is the sixth hall on this site since 1525, and although the fifth, by Charles Fowler in the 1850s, was burnt out in the Blitz, its ground floor survived, and this heavily rusticated granite base gives the building visual 'bottom' that sits rather well with the new design by Seely & Paget. This followed the general lines of the 1850s building, but with a typically 1950s palette of pinkish brick and light green oxidized-copper roof. Inside the hall everything is on a small scale except the hall itself, lit by the tall windows that dominate the front, but a low-key luxury makeover by FLACQ in 2004–7 (limestone floors, solid oak doors, bronze handles) has transformed the character of the interior.

St Anne and St Agnes in 1955, when the church was more hemmed in than it is now. A garden has since been made on the site of buildings cleared after war damage.

4 ST ANNE AND ST AGNES

Gresham Street EC2 • Sir Christopher Wren and Robert Hooke
1677–81, 1686–7

While there may be no such thing as a 'typical Wren church', St Anne and St Agnes is not even obviously a church. You must stand far back to see that there is a tower, and the two most visible frontages, to east and south, are of red brick and near-identical, giving it a boxy look relieved by the tall Dutch gables over large round-headed windows. St Anne and St Agnes owes its short tower to the earlier church, known from the 12th century, which burnt in the Great Fire: a 14th-century doorway to it is visible inside, under the tower. The interior is as symmetrical as outside, the result of an unusual 'cross-in-a-square' plan also used at Wren's St Mary-at-Hill (historically the Watermen's church). The central plan enabled Wren – or plausibly his assistant Robert Hooke, who is known to have worked at both and had been looking at the centralized Nieuwe Kerk in Haarlem – to squeeze the maximum accommodation on to these small sites. The effect within is serene and spacious, the central dome and cross-vaults supported on four surprisingly light Corinthian columns, with saucer domes at the corners. Although the reredos has always been here, most of the fittings are reused from other

The clear, open interior of St Anne and St Agnes designed by Wren (or his assistant Robert Hooke) on a 'cross-in-a-square plan', perhaps derived from Dutch examples, now serves London's Lutheran community.

churches destroyed in the Blitz, but they are of the right late 17th-century period – the Moses and Aaron paintings on the east wall were from St Michael Wood Street. Blitz damage to St Anne's was only finally made good in the 1960s, in an unsparing restoration by Braddock & Martin Smith that stripped away the remains of more vibrant 19th-century interventions by Ewan Christian among others, but this left the church appropriately plain for the Lutheran congregation that has used it ever since.

The most striking feature of no. 25 Gresham Street is the frontage cantilevered over the lob on huge diagonal struts.

5 NO. 25 GRESHAM STREET

EC2 • Nicholas Grimshaw & Partners 2000–02

A new street in the 1840s and badly hit in the Blitz, Gresham Street has seen most of the office developments that made good that wartime apocalypse in the 1950s swept away in the past decade for something bigger and better. No. 25 is rather special for a number of reasons. It has certain similarities with no. 5 Aldermanbury Square, notably the tipping back of the frontage – much sharper here – but while it lacks the purity of Parry's building, it has instead a rich materiality, the whole building textured with ranks of fixed louvres in green Cumberland slate. The central portion of the Gresham Street frontage is deeply recessed, with four super-sized window-boxes or 'hanging gardens', and the whole frontage is cantilevered over a frameless glass lobby, held by huge diagonal struts on the side elevations.

No. 25 Gresham Street overlooks Goldsmiths' Garden, first created by firewatchers during the war, and incorporating the site of the church of St John Zachary and its churchyard.

6 ROMAN WALL

Noble Street EC2

The ruined walls that stand in the sunken garden running along the west side of Noble Street are mostly not Roman at all – they are just-as-rare survivors of 19th-century buildings lost in the war, when Noble Street was entirely destroyed in the Blitz. The Roman remains are in front of these, consisting of parts of the 1st-century fort – a square turret and its curving south-west corner can be seen at the south end of the displayed remains, and another in the middle – and the City's perimeter wall, added in the 2nd century and incorporating the existing fort. Roman fragments crop up all over the City and are nowadays lovingly preserved, but our ancestors were more likely to plunder them for building materials. Most of the surviving portions are still here only because they were built into later buildings, since destroyed.

Detail of the swooping curve of One London Wall recalls the glamour of 1930s moderne, such as Owen Williams's *Daily Express* building in Fleet Street.

7 ONE LONDON WALL AND PLAISTERERS' HALL

EC2 • Foster & Partners 2001–4 and Ronald Ward & Partners 1970–73

This 21st-century curved glass building, which runs around London Wall from Noble Street to Aldersgate Street, is a welcome break from the sharp angles and solid surfaces of most of the buildings hereabouts. The swooping curve and glass recall

These remains of Victorian warehouses, preserved along with parts of the Roman City walls, remind us of what most of this area looked like after the Blitz, before the ruined buildings were cleared.

Tucked inside a 21st-century office building is Plaisterers' Hall, the largest livery hall in the City. A mystery inside an enigma, it is of the 1970s.

A detail of the Adam-style plasterwork in the hall, used as a showcase for the work of the live company's members.

Norman Foster's first landmark building in the early 1970s, the Willis building in Ipswich. The manner here, with the upper-floor setbacks and fine metal streamlining, pays more overt homage to the 1930s – Owen Williams's *Express* building in Fleet Street and William Crabtree's Peter Jones department store in Sloane Square. But inside this high-spec office building is a surprise: the livery hall of the Worshipful Company of Plaisterers, which has been on this site since the 1960s after having been burnt out three times in 300 years from its old premises (approximately where no. 5 Aldermanbury Square is now). The Great Hall (designed in the early 1970s by John Davies of Ronald Ward & Partners) is the largest livery hall in the City, and in some ways the strangest. Far from reflecting its time like, for example, Salters' Hall, it transports the visitor back to the 18th century with a dazzling virtuoso display of candy-coloured plasterwork to ceilings and walls in the Robert Adam manner.

8 NO. 88 WOOD STREET

EC2 • Richard Rogers Partnership 1993–2001

Stepping up or across is a common feature of Richard Rogers buildings, from Marco Goldschmied's Montevetro in Battersea in the 1980s to the planned Graham Stirk-designed British Museum north-west extension. Here the reason is entirely practical. The building faces the listed Wood Street Police Station and what was left of Wren's St Alban Wood Street after the demolition of wartime remains in 1954. Therefore the front of the building is only eight storeys, the two sections behind narrowing along a triangular site and stepping up to 14 then 18 storeys in what are almost three separate buildings, with the deep cuts between them allowing more light to be drawn into the building. Enhancing this effect is the old Rogers trick of banishing the services to the outside (or the basement) of the building: lessons learned from the maintenance issues at the Lloyd's Building mean the services here, the lifts and stairways, are enclosed for protection, like the rest of the building, in highly evolved super-clear glass.

The separation into three sections, the slimline service towers that rise above each and the glass all contribute to a bulk-defying delicacy all the more evident next to the monstrous bulk of Alban Gate. The lobby is a space of calm emptiness, punctuated by cylindrical monolithic columns – its great height is all the more surprising as this was designed as a speculative office building. Memories of Rogers's high-tech origins are present in the building's cross-bracing and there are also playful allusions to his first major success – the Pompidou Centre in Paris – in the red and blue funnels poking up round the perimeter, although these are practical: the blue ducts take in fresh air and the red ones exhaust the used air.

A typical Richard Rogers trick, having the services on the outside of the building, is evident here at no. 88 Wood Street, which seems slim and light next to the bricky bulk of Alban Gate.

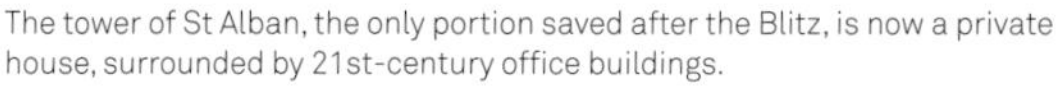
The tower of St Alban, the only portion saved after the Blitz, is now a private house, surrounded by 21st-century office buildings.

The neo-Gothic interior of Wren's St Alban Woo Street, seen around 1890. There has been a church on this site since the 8th century.

9 ST ALBAN WOOD STREET

EC2 • Sir Christopher Wren 1682–7, 1696–8; Frederick Burn, Smith & Partners 1984–5

Marooned in the middle of the road like a traffic policeman, the severed tower of St Alban sits oddly beside the showy early 21st-century offices around it. Although Perpendicular in style, it dates from Wren's time (and he, not Hooke, was almost certainly the designer) and was not a reuse of a medieval tower as at St Anne and St Agnes and St Olave Jewry. Excavation shows the site had been built on since Roman times, with a church there since the 8th century, possibly a chapel to the nearby Anglo-Saxon palace. After the Great Fire the parish was evidently not ready for something in up-to-the minute classical so Wren supplied a late-Gothic design. St Alban was not totally destroyed in the war, but the burnt remains were demolished for road widening in 1954. In 1984–5 the tower was converted by Frederick Burn, Smith & Partners into a private house that must be challenging to live in. A glimpse of its interior and staircase may often be had through the glass inner doors, when the main door is open.

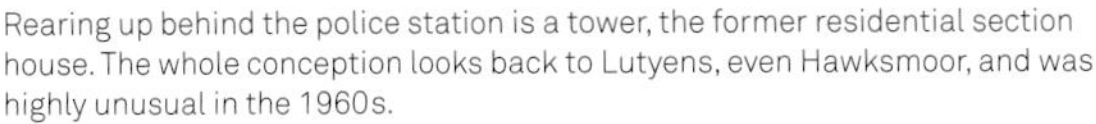
Rearing up behind the police station is a tower, the former residential section house. The whole conception looks back to Lutyens, even Hawksmoor, and was highly unusual in the 1960s.

The precision-cut rusticated stonework of the lower floors is especially arresting on a sunny day. The severity of the conception makes the traditional blue police lamp look very froufrou against it.

10 WOOD STREET POLICE STATION ➲

Wood Street EC2 • McMorran & Whitby 1962–6

This 1960s police station is just as important as Lutyens's Midland Bank, and more unusual. The City of London Police are independent of the Metropolitan Police and their buildings show an appropriate independence of mind: each is a one-off. As a small organization they have not traditionally employed a house architect, unlike the Met, whose stations have tended to have a 'house style' reflecting that of the police surveyor at the time. This one is unusual in that it is a recognizably classical building, designed at a time when classicism was anathema, and yet it is unimpeachably modern and in its own style – the result of a carefully considered rendering down of classicism to its fundamentals by Donald McMorran, who fully understood its rules and could use them to create something new and coherent. It was designed as the headquarters of the City Police and so incorporated some features unusual in a police station, including a museum, a tailor, Turkish baths and restaurant, as well as stables and cells, all fitted by McMorran's partner George Whitby into low blocks around a courtyard. From the north side rises up a slim tower providing an extra nine floors of offices and a residential section house topped with a simple double-pitch roof. The arresting Wood Street frontage is dominated by tall windows that light the first-floor lecture room. The outer faces are all Portland stone, which suits the abstract classicism; the tight arrangements of solid and void are given precision-controlled texture by the sharp-cut bands of rustication on the lower floors and massive chimney stacks. There may be echoes of Sanmicheli, Boullée and Ledoux, even Hawksmoor, but there is nothing else quite like it.

11 ST MARY ALDERMANBURY

EC2 • Sir Christopher Wren 1671–5

To sit in this garden is an eerie experience: it feels like a medieval church. This is all the stranger as its walls rise only a couple of feet from the ground, and it is, putatively, the Blitzed remains of a Wren church and its churchyard. The explanation is that after the Great Fire, Wren (or possibly Robert Hooke, his chief assistant in the City, who was also paid for the work) built his new church reusing the west tower of the 15th-century church as well as parts of the walls. It was not an adventurous design (round-headed windows, that at the west end with immense scrolled volutes) and it followed the plan of the old church. In 1940 the Wren church was burnt out but the walls and tower remained, and it could have been restored, like St Vedast. Instead these remains were cleared and in 1966 were re-erected at Fulton, Missouri, as a memorial to Winston Churchill. The stones that remained here are indeed, largely, medieval: the old footings left behind when the Wren church was boxed up for its transatlantic afterlife.

The atmospheric garden on the site of the church contains remnants of the medieval predecessor to Wren's church.

The striking east end of the church, seen in 1897. After Blitz damage it was dismantled and shipped to Fulton, Missouri.

There is a delicacy in the gentle curve and setting forward of the stainless-steel frontage of no. 5 Aldermanbury Square which means it does not bully its smaller neighbours.

12 NO. 5 ALDERMANBURY SQUARE

EC2 • Eric Parry 2001–7

This 18-storey office building replaced one of the 1960s slab blocks that lined London Wall. It is in an area that has seen intense redevelopment since the mid-1980s, starting with the neighbouring Alban Gate. No greater contrast could be imagined with that great bruiser than Eric Parry's building, its edges tapering upwards in a subtly modulated curve. The main material is a grid of stainless steel with a soft sheen that contrives to play nicely both with Alban Gate and the Wood Street Police Station. This structural steel envelope, its elements arranged in a major and minor rhythm, is set forward from the glazing, creating a texture almost like some hi-tech woven cloth. At ground level the building works on a human scale, with its lowest storeys opening up into a high colonnade over the pavement.

In the 1980s City Place House and Alban Gate, with their bulk and colour, put paid to the postwar Modernist conception of London Wall.

13 CITY PLACE HOUSE

55 Basinghall Street EC2 • Swanke Hayden Connell 1988–92

As a big brash example of Postmodernism, this is a fantastically vulgar building, cheerily careless of the classical tradition it blithely plunders. What is perhaps most striking now is how colourful it is, with its red and white stone cladding. The shiny balconies and tiers of bronzed panels between the windows give it an Art Deco glitz, as does the pyramid-topped entrance block at the junction of Basinghall Street and Avenue. Its shameless attitude is rather enjoyable.

14 ONE COLEMAN STREET

EC2 • Swanke Hayden Connell with David Walker 2005–7

Nothing could be further from the aesthetic character of the buildings planned for London Wall in the 1950s – a rank of near-identical Corbusian slab blocks stacked along the road – than

The view along the south side of London Wall from Armourers' Hall of the 1840s shows the street's architectural variety. Swanke Hayden Connell's One Coleman Street and City Place House are either side of City Tower, one of the surviving curtain-walled tower blocks of the 1960s.

this shiny white pineapple of a building. It almost seems specially calculated to thumb its nose at the ascetic sensibilities of those planners. But there is no doubt that it is a more cheery architectural presence than Austral House, the block it replaced – slab blocks tend not to age well. One Coleman Street bookends the south side of London Wall with Foster's similarly rotund One London Wall, but the glistening white surface (precast polished concrete, using much recycled material, on a steel frame) here is notably textured. The windows are a series of cells created by projecting shallow, irregularly triangular elements that change orientation on each floor. It is an arresting conceit. The effect is almost Expressionist and could hardly be more different from the same architects' City Place House from twenty years ago. The project included a new adjoining garden, in front of Girdlers' Hall.

Walls bristling with armour lend the livery hall of the Worshipful Company of Armourers and Brasiers an air of Hollywood baronial style.

15 ARMOURERS' HALL

81 Coleman Street EC2 • J. H. Good 1839–41

Armourers' Hall is an oddity, a domestic Victorian presence on London Wall – it is as if a prosperous provincial merchant's house had been dropped into the hurly-burly of the 21st-century metropolis. The site has in fact been home to the Worshipful Company of Armourers and Brasiers since 1346, and although the present building dates only from the early 1840s its survival was pure luck: an anonymous fireman broke in on 29 December 1940, the most terrible night of the Blitz, and extinguished the burning curtains while so many neighbouring buildings were reduced to ashes. The stock-brick hall was old-fashioned even when it was built, a late work by Good, the company's surveyor. The main frontage to Coleman Street is stiffened with Doric pilasters, with armorial decorations in the metopes of the frieze. The plain north front was never intended to have the exposure it has had since London Wall was opened up after the war. Inside it retains its old-fashioned air, a sober imperial staircase rising and dividing beneath a lantern light added in the 1870s. Throughout the building the walls bristle with arms and armour. The livery hall itself upstairs is entered through doors embellished with surprisingly light 1950s glass panels engraved with armorial motifs by Laurence Whistler – a contrast to the hall itself, with panelling and curving wooden wagon-roof added in the 1870s when various rooms were altered in High Victorian style by

The entrance frontage to Armourers' Hall on Coleman Street is now far less visible than the plain-Jane side facing London Wall. The buildir had the luckiest of escapes in the Blitz.

Woolgate House replaced a Modernist office complex on the site of the old Exchange with this unusual design in a kind of interwar classicism featuring Egyptian-inspired columns.

Alexander Graham, giving the hall an appropriately baronial atmosphere. Next door the 18th-century townhouse at no. 80 Coleman Street is worth a look (though the ground floor is a facsimile from the 1980s restoration).

The Victorian Wool Exchange that gave the new building its name is seen here awaiting demolition in 1962. One of its more unusual amenities was a Turkish bath.

16 WOOLGATE EXCHANGE

Basinghall Street EC2 • Sidell Gibson 1997–2002

Like the same architects' no. 30 Gresham Street, Woolgate Exchange has a relatively traditional appearance, here made more explicit by the unusual giant columns with flaring fluted capitals – the style recalls the Art Deco Egyptian in vogue in the 1920s after the discovery of Tutankhamun's tomb. This, and the building's bulk, relates it to Sir Giles Scott's lump of offices on the other side of Basinghall Street which, although built in the 1950s, were extremely old-fashioned for the time. Woolgate Exchange owes its name to the Victorian Wool Exchange building on the site, demolished in the 1960s. It is set back with an L-shaped colonnade ending in a kind of tempietto and placed around a garden on the Basinghall Street frontage, which had to sit comfortably with the scale and varied historic character of the street. This was achieved by a novel system of cladding in Portland stone only 75 mm (3 in) thick, which kept the walls thin; aluminium windbraces that mimic the giant columns allow large areas of glass, needed to flood the deep floor spaces with light.

A satirical cartoon of 1821 caricaturing a 'loyal address' made to King George IV by one Thomas Tegg of 111 Cheapside reminds us that politics in the City was just as lively 200 years ago as it is today.

THE GOVERNMENT OF THE CITY OF LONDON

The City has a claim to be the oldest continuous municipal democracy in the world – its proud boast is that it is older than the British Parliament. Like the British Parliament, the Mayor and Commonalty and Citizens of the City of London – to give the City of London Corporation its official title, which includes the Lord Mayor, the Court of Aldermen, the Court of Common Council and the Freemen and Liverymen of the City – lacks a written constitution, its authority having grown by custom. The City Corporation's structure and the way it operates is unlike any London borough as it is apolitical – at least in the party-political sense.

The City Corporation received its first charter from William I in 1067, but this merely confirmed rights and privileges established under his Anglo-Saxon predecessors. Its first elected body was the Court of Aldermen, established in the Guildhall with a Lord Mayor and two Sheriffs by the end of the 12th century: each alderman ('elder man') represented a ward, or collection of parishes, within the City, a system that has hardly changed in 800 years. Today the local authority is the Court of Common Council, which augmented the Court of Aldermen from the 14th century, with between two and ten councilmen elected by each ward. The Court of Aldermen survives, although today its functions are limited. The Lord Mayor is chosen from among the aldermen each year and takes office at the Lord Mayor's Show.

For most of its history, Guildhall Yard was a narrow space hemmed in by court and administrative buildings, as seen in a view by T. H. Shepherd from 1855. Since the war, when the Yard was opened up, Guildhall itself is much more visible.

The Freedom of the City is a privilege first recorded in 1237 and now largely symbolic. New Freemen are enrolled in a ceremony in Guildhall, when they receive a copy of *Rules for the Conduct of Life*, written by the Lord Mayor in 1737–8. There is a mythology surrounding the rights of Freemen of the City, most famously the right to drive a flock of sheep over London Bridge. More useful but just as apocryphal is the belief that, if a City of London Police officer finds a Freeman drunk and incapable, he will send him home in a taxi rather than putting him in the cells.

This Council Chamber (shown here as it looked in 1880, shortly before it was destroyed) in Guildhall was built in the 1770s to the designs of George Dance, whose celebrated porch survives on the Guildhall Yard frontage.

Because of the decline in the City's residential population – from 130,000 at the time of the first census in 1801 to about 9,000 today (around half of whom live in the Barbican) – the City, unlike the rest of the country, allows businesses to nominate voters. Voters are nominated from among employees, according to the size of the company: 15,000 of the 21,300 City voters are appointed by businesses within the City.

Today the City of London Corporation, which still has its offices in Guildhall, provides the usual local government services for the City, and supports and promotes 'The City' as the world leader in international finance and business services. It also maintains open spaces far beyond its boundaries at Epping Forest and Hampstead Heath, runs the Port Health Authority along 151 km (94 miles) of the Thames, as well as the wholesale food markets of Smithfield, Spitalfields and Billingsgate, and is one of the country's biggest funders of the arts, including the Barbican Centre.

17 GUILDHALL COMPLEX ➲

Guildhall Yard, Gresham Street EC2 • John Croxton 1411–c. 1429; George Dance the Younger 1777–8, 1788–9; Sir Horace Jones 1864–8, 1870–72, 1883–4; Sir Giles Gilbert Scott 1953–4; Richard Gilbert Scott 1966–9, 1969–75, 1984–99

The atmospheric east crypt beneath Guildhall was built by the mason John Croxton in the ea 15th century. Its exact use is unknown but the complex vaults and dark Purbeck marble piers suggest it was not just for storage.

The history of Guildhall, seat of the City of London Corporation, is the core of the history of this entire area and makes sense of the complex, much-altered array of buildings that remain around Guildhall Yard, despite Fire, Blitz and changes in fashion: it is an essay in every manner of Gothic and its reinterpretation. Dominating the Yard is the 15th-century Guildhall, itself dominated by George Dance the Younger's four-storey porch of 1788–9, a Georgian fantasy that mixes classical, Gothic and Oriental (the earliest example of Indian influence in British architecture) motifs without fear or favour, swallowing up the 15th-century porch in its lower storeys. The ranks of windows on Dance's porch conceal the vast single space of the hall itself, the largest civic hall in medieval England, built by the mason John Croxton from 1411 to *c.* 1429 as the third guildhall on this site. We cannot know for sure what the original roof was like, but evidence suggests it was likely to have been stone-vaulted, steeper and richer than today's simple, pointed-stone arches which, like many of the fittings – the chandeliers, panelling, stained glass and wooden galleries – were designed during the restoration of 1953–4 by Sir Giles Gilbert Scott, architect of Liverpool's Anglican Cathedral and the Battersea and Bankside (now Tate Modern) power stations. But the walls and windows, including huge traceried extravaganzas at each end, are largely Croxton's, though often repaired. The Perpendicular Gothic sits rather oddly with the huge 18th- and 19th-century stone sculptured groups commemorating, among others, Pitt the Elder (by John Bacon the Elder), Nelson (the naked figure is Neptune, not the Admiral) and Wellington. Beneath the hall is an undercroft divided into two crypts: the west one is even older than the hall – probably early 14th century, restored in 1973 after three hundred years hidden within brick vaults. Octagonal piers rise organically without capital into the vaults, the whole atmospherically uplit. Still more impressive is Croxton's east crypt, where clusters of dark Purbeck 'marble' piers hold up the complex chamfered-stone tierceron vaults above.

Nothing else in Guildhall Yard quite lives up to Guildhall itself. Pinning the north-east and south-east corners of the yard are two similarly unadventurous rock-faced Victorian Gothic buildings. The first, better seen from Basinghall Street, is the former museum and library, a Perpendicular Gothic building by Sir Horace Jones, the City Surveyor, from the early 1870s, with a crusty ragstone exterior – it looks like a mid-Victorian church. The old library, now a reception hall, is on an impressive scale, as is the open staircase, though the most atmospheric room is the dark wood and gold wagon-ceilinged meeting room, with curved apsidal end and Gothic bookcases. The second building is a disused Court House of 1887–94 by Andrew Murray.

Opposite
Guildhall's roof supported on simple stone arches dates only from Sir Giles Gilbert Scott's restoration of 1953–4. Much of the walls and spectacular traceried windows are 15th-centu survivors of the Great Fire and Blitz, however.

This panorama of Guildhall Yard swings through every flavour and date of Gothic. Richard Gilbert Scott did it in spiky concrete for the 1960s glazed cloister at the far left and more gently in the 1980s for the new Guildhall Art Gallery in the centre. Either side of this are glimpses of the Victorian Gothic of the former library and museum, left, and court house, right. Most sublime is the 'Hindoo-Gothic' porch of Guildhall, to the left, though the little Irish Chamber, far right, is more obviously Georgian.

By the 1970s the old museum had been rehoused in the Museum of London and the library had moved to the other side of Guildhall Yard, into the long extension in concrete and glass by Sir Giles Scott's son Richard Gilbert Scott which wraps round the north and west sides of the Yard. Opinions are divided on this building, which not only houses the Guildhall Library but also the Clockmakers' Museum and offices. Until the late 1960s Guildhall Yard was much less open, with a range of buildings immediately west of the porch, but Scott's addition opened up the Yard – and so the Guildhall – to view. The glazed cloister with pyramidal roofs leading from Guildhall to the new range is perhaps the most appealing aspect: Scott's novel Modernist take on Gothic in light spiky concrete works well on this scale.

Opposite this, filling the east side of the Yard, is the Guildhall Art Gallery, which finally opened in 1999, replacing a former court house damaged in the Second World War. It is also by Richard Gilbert Scott – but what a difference a quarter of a century makes. Guildhall Art Gallery could be described as Postmodern, but it is a refined take on architecture's past (in this case Gothic more than classical), more in the spirit of Dance's porch than Scott's own 1970s extension. The recurring motif inside and out is square arches with canted corners. Outside this is used in a quasi-Gothic manner with six main windows divided up by similar smaller 'lights' topped by light tracery-like stone mullions, the creamy facing stone banded with darker fossil stone

This seated bronze figure of Winston Churchill by Oscar Nemon was added in 1955 to the array of memorials inside Guildhall commemorating, among others, Wellington and Nelson.

A watercolour of the 1890s shows St Lawrence Jewry, left, with, to the right of Guildhall, the pedimented court house of 1822, whose blitzed remains were replaced by the new Guildhall Art Gallery in 1999.

– an unusually restrained neo-Victorian touch. Inside the motifs are the same but the character is different. A huge double-height room was built around John Singleton Copley's vast painting *The Defeat of the Floating Batteries at Gibraltar* (1783–91), which is 7.5 m (24½ ft) wide and 5.5 m (18 ft) high, lit from above by a grid of tented lights as might be found in a 1930s ocean liner.

Down in the basement is the reason this building took more than fifteen years from commission to opening – the Roman amphitheatre, found during routine archaeology before the gallery's foundations could be dug. It had to be supported on a huge concrete slab beneath which another two storeys of basement were built. The display of the amphitheatre makes the most of what was found: walls just 1.3 m (4¼ ft) high of one end of an elliptical building, rebuilt *c.* AD 120, with an entry and two rooms either side that might have been pens for animals to be released into the arena for gladiatorial combat. The dark room displays the surviving stone walls and, amazingly, wooden drains with clever silt traps to stop them blocking up. The missing area of amphitheatre and the gladiatorial combatants are 'drawn in' as lines of green light against a black ground (see p. 203). As the visitor progresses into the arena the silence is broken suddenly by the sounds of a crowd baying for blood. Up in Guildhall Yard the outline of the amphitheatre is picked out in the paving. The south side of the Yard is mostly taken up with the City Corporation's official church, St Lawrence Jewry, and a solitary Georgian survivor – the former Irish Chamber of 1824–5 by Joseph Walker.

Two views of the interior of St Lawrence Jewry – in 1891 and as it is today, with new plasterwork and woodwork that replaced what was destroyed in the Blitz. It is appropriately rich for the City Corporation's official church.

18

ST LAWRENCE JEWRY

Gresham Street EC2 • Sir Christopher Wren 1671–80; Cecil Brown 1954–7

Architecturally this is the grandest Wren church in this area. Although Robert Hooke may have been in charge of the general design, the magnificent pedimented east front, with its grand but tightly controlled ensemble of Corinthian columns and pilasters, niches and festoons, must be Wren's, so close is it to one of his St Paul's designs. This front was designed to be seen from the newly created King Street, which provided a processional route to Guildhall. The north and west fronts, respectively rather awkward and plain, originally faced narrow lanes rather than the current echoing spaces of Guildhall Yard, but the south side makes up for it, with its five arched windows continuing the theme of the west front in a simpler manner. Once again, the incendiary bombs of 29 December 1940 almost did for a Wren church. It was rebuilt in a faithful manner (though the lead steeple is now fibreglass) by Cecil Brown in 1954–7 to become the official church of the City of London Corporation – in John Betjeman's words, 'very municipal, very splendid' – which accounts for the grand furnishings in what has also been called a 'sumptuous barn' of an interior. The pictorial stained glass is by Christopher Rahere Webb (his father was churchwarden at St Bartholomew-the-Great, hence his unusual middle name). The north aisle is the Commonwealth Chapel. Sombre and pleasing though Cecil Brown's dark oak fittings are, set off by the white and gold-leaf decoration, photographs displayed inside the church showing it before the Blitz are a reminder of the terrible losses: a panelled vestry at the north-west corner of the church which had a richly plastered quatrefoil ceiling, with a painting by Isaac Fuller, has become the Tower chapel, a serene void designated for 'private contemplation'. The vast, two-tier organ squatting over the west end of the nave was rebuilt again in 2001 as a millennium project by Johannes Klais of Bonn, using the existing cases. The late 17th-century monument to Archbishop John Tillotson with weeping cherub is attributed to Grinling Gibbons.

Opposite
The east end of St Lawrence Jewry is a tour de force, obviously by Wren, designed to be seen from King Street, part of a new processional route leading to Guildhall.

GUILDHALL
YARD

19 NOS 42–44 GRESHAM STREET

EC2 • Sancton Wood 1850–52

Gresham Street was only created out of several narrower existing streets in 1845 and this grand commercial palazzo, built for an insurance company on the corner with King Street, is a rare survivor from that period, all the rarer in an area where much has been rebuilt twice in fifty years. The architect Sancton Wood – best known for designing railway stations – was a pupil of Robert Smirke, and this represents an appropriately scaled commercial take on Smirke's Oxford and Cambridge and Carlton Clubs in Pall Mall, but with the windows closer packed, looking forward to the 'wall-of-glass' offices of the later 19th century. The retention of the window surrounds, with appropriate new frames, on the ground floor shows just how important these are to the streetscape, as do the adjoining later Victorian commercial buildings at nos 46 and 48 Gresham Street and 16–17 King Street (all from the 1860s, the last rebuilt behind the retained façade). None of these is individually outstanding, but the mix of styles and window rhythms adds up to a dynamic and pleasing streetscape, easily ruined through thoughtless changes by individual owners. Unfortunately the extra storey on nos 42–44, added in the 1970s, looks like a layer of royal icing above the bold cornice.

The regular close-packed windows of nos 42–44 Gresham Street of 1850–52 look forward to the wall-of-glass office buildings of the later 19th century. It is a shame about the ugly top floor added in the 1970s.

20 ST OLAVE JEWRY

Ironmonger Lane EC2 • Sir Christopher Wren 1671–9; Swanke Hayden Connell 1986–7

St Olave is one of several Wren churches in the City reduced to its tower – but not, for once, as the result of the Blitz. Depopulation of the City of London during the 19th century had put paid to a dozen Wren churches half a century before the

The surviving tower, augmented with a Wren-style building tacked on the back in the 1980s, is now used as offices.

John Crowther's atmospheric watercolour of 1887 shows the church a few years before most of it was demolished owing to depopulation in the City.

Luftwaffe arrived. The tower and west wall of St Olave were retained and a new building tacked on to the back in the 1890s. The Wren church, an early rebuilding after the Great Fire of a much-altered 12th-century church, was certainly not the showiest, and the tower has gently sloping sides and obelisk pinnacles. In front of it is a leafy garden on the site of another lost church, St Martin Pomary. In 1986–7 Swanke Hayden Connell replaced the 1890s conversion with a quiet neo-Wren addition – no greater contrast is imaginable than with the same architects' shiny white pineapple of a building at One Coleman Street.

The vigorous stonework of the former Atlas Assurance building of the 1830s contrasts with the bloodless classicism of some of its mid-20th-century neighbours.

21 NO. 3 KING STREET/92 CHEAPSIDE

EC2 • Thomas Hopper 1834–6; E. N. Clifton 1857; Alfred Waterhouse 1893–4; Michael Waterhouse 1927–9; Waterhouse & Ripley 1952

This survivor of the Blitz and the relentless drive to redevelop the City sits right over the pavement on the north side of Cheapside. It more than holds its own among its giant interloper neighbours by virtue of its Italianate vigour, with rusticated Cornish granite base and a profusion of pedimented and pilastered windows above. When originally built for Atlas Assurance in the 1830s it stretched back only four windows along King Street, but it was altered and extended northwards by E. N. Clifton in the 1850s and three generations of the Waterhouse family from the 1890s. The arcaded ground floor dates only from Michael Waterhouse's restoration of the Blitzed shell in the 1950s, a clever response to road widening that preserved the building and nods to the lost Inigo Jones arcades of Covent Garden.

Iron railings are a rarity now in the City and add to Frederick's Place's domestic charm and scale

22 FREDERICK'S PLACE

Nos 3, 4 and 6–8, and 35 Old Jewry EC2 • Robert and James Adam 1770s

This little close off Old Jewry is unique in this part of the City, which has so often been built and rebuilt on an ever larger scale. Although its buildings are 18th- and 19th-century, the general form of Frederick's Place recalls the time when important City houses were built round courtyards, hidden behind modest street frontages, as can still be seen more widely in Paris. But the buildings that now line it are also interesting as a speculative development by the architect Robert Adam and his brothers James and John, who pulled down a 17th-century house in 1773–4 to build what they called 'eight capital dwellings', probably to the designs of James Adam. Architecturally it is unexceptional, a reflection of the commercial nature of the enterprise and the fact that the Adams handed over the scheme to Samuel Dowbiggin, a builder-architect who built the north side. Least altered is the big no. 6 on the south side, with a plaque recalling Benjamin Disraeli's apprenticeship there as a solicitor in the 1820s, where an Adam ceiling survives on the first floor. Most of no. 4's staircase, its lantern light and some decoration were alterations of 1806–9 by Sir John Soane, his only intact surviving work in the City. Though Frederick's Place cannot compare with the Adams' Adelphi development off the Strand, its survival is remarkable and the atmosphere is enhanced by 18th-century railings and overthrows – the iron archways to the doors.

A photograph taken in 1963 of the north side of Frederick's Place, the portion built by Samuel Dowbiggin after the Adam brothers lost interest in the development. No. 4, at the far left, has interiors that were partly remodelled by Sir John Soane in the early 19th century.

Part of the Poultry frontage of Lutyens's Midland Bank, with some of his favourite features, such as the recessed entrance and windows in round-arched niches.

23 MIDLAND BANK HEADQUARTERS (*former*)

27–35 Poultry and 5 Prince's Street EC2 • Sir Edwin Lutyens with Gotch & Saunders 1924–39

This magnificent building, which arches across from Poultry to Prince's Street behind Sir Edwin Cooper's National Westminster Bank on the corner, was the second of Lutyens's Midland Bank designs after the perfect little 'Wrenaissance' box next to St James Piccadilly in the West End. Lutyens got the job through his friend Reggie MacKenna, whose predecessor as Midland Bank chairman had built five hundred new branches on the policy that 'a good bank with poor premises does not attract deposits'. The job suited Lutyens as he could concentrate on the frontages and the important interior rooms, leaving the practical business of putting up good working offices to the experienced bank designers Gotch & Saunders.

Despite its classical garb it is steel framed. The frontages to each street are almost identical (that on Poultry is easier to see), managing to look quite spare despite the variety of forms and decoration. The setback corners and top floors lend texture without bulk. Lutyens features include the recessed entrance and windows in round-arched niches, and the storeys are tied together visually with his typical control – their heights and the courses of rusticated stonework that make them up diminish very subtly up the building. The consulting engineer recalled Lutyens 'lying on the floor smoking his pipe' while he drew the façades 'more or less freehand…they were a dream to work with'. Inside is also very special, with Lutyens-designed fireplaces, friezes, panelling and doorcases surviving in many rooms. The monumental banking hall on the ground floor is articulated with simple but luxurious square columns in African verdite (a green serpentine) set against white marble. On the fifth floor, less monumental but equally striking, is a directors' suite of panelled and tapestried boardroom, directors' dining room and (quaintly) a smoking room with black-marble-pilastered lobby. The rooms are connected by long straight corridors, each with ingeniously varied vaulted plaster ceilings, as distinctively Lutyens as anything in the building. A stone service stair corkscrews vertiginously down to the basement at one end. Lutyens-designed chairs, tables and a cabinet in which the directors could store their top hats survive here.

A view down the service stair that plunges all the way from the top floor to the basement of Lutyens's Midland Bank.

Such buildings are no longer considered suitable for banks. At the time of writing, the building is locked and empty, its windows dusty, although plans by EPR Architects have been accepted for its conversion to a luxury hotel (a suitable use) with 172 suites and retail use for the original banking hall. The safety deposit vaults, whose 25-ton door (see p. 156) stood in for Fort Knox in the James Bond film *Goldfinger* (1964), are also intended for retail development.

24 NATIONAL WESTMINSTER BANK

1 Prince's Street EC2 • Sir Edwin Cooper 1929–32; T. P. Bennett Partnership 1994–7

It cannot have been easy for Edwin Cooper to design a building tucked into the corner of Lutyens's Midland Bank, but he made a fair job of it. He knew what he was doing – his obituaries in 1942 claimed he had designed more buildings in the City than any other architect. This one is a trifle unsubtle in its treatment of the corner site – cut off blunt, slightly convex – but it had to make a bold statement, sitting as it does in company with the Bank of England, the Mansion House and the Royal Exchange, and Cooper achieves this with its simple assemblage of giant order and rustication. There is also more than a nod to Hawksmoor's St Mary Woolnoth opposite, in the rusticated blockiness and

A female figure representing Prosperity, by Charles Doman, a favourite sculptor of Cooper's, adorns the Poultry frontage of the National Westminster Bank building.

Edwin Cooper's National Westminster Bank turns the corner between the Poultry and Prince's Street's fronts of Lutyens's Midland Bank, opposite the Bank of England – a difficult site for any architect.

Corinthian columns. Round the walls are four figures representing Courage, Integrity, Security and Prosperity by Cooper's favourite sculptor, Charles Doman. These Renaissance-style figures were very old-school in the 1930s, a quarter of a century after Jacob Epstein had produced his controversial figures for Charles Holden's BMA building in the Strand. More obviously of the 1930s is the group on the parapet, with Britannia and allegorical figures representing Commerce and Truth and Higher and Lower Mathematics by Ernest Gillick. Inside, Cooper's pale marble banking hall survived the 1990s rebuild, as did bronze versions of Doman's Integrity and Prosperity sculptures, and it is still in use for banking.

The Corn Exchange, seen here in Pugin and Rowlandson's view of 1808, was once the wholesale market for all kinds of grain. It operated from a site in Mark Lane until 1987.

MARKETS AND COMMODITY EXCHANGES

The high-tech world of today's City, with 24/7 electronic trading, is a world away from the coffee houses of Georgian London, where stock trading began. But it is almost as far from the face-to-face trading, with men in coloured jackets shouting and gesticulating, that occurred on the floor of the Stock Exchange until only twenty-five years ago. Equally, nothing could be more 21st-century than the new One New Change shopping mall by the French architect Jean Nouvel, all angles and dark windows inspired by the 'stealth bomber', yet its location of Cheapside has been a market for Londoners for nearly 1,000 years. Of such unexpected continuities and discontinuities is London's history made.

Trading in stocks began in the 17th century as a way of funding trading expeditions to China and India, and by the end of the century there were more than a hundred companies trading stocks in the City's coffee houses. By the mid-18th century there were eighteen coffee houses in Exchange Alley and the other streets between Cornhill and Lombard Street, home of banking since the 14th century. Most famous were Garraway's and Jonathan's, established by Jonathan Miles in 1680. Jonathan's was rebuilt three times in the 18th and 19th centuries as it became the Stock Exchange before moving into a vast and ugly new building beside the Bank of England in 1972. The 'Big Bang' of 1986 that deregulated trading meant trades no longer had to be made face to face, so large numbers of office and trading floors were no longer needed. Leaving its Threadneedle Street premises in 2004 for a gentler building with a loggia running along its front in the new Paternoster Square development next to St Paul's, the London Stock Exchange resisted a takeover by the American

NASDAQ in 2006–7, merged with the Italian Borsa in 2007 and today has a market capitalization of more than £2.5 trillion, making it the largest in Europe.

Although the Stock Exchange became the dominant commercial enterprise in London, it was an upstart compared to the Royal Exchange, opened by Queen Elizabeth I in 1565 – stock dealers were expelled from the Royal Exchange for rowdiness in 1698. It was, and remains, essentially a high-grade shopping centre with small shops around a colonnaded piazza, rebuilt after the Great Fire and once again with the huge pedimented building by William Tite in 1840–44. Increasingly, specialized exchanges came to dominate the City – the Corn Exchange in Mark Lane (1747–50, 1827–8), the Wool Exchange in Basinghall Street (1873–4), the Metal Exchange in Whittington Avenue (1882), the Coal Exchange in Lower Thames Street (rebuilt 1897–9) and the Baltic Exchange in St Mary Axe (1900–03). Of these only the Baltic Exchange and the London Metal Exchange still operate in the City. The headquarters of the Baltic, a specialist maritime exchange, were destroyed by an IRA bomb in 1992. The 'Gherkin' building is on the site. The Metal Exchange in Leadenhall Street is Europe's last 'open outcry' exchange, where traders shout and gesticulate to establish prices.

Although today only around 9,000 people live in the City, mostly in the Barbican, street markets and shopping were a major feature of the City until the late 19th century. Roman London had its forum on Gracechurch Street, and by the 12th century Cheapside, the widest street in the City, was a focus for markets, the names of its side streets recalling their specialist function – Milk Street, Bread Street, Poultry. The word 'cheap' means market – Eastcheap was the eastern market of the City. Cheapside has always remained the City's main shopping street, its status receiving a boost with the opening of One New Change in 2010.

The great wholesale markets at Billingsgate (fish) and Smithfield (meat), also with medieval origins, were rebuilt in the 19th century, and while Billingsgate moved out to new premises next to Canary Wharf in 1982, Smithfield remains on the site it has occupied for nearly 1,000 years. Smaller markets have come and gone – for example, in the mid-18th century the Stocks Market, then located where Mansion House is now, removed to the Fleet Market where Farringdon Street now is – but two great survivors are Petticoat Lane and Leadenhall Market. Petticoat Lane market, held around Middlesex Street, is a rare survivor of the old working-class City (Alan, Lord Sugar started in business on a stall here), selling cheap and second-hand clothes and bric-a-brac since the early 17th century; it is similar in character to Brick Lane in Whitechapel to the east. Leadenhall Market, off Gracechurch Street and built on the site of the Roman forum, was a meat, fish and poultry market by the 14th century. The present late-Victorian building is an atmospheric series of cobbled arcades of iron and glass between buildings, its market spaces converted to retail, though a good number are still food-related.

Billingsgate fish porters in 1910. There had been a market on the site since Saxon times, but the location was no longer practical by the late 20th century and the market moved to Canary Wharf.

The Billingsgate building, seen here in 1973, a decade before the fish market moved out, survives on Lower Thames Street. Much cleansed, no doubt, it has been converted to office and conference use.

Additional Places to Visit

○ a **Aldersgate**

The principal northern entrance to London was one of eight gates to the City before they were demolished (except Temple Bar) in the 18th century. The name Aldersgate is probably Saxon in origin: the gate was built in Roman times, rebuilt in 1617 and again after the Fire, and demolished in 1761. The blue plaque is on no. 1 St Martin's le Grand, where it joins Aldersgate Street, north from St Paul's Tube station, south of the Museum of London roundabout, opposite the entrance to Postman's Park (pp. 204–5).

○ b **St Olave Silver Street**

In the small open space at the corner of Noble Street and London Wall, a skull-and-crossbones tablet set into the low wall commemorates the site of St Olave's church, burnt down in the Great Fire. Opposite, another stone records that the churchyard was 'thrown back' to allow for road widening in 1862 by the Commissioner for Sewers. Just near here, on vanished Silver Street, Shakespeare stayed, as described with much contextual detail in Charles Nicholl's excellent book *The Lodger* (2007).

○ c **St Mary Staining Garden**

This very quiet garden, on the site of another destroyed church, nestles under the shadow of the massive no. 100 Wood Street (introduction, pp. 108–9), and is accessed through the archway of St Alban's Court or up Staining Lane.

○ d **Aldermanbury Square**

Behind no. 5 (p. 121), next to the Brewers' Hall, is a fine landscaped open space with small fountains and shady trees. A carved standing stone and bench (2000) by Richard Kindersley records that 'near this spot stood the Augustinian Priory of Elsing Spital 1329 to 1536 and since circa 1400 Brewers Hall', which was rebuilt after the war. On the other side of the Hall, by London Wall, the gentle 1972 sculpture by Karin Jonzen (1914–98), *The Gardener,* a kneeling young man tending the earth, is a tribute to the work done 'greening' the City's open spaces.

○ e **Aldermanbury Garden**

South of the square, at the top of Aldermanbury by the Guildhall complex, is this garden that has the foundations of the bombed Wren church of St Mary Aldermanbury (p. 120). Nearby there is a tribute to two of Shakespeare's actors who brought to print the First Folio (of which there is a precious copy in Guildhall Library), John Heminge and Henry Condell, with an 1895 bust not of them but of the poet, by Charles J. Allen (1862–1950).

○ f **Wood Street**

South from Gresham Street to Cheapside, several new buildings (nos 1 and 125 Wood Street) have preserved cheerful boundary marks. On the south corner are old shops of 17th-century origin at nos 124–126 Cheapside, and the tiny pocket garden of St Peter Cheap (see introduction, p. 105), rather dank and gloomy now but mentioned by William Wordsworth in his 1797 'Reverie of Poor Susan', with a tree that swings atmospherically over the old buildings.

○ g **Milk Street; St Olave's Court; Old Jewry**

Milk Street is one of the small streets off Cheapside named after the local trades (first recorded about 1140); the south end is now pedestrianized, with stone seats and a blue plaque on the site of the City of London School, 1835–82. At the north end of Milk Street, a plaque on no. 20 Gresham Street marks the birthplace of Thomas More in 1478. Moving east to the north of Cheapside via Russia Row and Trump Street, the plain-tiled alley Prudent Passage leads to Ironmonger Lane and the very attractive St Olave's Court, a garden by the Wren tower of St Olave Jewry (pp. 134–5), now offices. In Old Jewry, a blue plaque marks the site of the Great Synagogue that was here in the centre of the old Jewish community until 1272, when it was attacked and destroyed. The Jews were expelled by Edward I in 1290, and did not resettle in the City until the 1650s; in 1701 the community moved to the fine new synagogue in Bevis Marks, which still survives (pp. 271–2). Just off Old Jewry is the civilized enclave of Frederick's Place (p. 136), where Benjamin Disraeli (1804–81) worked as a solicitor.

○ h **Thomas Becket**

Complementing the statue in St Paul's Churchyard (p. 99), there are two markers of the spot near where Thomas Becket was born around 1118: a City blue plaque at no. 86 Cheapside and a striking small portrait high in the wall of no. 90 Cheapside. Nearby, there is an inscription in the unobtrusive but prosperous Mercers' Hall which points out that Becket was the son of a Mercer, Gilbert Beket, who at one time was a sheriff of the City and was buried in Old St Paul's.

BVLGARI
Cartier

The Bank of England & The Royal Exchange

Despite the cycles of destruction and rebuilding that have punctuated the City's history, its centre has barely shifted at all. In the 1st century AD the Romans laid out a forum on the high ground east of the Walbrook stream. Centred on what is now Gracechurch Street, its southern edge was aligned with Lombard Street and Fenchurch Street. A modern visitor standing in the middle of the site need walk for only a minute to the west along Cornhill to enter the forum's modern equivalent, the triangular space overlooked by the porticoes of three great buildings designed in the grand Roman manner: Mansion House, the Royal Exchange and the Bank. At its centre is Chantrey's bronze equestrian statue of the Duke of Wellington, and it is a reasonable conjecture that he too is a successor of Roman memorial sculpture: a 2nd-century bronze head of the emperor Hadrian, found in the Thames near London Bridge in 1834 and now in the British Museum, almost certainly came from a statue in the forum.

The City's modern forum is largely a creation of the 19th century, as its southern edge is defined by King William Street, cut through in 1829–35, and Queen Victoria Street, which followed in 1867–71. The former linked the Bank to London Bridge, while the latter created a route into the City from the new Victoria Embankment. When they were joined to the ancient roads that converge here – Poultry, Cornhill and Threadneedle Street – the result was the great traffic interchange, inducing the feeling that in the City all roads lead to the Bank of England. The Bank itself lies largely hidden behind its mighty screen wall; with the exception of its museum, all entrances are barred. As a result, it is a building that invites circumambulation. The mood shifts as the pavement leads away from the broad streets at its front to the narrow Lothbury behind it, densely lined with offices that are interrupted only by a Wren church, struggling to assert the needs of the spirit in the very shadow of Mammon's crushing bulk.

St Margaret Lothbury once stood on the banks of the Walbrook, which ran down to the Thames from Finsbury. It was the principal source of fresh water for the Roman city but was never navigable and had been covered over by the 16th century, when its precise course had already been forgotten; the modern street called Walbrook probably followed its east bank. London Wall still marks the approximate route of the Roman wall, the City's northern boundary; Bishopsgate was a Roman gate, and Moorgate was made in the 15th century. The varied uses of the area before the Great Fire are evident in the archaeology of street names. To the south, around what is now the Bank of

Opposite
The interior of the Royal Exchange today, home to restaurants, bars and shops following refurbishment in 2001. The top storey and a new glazed roof were added in 1986–91; the original roof is illustrated on p. 172.

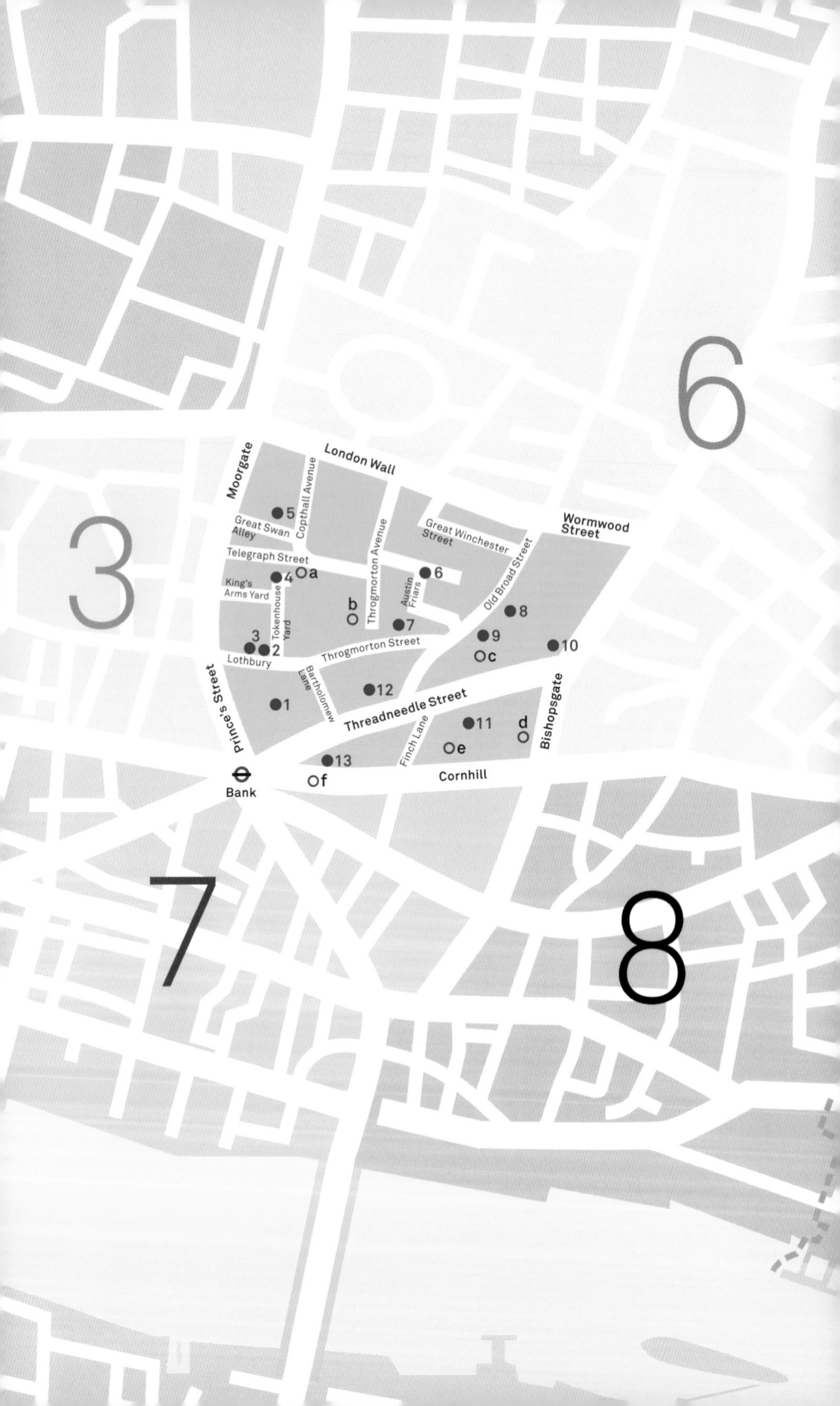

London Wall
Moorgate
Copthall Avenue
Great Swan Alley
Telegraph Street
King's Arms Yard
Tokenhouse Yard
Throgmorton Avenue
Austin Friars
Great Winchester Street
Old Broad Street
Wormwood Street
Throgmorton Street
Lothbury
Bartholomew Lane
Prince's Street
Threadneedle Street
Finch Lane
Bishopsgate
Cornhill
Bank
1
2
3
4
5
6
7
8
9
10
11
12
13
a
b
c
d
e
f
3
6
7
8

KEY TO AREA 4

● 1 Bank of England
● 2 Overseas Bankers' Club (former)
● 3 St Margaret Lothbury
● 4 Tokenhouse Yard
● 5 Institute of Chartered Accountants
● 6 Austin Friars
● 7 Drapers' Hall
● 8 Tower 42
● 9 City of London Club
● 10 Gibson Hall
● 11 Merchant Taylors' Hall
● 12 Stock Exchange (former)
● 13 Royal Exchange

○ a Moorgate alleys
○ b Angel Court
○ c Adams Court, Fountain Court; White Lion Court, Sun Court
○ d No. 1 Bishopsgate
○ e Cardinal Newman; Thomas Gray
○ f Royal Exchange Buildings

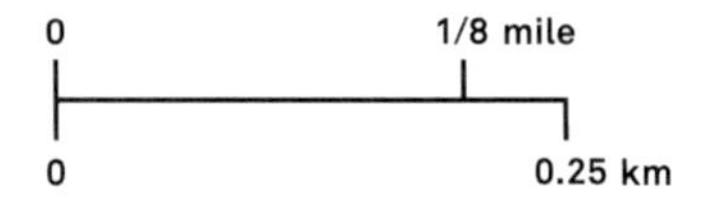

A view up Great Winchester Street towards London Wall in a print of 1814. Nothing survives of these modest timber-framed terraces, which were typical of the redevelopment of the City's minor streets after the Great Fire.

England, were trades: Threadneedle refers to the tailors, whose livery hall has been in the street since the 14th century, and one of the many possible explanations of the name 'Lothbury' is that it was originally 'Lottenbury', a street of copper foundries. Further north was London's Augustinian friary, commemorated today by Austin Friars, which preserves a sense of enclosure. Large houses were built in its neighbourhood, and these too have given their names to streets: Copthall Avenue is derived from a medieval mansion known as Copped Hall; Great Winchester Street recalls the house of the Marquess of Winchester. Livery company halls were often converted from such houses: Drapers' Hall, for example, is on the site of the house of Thomas Cromwell, Henry VIII's chief minister, and preserves not only its layout but also part of its garden. Throgmorton Street derives its name from Sir Nicholas Throckmorton, Elizabeth I's ambassador in France; he was a benefactor of the Protestant Dutch congregation who had taken over the church of the Austin Friars – where, 450 years later, they still remain.

To anyone who remembers the area before the late 1980s, its peacefulness is almost eerie. For centuries the Bank was choked by traffic jams and its narrow pavements were engulfed by pedestrians. The great change was the severe limitations imposed on traffic in the City as a security measure following the bomb planted in Bishopsgate by the IRA in 1993. That intensified the

Looking north from Mansion House in 1890, top, and 2011, above. In 1890 Soane's Bank of England, on the left, was still intact. Today only its screen wall survives, the rest having been rebuilt in 1923–39. The portico of the Royal Exchange is unchanged – although now free from Victorian soot – but has been overshadowed by the bulk of the former Stock Exchange building rising above it. In the distance is Tower 42.

hush brought about by the deregulation of the markets in 1986 and the introduction of electronic trading, which brought to an end the crowds of traders who would spill out of the Stock Exchange, just to the north of the Bank. Even on a weekday Threadneedle Street, lined with the Victorian palazzi of the joint-stock banks, can be as peaceful as an Italian town at siesta time; apart from rush hours and lunchtime, the modern City of London is overwhelmingly an indoor world.

Between the Bank and London Wall a dense network of small streets and alleys weaves between the main thoroughfares, creating a layout that has been very little affected by 20th- and 21st-century development. This good fortune can be explained largely by maps of the destruction wrought by the Blitz: almost no major damage was done east of Moorgate or north of the Bank. There was bombing at the edges – Merchant Taylors' Hall was badly damaged, and only the rich Victorian façade of the Carpenters' Hall survived a raid in May 1941 that ignited a gas main in London Wall – but otherwise the area's historic buildings were largely untouched. Despite great changes since the Second World War, there have been no losses to compare with the replacement of Sir John Soane's Bank of England between the wars.

Carpenters' Hall, from London Wall, photographed after an air raid in 1941. Bomb damage left only this rich classical façade of t 1876–80 livery hall designed by W. W. Pocock.

This would not have been the case if the redevelopment in the 1970s of the Bishopsgate site of the National Westminster Bank, resulting in what is now Tower 42, had gone ahead as initially planned. The City of London Club and John Gibson's National Provincial Bank, perhaps the most distinguished Victorian bank building in the City, were spared demolition only after a fiercely fought conservation battle. That episode marked a major shift in public appreciation of the City's historic fabric. Although the area is overlooked by new towers – notably the Heron Tower on the far side of Bishopsgate – it now contains only one, since the National Westminster Bank's other postwar intruder, Richard Seifert's Drapers' Gardens skyscraper built in 1962–7, was replaced in 2008–10 by low-rise offices, and even Tower 42 has survived only because planned demolition in the 1990s proved too expensive. A stroll from London Wall to the Bank demonstrates perfectly why, in the words of one historian of city planning, Michael Hebbert, 'the compactness of a 2000-year-old urban core is fortuitously well suited to the operation of a globalised financial service centre'.

Opposite
Tower 42, built in 1970–81 as the NatWest Towe and for thirty years the City's tallest building, at 183 m (600 ft) high. It was repaired and reclad following damage by a terrorist bomb in 1993.

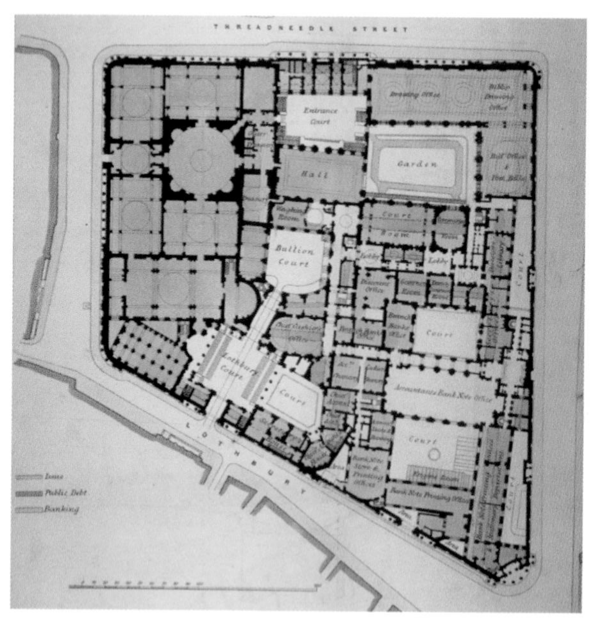

A plan of the Bank of England as it appeared in 1840, showing the full extent of the rebuilding and extensions carried out by Sir John Soane between 1788 and 1827.

1 BANK OF ENGLAND

Threadneedle Street EC2 • Sir Herbert Baker 1923–39

At the heart of the City, six streets – Cheapside, Prince's Street, Threadneedle Street, Cornhill, King William Street and Queen Victoria Street – radiate outwards like the spokes of a wheel. The axle around which they (and the City) revolve is the Bank of England, ceaselessly turning in its task of maintaining the monetary and financial stability of the nation. The building from which it operates occupies some three and a half acres (14,000 sq. m) between Threadneedle Street and Prince's Street, encircled by a high, blank screen wall that is the chief survivor of one of the great masterpieces of British architecture.

Founded in 1694 as the Government's banker, a role it still fulfils, the Bank is also the sole authorized issuer of banknotes in England and Wales, guardian of the country's gold reserves and, since 1997, although wholly owned by the Government, it independently sets monetary policy. It moved to George Sampson's purpose-built Palladian premises in Threadneedle Street in 1734 and rapidly developed a complex layout that reflected its multiplicity of roles: as well as a printing house for banknotes, it incorporated the Stock Exchange (from 1774 until 1802), a busy commercial bank and a barracks for the Brigade of Guards that until 1973 provided overnight security.

When Sir John Soane was appointed architect to the Bank in 1788 he at once began to remodel and extend the loose-knit mixture of buildings by his predecessor, Sir Robert Taylor, and others. Soane had an extraordinarily personal neo-classical

Opposite
Tivoli Corner, at the north-west tip of the Bank. Designed by Soane in 1804 on the model of the circular Temple of Vesta at Tivoli, it was remodelled in 1936 by Baker, who opened it up to create a top-lit pedestrian passage. High up on Baker's cupola is a gilded statue of Ariel by Sir Charles Wheeler.

architectural language, taut in its forms, spare in decoration, yet with a powerfully theatrical use of space and light. The Bank's need for security had encouraged the use of blank exterior walls combined with top lighting, ideas that Soane exploited with brilliant flair. He worked on and off for the Bank until 1833, during which time its premises doubled in size to their present extent, all eventually encircled by the windowless, rusticated screen wall. One of its immediately famous features was 'Tivoli Corner' (1804–7) where, inspired by the circular Roman temple of Vesta at Tivoli, Soane placed an open screen of close-set Corinthian columns curving between Lothbury and Prince's Street.

Thanks largely to the great increase in its responsibilities during the First World War, the Bank resolved in 1916 on a major redevelopment that would fundamentally break with its essentially single-floor structure. Plans were produced by the Bank's architect, F. W. Troup, but by 1922 he had been pushed aside by Herbert Baker, a friend of the Deputy Governor. Work on the rebuilding began in 1923 and was complete externally by 1939. Neither Baker – a conventional designer and self-satisfied man – nor his building have ever had a good press, and their

Reid Dick's statue of Soane, set into a niche in north front of the Bank's perimeter wall. By the time it was erected, in 1932, very little of Soan work survived inside.

Herbert Baker's towering entrance façade of the Bank on Threadneedle Street. Below the columns of the raised portico are six massive statues by Sir Charles Wheeler, who was responsible for most of the rebuilt Bank's exterior sculpture. On the right is the portico of the Royal Exchange; on the left is a First World War memorial designed by Aston Webb, with sculpture by Alfred Drury.

reputations have declined further as Soane's has soared. It is difficult to judge what Baker did, since there is such limited public access to the Bank, and the decision to retain as far as possible Soane's retaining wall, while welcome in itself, means that from close up the new buildings poke uncomfortably over the top; only from an elevated position can one see that Baker has used the wall as a visual platform from which the new bank rises. Although it was the Bank itself, by its decision to build upwards, that made the destruction of Soane's interiors all but inevitable, Baker had no great regret about replacing most of what his predecessor had done. He retained the form of some of Soane's banking halls, but took more care over two interiors by Taylor, the Court Room and Committee Room of 1767–8, which were dismantled and re-erected on the first floor.

The new buildings are designed in an accomplished if conventional streamlined neo-classical manner, in which sculpture is given an integral role. Baker's collaborator was Sir Charles Wheeler, who carved all the external sculpture and modelled the bronze external doors. Most prominent are the six mighty figures over the main entrance on Threadneedle Street, which exemplify Wheeler's wish that sculptors should 'cull from the Chinese or Negro or Egyptian or Greek those lovelinesses which seem good to us'. The lost interiors are well recorded not only in photographs but also in six hundred or so drawings in Sir John Soane's Museum in Lincoln's Inn Fields, and this evidence was used by the Bank in 1988 when it commissioned a reconstruction (by Higgins Gardner) of Soane's domed Bank Stock Office of 1792–3. This is part of the fine Bank of England Museum, which also displays gold bars among its other treasures.

The Lothbury façade of the Venetian Gothic former Overseas Bankers' Club, commissioned by the General Credit Company and built in 1866. Its main entrance was originally on the right-hand flank of the building, in Tokenhouse Yard; it was moved in the late 19th century.

2 OVERSEAS BANKERS' CLUB (*former*)

7 Lothbury EC2 • George Somers Clarke Sr 1866

It is always startling to encounter a Victorian commercial building in the City that is not classical, yet Ruskin's comparison in the *Stones of Venice* (1851–3) between the maritime empires of modern England and medieval Venice may explain why a revival of Venetian Gothic became briefly fashionable. No. 7 Lothbury looks as though it should face onto the Grand Canal, but in fact this palazzo sits between St Margaret's and Tokenhouse Yard, overlooking the back of the Bank of England. Its single-bay Portland stone façade on Lothbury is extraordinarily lavish: above a round-arched doorway with three orders of black marble columns and voussoirs banded with pinkish sandstone (used also for the building's plinth) rises a four-light Gothic window and balcony. Between the second and third floors is a large carved relief by James Redfern: its iconography has been interpreted by Philip Ward-Jackson as credit facilitating transport, commerce and industry. In 1962 the building, which was commissioned by the General Credit and Discount Company, was divided between stockbrokers' offices and a club for overseas bankers. In 2005–7 it was converted into one- and two-bedroom flats.

The carved relief by James Redfern on the façade of the former Overseas Bankers' Club.

The door to the principal vault in the former headquarters of the Midland Bank in Poultry, designed by Edwin Lutyens with Gotch & Saunders and built in 1924–39. There are plans to convert the building into a hotel.

THE ARCHITECTURE OF BANKS

It might be assumed that since it is the centre of the country's financial life the City should be able to demonstrate better than anywhere the historical development of banks as buildings. In fact, its earliest surviving banks of architectural significance date from as late as the 1850s. This is only partly a consequence of redevelopment. Because of the Bank of England's special status, protected by legislation, no rivals of equal architectural ambition were able to establish themselves in London for nearly one hundred and fifty years after its foundation in 1694.

As elsewhere in Europe, banking in London emerged from the goldsmiths' trade. Until the creation of the Bank of England, all banks were private businesses, usually family concerns, and there was little to distinguish their buildings from the premises of other tradesmen – they had a banking hall, usually called 'the shop', a room for private interviews, and accommodation for the banks' owners. Only one bank of this type survives in operation in the City today: Hoare's Bank in Fleet Street. The Bank of England, however, was a joint-stock company – a public company with shareholders. Since it was (as it remains) the Government's bank, legislation was passed to help ensure its sustainability by forbidding the founding of other joint-stock banks.

A photograph from 1913 of one of the City's earliest buildings for a joint-stock bank, the London, County and Westminster Bank in Lothbury, designed by C. R. Cockerell and William Tite and built in 1837–9. It was replaced in 1921–32 by the present much larger building by Mewès & Davis.

A. C. Pugin and Thomas Rowlandson's aquatint from 1809 of the Great Hall at the Bank of England. There were to be no other banks of comparable magnificence in the City for another fifty years.

Initially protected in a similar way, the Bank of Scotland lost its monopoly as early as 1716, leading to a flourishing of rival joint-stock banks in Edinburgh and Glasgow. In architectural terms, their needs were the same as the private banks, although domestic accommodation was not usually required. However, motivated by competitive display as well as a desire to impress potential investors, they spent heavily on magnificent premises with splendid banking halls. In 1826 the Bank of England lost its monopoly outside London, prompting a wave of new bank buildings in England's county towns and manufacturing cities. Legislation in 1833 permitted joint-stock banks to open in London for the first time, but the private banks managed to exclude them from the Bankers' Clearing House, where cheques and orders were exchanged, until 1854, and it was only then that joint-stock banks were able to compete on equal terms; soon they had routed the private banks. However, the private banks' tradition of architectural reticence survived for at least a century in the premises of merchant and investment banks, such as N. M. Rothschild, many of which remained private and even family concerns well into the postwar period.

At first the joint-stock banks copied the predominantly Palladian style of the original Bank of England, which had been taken up in the 18th century by private banks. By the 1860s, the High Renaissance palazzo style pioneered by Charles Barry's West End clubs had become the norm; a fine surviving early example is E. N. Clifton's 1861 building for the National Bank at nos 13–17 Old Broad Street. The style had obvious historic resonances with the urban palaces of the great Renaissance banking families, most famously the Medici. John Gibson's exceptional National Provincial Bank in Bishopsgate inaugurated a new fashion for sculptural ornament and freer forms of classicism, which by the end of the century had merged seamlessly with the enthusiasm for Baroque architecture. After the First World War, specialist firms of bank architects emerged, but the façades of their principal projects were often entrusted to celebrated names, most famously Lutyens (at the Midland Bank in Poultry, 1924–39) and Mewès & Davis, architects of the Ritz (at the London, County and Westminster Bank in Lothbury, 1921–32, and elsewhere).

Following deregulation of the financial markets in 1986, banks were able for the first time to trade in stocks directly, and so needed large dealing floors. This was one reason why the NatWest tower did not become a model for other bank buildings, most of which have since deregulation been comparatively low and spreading. Externally at least, they are now indistinguishable from other large commercial buildings. Although they are still making a fundamental contribution to the development of the City's appearance – for example, Deutsche Bank's large headquarters at Throgmorton Avenue, designed by Swanke Hayden Connell and completed in 1999, greatly improved a grim stretch of London Wall – it is arguable that banks are no longer an independent building type.

St Margaret's chancel fittings, which form a sumptuous ensemble of Wren-period woodwork, although little is indigenous to the church. The three east windows have been blocked for the reredos and the flanking paintings of Moses and Aaron. The latter were made around 1700 for St Christopher le Stocks, a church in Threadneedle Street demolished in 1782 when the Bank of England was extended.

3 ST MARGARET LOTHBURY

EC2 • Sir Christopher Wren 1683–92, 1698–1700

So devastating were the effects of the Blitz on the City's churches that an earlier phase of destruction, in the 19th century, is often forgotten. It was led by the Church of England itself which, following the steep mid-century decline of the City's resident population, wished to reduce the number of buildings for which it was responsible and make money from the sale of their sites. Between 1860 and 1905 some twenty City churches were demolished, among them masterpieces by Wren. As disquiet over this process grew, attempts were made by architects and others to preserve at least the major fittings of the demolished churches, and as a result St Margaret Lothbury was greatly embellished. Fortunately, what is almost a museum of 17th-century church fittings came through the Blitz unscathed.

The church hugs the street line on a tightly confined site immediately north of the Bank of England. Wren reused the foundations of the medieval church destroyed in the Great Fire, which explains why the west tower functions also as a porch and the unusual plan of a nave with a single wide south aisle. As so often with Wren's churches, the tower was completed a decade or so after the main body of the church; the design of its obelisk-like lead spire is attributed to his colleague, the scientist Robert Hooke.

The interior is dominated by the chancel screen, one of only two by Wren to have survived (the other is at St Peter upon Cornhill). Of great openness and delicacy, it is crowned by an eagle with spread wings below a broken segmental pediment bearing the royal arms. It was carved in 1683–4 (by William

The font, originally in Wren's St Olave Jewry, is finely carved by an unknown sculptor with cherubs' heads and biblical scenes, including Adam and Eve, shown here.

Woodruffe and an assistant, Thornton) for All Hallows the Great, All Hallows Lane. Demolished in 1894, that church was also the source of the chancel's brass candelabra and the pulpit's magnificent tester, busy with cherubs and flowers. St Margaret's marble font, the communion tables and the reredos in the south aisle all came from Wren's St Olave Jewry, Ironmonger Lane, torn down (apart from its tower) in 1892. Among the monuments are two fine portrait busts in marble, quite a rare sight in the City churches: Ann Simpson by Joseph Nollekens (1795) and Alderman Boydell, designed by Thomas Banks and executed by F. W. Smith (1820).

St Margaret Lothbury. Since this engraving was made, in about 1815, the three arched windows have been extended downwards and the south-east door removed.

4 TOKENHOUSE YARD

EC2

'Passing through Token House Yard in Lothbury, of a sudden a casement violently opened just over my head, and a woman gave three frightful screeches, and then cried, "Oh Death, Death, Death!"' That was how Daniel Defoe imagined the disaster that struck London in 1665 in his *Journal of the Plague Year*, a chilling echo in what is now an intimate L-shaped alley lined with mostly 19th-century banks and offices. Laid out in the early 17th century on the site of a mansion of the Earl of Arundel (who had moved to the Strand), it takes its name from an office dispensing privately issued copper tokens that compensated for the fact that until 1672 there was no legally authorized farthing coin. At no. 19, next door to the former Overseas Bankers' Club, is another former club, the Bank of England Dining Club, a steel-framed building of 1924–5 by F. W. Troup, whose designs for the rebuilding of the Bank were superseded by Herbert Baker's. Troup was in essence an Arts and Crafts supporter who in the 1880s had been an assistant in the office of J. J. Stevenson. There are no buildings by Stevenson in the City, but the impact of the 'Queen Anne' style with which he helped to revolutionize English architecture is evident in the delightful redbrick at no. 12 Tokenhouse Yard, designed in 1869–71 by E. A. Gruning for a merchant bank: a vision of the Restoration period very different from Defoe's. A narrow passage cuts through the building to link Tokenhouse Yard with a small network of alleys to its north, including the tiny Whalebone Court, which presumably takes its name from corset-makers rather than fishmongers.

Looking north up Tokenhouse Yard to the red-brick no. 12, built for a merchant bank in 1869–71. It is in the new Queen Anne style that was a reaction against the heavy opulence of much mid-Victorian City architecture. Note the recessed ground floor of the 1880s office building on the right, designed to make the most of the light in this narrow street.

5 INSTITUTE OF CHARTERED ACCOUNTANTS

Great Swan Alley and Moorgate Place EC2 • John Belcher 1890–93; J. J. Joass 1930; William Whitfield 1964–70

Even its greatest admirers would agree that the profession of chartered accountant is rarely associated with the words 'festive' or 'Baroque'. That makes its London headquarters all the more of a surprise: tucked away in a narrow street off Moorgate, this is a building that never fails to lift the spirits. In 1888 a limited competition for its design was won by John Belcher in collaboration with his assistant Beresford Pite. His choice of an Italianate Baroque style was not especially innovatory, although he manipulates its forms with great confidence and imagination; what made the building immensely influential was the special place that he and Pite gave to sculpture.

In 1884 Belcher had been on the committee that inaugurated the Art Workers' Guild, an association based on Arts and Crafts principles that sought to promote closer links between architects, artists and designers. At the Institute of Chartered Accountants, Belcher was able to demonstrate his belief that architecture should give sculpture 'loving assistance and unobtrusive support' by treating it 'as a jewel whose beauty is to be enhanced by an appropriate setting'. He worked with two outstanding young talents, both fellow members of the Art Workers' Guild: Harry Bates, who carried out all the ornamental carving, and Hamo Thornycroft, responsible for the frieze that runs round the building above the first-floor windows. This, it was said when the building was opened in 1893, 'represents those varied interests which look to the Chartered Accountants for financial guidance and order' – the arts, education, commerce, manufactures and much more (when the sculpture was first proposed, one wag wrote that it should depict a 'row of figures balancing themselves'). The interiors are equally enjoyable, combining, in the words of the historian Susan Beattie, 'immense grandeur and… that air of sweet approachability which is the hallmark of Arts

The main front of the Institute of Chartered Accountants, in Moorgate Place. This is the earliest part of the building, a Baroque design inspired by the palazzi of Genoa (which simila occupy narrow streets). Its rich sculptural programme includes, on the corner of the top floor, a figure of Justice. In terms of architectu propriety, the frieze, by Hamo Thornycroft, sho be at the top of the building; Belcher dropped it to a position above the first-floor windows t ensure that it would be legible from the groun

Belcher carried the Italian Baroque theme into the interior: the coffered barrel vault of the entrance hall was inspired by Galeazzo Alessi's Palazzo Pallavicini-Cambiaso in Genoa, designed in 1558.

and Crafts design'; especially memorable is the little balustraded bridge that spans the former library, now the members' room.

In 1930 the building was extended six bays along Great Swan Alley; Belcher had died in 1913 and the work was carried out by his former partner, J. J. Joass, in close imitation of the original. By contrast, William Whitfield's extension, completed in 1970, is unmistakably of its time in both its materials – concrete, glass and polished stone – and its aggressively hard-edged forms (no 'sweet approachability' here). However, it is linked to Belcher's building with uncommon sensitivity by a new bay and portal in his manner, complete with a carved frieze by David McFall. Whitfield's principal interior is the hall, where the building's Arts and Crafts tradition is continued by David Kindersley's engraved glass overdoors and a tapestry by Eduardo Paolozzi.

Built in 1950–54, the Dutch Church occupies a historic site in Austin Friars, home until the Dissolution of the monasteries of London's Augustinian friary. The houses and offices that tightly hem in the church have preserved a sense of the original monastic enclosure.

6 AUSTIN FRIARS

EC2

Many people passing no. 4 Austin Friars must be startled by the apparition in this narrow alley of a life-size statue of a friar writing in a book, carved by Tim Metcalfe in 1989. It is a reminder that the close that winds around the Dutch church was once the site of London's Augustinian friary, founded here in 1253. After being surrendered to the Crown in 1538, it was acquired by William Paulet, Marquess of Winchester, who built a house for himself on the northern part of the site (Great Winchester Street was later developed over its garden). In 1550 the nave of the friars' church, which had been rebuilt in the mid-14th century, was given by Edward VI to London's Dutch Protestant community, and the rest demolished. The church's tall, spare interior, restored in 1863–5 by Edward I'Anson and William Lightly after it was badly damaged by fire, had a significant influence on the later Gothic Revival in England. Destroyed in 1940, it has been replaced by a smaller, sober Portland stone building by Arthur Bailey, completed in 1954, which remains the home of the oldest Dutch Reformed congregation in the world. Its simple, cubic forms are relieved externally with carving by John Skeaping and internally by a blaze of colour from the west window's stained glass, designed by the Dutch artist Max Nauta.

The church stands in the middle of what is almost a small square, which until the 19th century was lined with substantial houses. It was rebuilt as offices, largely by the Drapers' Company, whose nearby hall is on the site of the mansion built by Thomas Cromwell on land leased from the friars. Many of the office buildings (for example, nos 2–6, 22 and 28) were designed by the Drapers' architect, Charles Reilly Sr, but the most striking, no. 23, an eccentric round-arched design of 1888, is by Aston Webb and Ingress Bell. In 2005 the Worshipful Company of Furniture Makers became only the fourth livery company since 1632 to acquire a hall in the City when they bought no. 12 Austin Friars, a domestic-looking redbrick building, designed in 1881 by E. A. Gruning.

For all the characteristically mid-Victorian opulence of its rebuilding in 1866–70, Drapers' Hall preserves the courtyard plan of the house of Henry VIII's minister Thomas Cromwell. The tympana over the ground-floor arches contain sculpture by Edward Wyon with scenes depicting commerce, industry, religion and science. The present layout, centred around a copy of the celebrated Hellenistic or Roman bronze of the boy removing a thorn from his foot, dates from the 1970s.

A corner of the Drapers' garden, which overlo Throgmorton Avenue. Shaded by mulberry tre it dates back to Tudor times.

7 DRAPERS' HALL

Throgmorton Street EC2 • John Gorham 1773–8; Herbert Williams 1866–70; T. G. Jackson with Charles Reilly Sr 1898–9

Screened from Throgmorton Avenue only by handsome gates and railings, the pretty garden of Drapers' Hall comes as a refreshing surprise in the cluster of narrow lanes and alleys immediately north of the Bank of England. As Walter Thornbury wrote in *Old and New London* (1878), this 'might be readily supposed the mansion of a person of rank'. Indeed, that is what it once was: Drapers' Hall is on the site of the mansion of Thomas Cromwell, Earl of Essex, whose life here has been so imaginatively recreated by Hilary Mantel in her award-winning novel *Wolf Hall* (2009). After Cromwell's execution in 1540 his house was forfeited to Henry VIII, and three years later the king sold it to the Drapers, then based in St Swithin's Lane. The arrangement of the building around a courtyard perpetuates the plan of the house, and the hall is on the site of Cromwell's. His 'Great Garden', extending northwards to London Wall, survived until 1873, when it was sold for development, but fortunately the part closest to the hall, the 'Upper Garden', was kept; shaded by five mulberry trees, it is a rare amenity for a livery company.

Founded to regulate the City's cloth trade, the Drapers' earliest royal charter was issued in 1364; it ranks third in precedence among the City companies (after the Mercers and the Grocers). No longer associated with textiles, it devotes its charitable activities primarily to education. Its building, destroyed in the Great Fire and rebuilt in 1668–71, was replaced in 1773–8, as a result of another fire, with a neo-classical design by the Company's surveyor, John Gorham. Most of his building

A detail of the hall's ceiling, painted by Herber Draper with scenes from Shakespeare: the central panel, shown here, is entitled *Prospero Summoning Nymphs and Deities*.

Opposite
The hall, which was built in two stages: the ceiling and the upper storey were added by T. G. Jackson and Charles Reilly Sr in 1899 to the palatial room designed in the 1860s by Herbert Williams.

survives but in 1866–70 it was remodelled out of recognition by Herbert Williams, who collaborated with the celebrated decorator John Dibblee Crace to create a sequence of splendid interiors in a free High Renaissance style. Having survived the Blitz, they wonderfully evoke the mid-Victorian City at its most plutocratically confident. The spectacularly large apsed hall, lined with pairs of full-height maroon marble Corinthian columns with gilded capitals, was given a new ceiling by T. G. Jackson in 1898–9 (its paintings, which depict scenes from Shakespeare's plays, are by Herbert Draper). This was part of a series of alterations by Jackson that involved the complete rebuilding of the Throgmorton Street front to provide lettable commercial accommodation. As a result, the original main staircase was replaced by a new one on the west side of the building, expensively lined with cipollino marble in an Italianate fashion, but tellingly in the Quattrocento style that fashionable taste by then preferred to the High Renaissance.

8 TOWER 42

25 Old Broad Street EC2 • R. Seifert & Partners 1970–81; GMW Partnership 1993–5

Although it has a secure place in history as the City of London's first skyscraper, Tower 42 – formerly known as the NatWest Tower – has had its architectural thunder comprehensively stolen

City high-rise old and new: on the left, the tip of the 'Gherkin' – no. 30 St Mary Axe – designed by Foster & Partners and opened in 2004; on its right, Richard Seifert & Partners' Tower 42, which opened as the NatWest Tower in 1981. The building in the foreground i an office development at O Coleman Street, designed b Swanke Hayden Connell wi David Walker and complete in 2007. In an interesting demonstration of changing architectural fashions, the chamfered geometry of the concrete window surround was influenced by some of Seifert's buildings from the 1960s, such as the Centre Point tower in Tottenham Court Road.

by the array of towers that have sprung up around it since 2004. Having lost its decade-long crown as Britain's tallest building to Cesar Pelli's One Canada Square in Docklands in 1990, its status as the City's highest building finally ended twenty years later with the topping-out of Heron Tower at no. 110 Bishopsgate.

The NatWest Tower had a long gestation. In 1959 the National Provincial Bank (which merged with the Westminster Bank in 1968) extended its site in Bishopsgate as the first stage in redeveloping its headquarters. In 1964 Richard Seifert prepared designs for a 197-m (647-ft) tower, but these had to be amended when permission to demolish John Gibson's banking hall was refused. Work finally started in 1970 on a tower 183 m (600 ft) high but was interrupted by a successful conservation battle to save the City of London Club and did not finish until 1981.

The tower is designed around a concrete core from which the floors are cantilevered, making it strong, but so greatly reducing the amount of space available that the bank could find room there only for its international banking division. Its appearance is largely determined by its narrow-set vertical stainless steel fins, but despite the tower's great size it has a weak silhouette and lacks memorable close-up detail. (There is a story, always denied by Seifert, that the plan was based on the three interlocking chevrons of the National Westminster Bank's logo.) In 1993 it was badly damaged by the IRA bomb in Bishopsgate: demolition was proposed but proved too expensive. Instead the tower was reclad and the interior refurbished. In 2000 it was sold by the bank and renamed Tower 42 (after the number of its cantilevered floors). It is now in multiple occupation; as well as offices it houses a restaurant on the 24th floor and, at the top, a champagne bar aptly named Vertigo 42, with what may well be the best views in the City.

Philip Hardwick's City of London Club, the only surviving club building in the City comparable with those of St James's and Pall Mall. Threatened with demolition in the 1970s as part of the National Westminster Bank's redevelopment of its Bishopsgate headquarters, it was saved after a conservation battle that proved a turning point in attitudes to the City's 19th-century architectural heritage.

9 CITY OF LONDON CLUB

19 Old Broad Street EC2 • Philip Hardwick 1833–4

Thanks to the presence of the livery companies, the City had less need of private members' clubs than the West End. The City of London Club was the first, founded in 1832, for directors or partners of City firms. Its Palladian premises, opened two years later, were designed by Philip Hardwick, who had many City connections – he was architect to the Goldsmiths' Company and designed their new hall, which opened in 1835. The club is far more restrained than either that great Baroque palazzo or the West End clubs of the same period, most of which had adopted a grand High Renaissance style, but Hardwick was also a master of a plain classical manner, evident in his buildings for St Bartholomew's Hospital. A hallway is screened by three arches from the impressive staircase, which rises in a single flight to a landing where it divides into two for the ascent to the main floor. The main dining room, a double cube, lies behind the staircase. No longer a private club, it functions as a venue for weddings and other events.

Commissioning royal portraits is a long-standing tradition for many of the livery companies. The Drapers have a particularly fine collection, of which part is shown here on display in the hall; it includes, on the far left, a portrait of George IV by Thomas Lawrence.

THE CITY LIVERY COMPANIES

Livery companies are an institutional link with the medieval past without parallel in Britain. They originated as guilds with three principal functions: to regulate trade, to provide fellowship and financial support for their members, and to offer masses for the souls of their deceased brethren. Their members were granted by the City authorities the privilege of wearing a distinctive uniform – livery. Each company is governed by a Master (sometimes known as a Prime Warden) and wardens, who elect the liverymen, chosen on the grounds of patrimony (a parent was a liveryman), apprenticeship in the trade, or 'redemption' – payment of a fee. To become a liveryman it is usual to apply first for the freedom of the City, and they then have the right to be involved in the election of the Lord Mayor and Sheriffs.

The companies' religious role came to an end at the Reformation, and their monopolistic control over their trades had largely died out by the 17th century. From then onwards they devoted their endowments to charitable purposes, the primary function of the livery companies today. Although some companies, such as the Goldsmiths, are still intimately involved with the trades that brought them into existence, many of the largest and most venerable, such as the Mercers and Merchant Taylors,

Most of the older livery companies have impressive collections of plate, designed primarily for use or display when dining. This silver table centrepiece was commissioned by the Leathersellers' Company as a First World War memorial: it is inscribed with the names of members who died. The Company, founded in 1444, still supports the leather trade in Britain.

are in effect educational charities. Others have reinvented themselves: the Tallow Chandlers, for example, are involved with the oil business. No companies were founded for over two hundred years after the creation of the Fan Makers in 1709, but since the establishment of the Master Mariners, who received livery in 1932, there has been a steady stream of new companies, including the Actuaries, granted livery in 1979, the Information Technologists in 1992 and the Tax Advisers in 2005.

There are currently 108 livery companies, and other companies await grants of livery. However, fewer than forty maintain traditional halls in the City (the others hire accommodation as necessary). These consist of at least a hall for dining and a court room for private business – in essence the hall and parlour that were the essential features of any substantial medieval house – but all have in addition suites of rooms for entertaining. Although most of the halls are on ancient sites, only Merchant Taylors' Hall has substantial medieval remains. Most were rebuilt after the Great Fire; a few, notably the Apothecaries', Skinners' and Tallow Chandlers' Halls, still date largely from the 17th century. A renaissance of the companies in the Victorian period produced some opulent buildings, of which those for the Goldsmiths, Fishmongers and Drapers are among the best survivors. Many halls had to be substantially reconstructed or wholly replaced after the Blitz; most companies favoured traditional styles, but from 1961, with the design of Bakers' Hall, Modernism became the accepted preference, at least for exteriors.

Where appropriate, the furnishings of a company's hall can demonstrate the trade that the company represented: this is the master's chair at Carpenters' Hall, photographed in 1917. When the company, which received its royal charter in 1477, built a new hall, opened in 1960, to replace one destroyed in the war, it commissioned new furnishings in eighteen different woods to display the skills of contemporary craftsmen.

10 GIBSON HALL

15 Bishopsgate EC2 • John Gibson 1864–5, 1878–9

In the vestibule of no. 15 Bishopsgate, built as the headquarters of the National Provincial Bank, is a bust by Carlo Marochetti of Daniel Robertson, its first manager. As his plaid cloak reveals, he was a Scotsman, and he was well aware of the architectural competitiveness between the great joint-stock banks of Edinburgh and Glasgow, a tradition that did not arrive in London until legislation in 1833 permitted banks funded by shareholders to open in the capital. Although the National Provincial Bank was relatively late in taking up the opportunity this offered – it was previously based in the Midlands – it set new standards in the City for architectural magnificence and, in particular, the prominent use of sculpture. Its designer John Gibson, a former pupil of Charles Barry, was the bank's official architect and had earlier designed its Glasgow premises.

The single-storey building, articulated by full-height attached fluted Composite columns alternating with round-arched windows, perfectly exemplifies Gibson's sensuous classicism, in which abstract detail is treated with the same plasticity as the sculpture with which it is integrated. The relief panels over the windows, carved by John Hancock, depict the arts and industries, and rising above the parapet are large figures by Henry Bursill and F. M. Miller that personify (from south to north) Manchester, England, Wales, Birmingham and Dover. The bank was extended to the north by Gibson in 1878–9, and the sculptural programme was continued, in a more naturalistic vein, by Charles Mabey. The principal interior – the original banking hall, 36 m (118 ft) long – is no less magnificent: lit by three saucer domes, its walls are lined with Corinthian columns of red Devon marble, below reliefs of putti engaged in banking operations.

In 1968 the bank merged with the Westminster Bank and the District Bank to become the National Westminster Bank, restyled NatWest in 1995. It inherited the National Provincial Bank's decision to redevelop its premises on Bishopsgate with a large tower (now Tower 42), but an application to demolish Gibson's bank as part of this scheme was refused. In 1980 the building was converted into a hall for the bank's social events, which involved stripping out its fittings. Despite its subsequent sale of the tower, NatWest has kept a branch at no. 15 Bishopsgate; the Gibson Hall, as it is now known, was restored in 2005 as a venue for corporate and private events.

The exterior of Gibson Hall. Its single-storeyed form imitates the Bank of England before its 20th-century reconstruction.

In Merchant Taylors' Hall, this rib-vaulted crypt, built in about 1375, was originally below a chapel, of which it does not appear to have been a part. It may have been constructed to provide secure storage for a shop in Threadneedle Street.

11 MERCHANT TAYLORS' HALL

30 Threadneedle Street EC2

At Merchant Taylors' Hall, the chefs still work in a great square kitchen built in 1425–33, the only substantial medieval interior to survive in any City livery hall. Even more atmospheric, although no longer in use, is a rib-vaulted crypt, built in about 1375, which probably once provided storage for a shop in

Opposite
A photograph from 1964 of the banking hall in the National Provincial Bank in Bishopsgate (now Gibson Hall), the finest Victorian bank interior in the City. Its fittings were removed in 1980 to allow it to be converted into a room for social events.

Despite its postwar appearance, a result of reconstruction after Second World War bomb damage, the hall is essentially a 14th-century structure, of extraordinarily large dimensions – 13 m (43 ft) by 28.5 m (94 ft). The organ came from Wren's St Dionis Backchurch in Fenchurch Street, demolished in 1878; the case was designed by Stephen Dykes Bower in 1966.

Edward I'Anson's courtyard buildings of 1878– for Merchant Taylors' Hall. The range on the left houses the Court Room; that on the right is the library.

Threadneedle Street. Few people walking along the street today would guess that they are passing a livery hall on a grand scale, since it has no façades: access is provided by modest doorways that lead into narrow hallways, exactly as would have been the case in medieval times. This is because the hall was built on the site of a large courtyard house belonging to John Yakeslee, the royal tent-maker. It was acquired by trustees in 1347 on behalf of the Merchant Taylors' Company, which soon afterwards rebuilt his hall.

Although nothing of the Middle Ages is visible in the hall now, its structure dates essentially from the 14th century, and its great size – 28.5 m (94 ft) long – is a powerful reminder of the wealth of the medieval Merchant Taylors, who were cutters and makers-up of cloth. The principal survivor of the building's reconstruction after the Great Fire is the courtyard's redbrick west range, built in 1681–3. The stone south and east ranges, containing the library and Court Room, are a late 1870s Gothic design by Edward I'Anson, best known as the architect of some of the earliest purpose-built offices in the City. He had been educated not only at Merchant Taylors' School (which helps explain how he got this commission) but also at the Collège Henri IV in Paris, which may account for the French flavour of his Gothic. His cloister on the north side of the courtyard, in front of the hall, was replaced in 1927 with a double-aisled Doric design by Herbert Baker. Repair of the buildings after the Blitz was entrusted to Albert Richardson, whose interventions are most evident in the attenuated but well-crafted 17th-century look of the remodelled hall and staircase.

12 STOCK EXCHANGE (*former*)

125 Old Broad Street EC2 • Llewelyn Davies, Weeks, Forestier-Walker & Bor 1964–72; Grimshaw Architects with VGMW Partnership 2004–8

London's stock exchange began in the coffee houses of the Restoration City and had no premises of its own until it moved to Threadneedle Street in 1774. Its first purpose-built home was in Capel Court, off Bartholomew Lane, completed in 1802 and greatly enlarged in two phases in the 1850s and 1880s. In 1972 it was replaced by a 26-storey heptagonal tower rising from a podium conforming to the planners' requirement that it had to allow access to the raised pedestrian walkways that were intended to replace street-level pavements throughout the City, a scheme first proposed in 1959 and not finally abandoned until the mid-1970s.

Clad in boldly modelled precast concrete panels, the tower was a prominent example of the Brutalist aesthetic of the 1960s, and almost as soon as it opened began to feature regularly in lists of London's ugliest buildings. Its large trading floor was a prominent attraction, but in 1992 this was closed to the public

A view along Old Broad Street towards the former Stock Exchange tower. Completed in 1972, it was remodelled out of recognition in 2004–8, following the move of the Stock Exchange to Paternoster Square. The City of London Club is visible on the far left; beyond it are two bank buildings of the 1860s.

Traders on the dealing floor of the Stock Exchange, photographed in 1968. Before the introduction of computers in the 1980s all trading was done in person. The man in the foreground is wearing a top hat, used to distinguish the runners, who delivered brokers' orders to the traders – all, at this time, men.

after a combination of deregulation in 1986 and the introduction of electronic systems had brought the furious excitement of face-to-face trading to an end.

In 2004 the Stock Exchange moved to a new building in Paternoster Square and its old home was redeveloped for mixed office and retail use. The tower was stripped of its cladding and its floors enlarged before being clothed in a new glass curtain wall that rises to hide the roof-top services; its corners are deeply recessed, producing the effect of a structure hung with seven separate sheets of glass. The podium was completely rebuilt and much enlarged as part of a joint development with the neighbouring building, which allowed a new pedestrian route to be opened between Throgmorton Street and Old Broad Street. Lined with shops and restaurants, it is a welcome reminder that, in the modern City, pavement life is precious.

An inscription in gilded letters in the frieze of Royal Exchange's portico records the building foundation in the reign of Elizabeth I and its reconstruction in the reign of Victoria. The wa memorial in front was designed by Aston Web and erected in 1920.

13 ROYAL EXCHANGE

Cornhill and Threadneedle Street EC2 • Sir William Tite 1841–4

Until the mid-16th century the City's merchants held their business meetings in the open air in Lombard Street. The completion in 1531 of a splendid bourse in Antwerp gave the merchant Sir Richard Gresham the idea of building something similar in London, but despite royal support no site could be found. The idea was later taken up by his son, Sir Thomas Gresham, and in January 1570 Queen Elizabeth I opened the Royal Exchange, in the prominent position on Cornhill that its successor still occupies. The first large-scale building in the City in a Renaissance style, it was replaced after its destruction in the Great Fire with a design by Edward Jerman. In 1838 this also burnt down, and a competition for its successor was won by William Tite, who, scandalously, was also one of the judges.

Like its two predecessors on this site, the Victorian Royal Exchange originally had an ope courtyard, but in 1883–4 it was given the glaze roof shown in this photograph of around 1900. the centre is a statue of Queen Victoria by Han Thornycroft, carved in 1896.

His building is much larger than its predecessors. It entirely fills its trapezoidal site, which widens from the west, where a mighty Corinthian portico faces Mansion House and the Bank, to the east, where a Baroque-looking tower rises above a statue of Thomas Gresham by William Behnes. The essentials of the original exchange's design, in which multi-storeyed ranges surrounded an open courtyard, was replicated in each of its successors, as were the small shops set into the ground floor of the external walls. Tite's courtyard, oblong in form, was also originally open, but in 1883–4 it was given a glazed roof by Charles Barry Jr.

The Royal Exchange has an imperious swagger that was new for the City's public buildings, emphasized by a rich programme of sculptural embellishment, notably the sculpture in the pediment, on the theme of 'The Earth is the Lord's and the Fullness Thereof', carved by Richard Westmacott Jr in 1842–4. The bronze equestrian statue of the Duke of Wellington in front of the building is by Francis Chantrey (completed after his sudden death in 1841 by Henry Weekes), a surprisingly quiet and reflective image of the Iron Duke. A sequence of mural paintings was

The Royal Exchange's tower, overlooking Royal Exchange Buildings, seen from the corner of Cornhill and Birchin Lane. The tower is capped with a weathervane of a gilded grasshopper – the device of Sir Thomas Gresham, founder of the Royal Exchange – which survives from the building's 17th-century predecessor.

La Maternité, a bronze sculpture by Aimé-Jules Dalou that forms part of a drinking fountain of 1877–9 in Royal Exchange Buildings, the open space to the rear of the Royal Exchange. Dalou's original sculpture was in marble, which weathered badly and was replaced by this bronze replica in about 1897.

commissioned for the internal courtyard; executed over a period of thirty years and now on display in the first-floor gallery, they include works by Lord Leighton (*Phoenicians Bartering with the Ancient Britons*), Stanhope Forbes and Frank Brangwyn. The Exchange continues to attract art: the strip of land behind it, Royal Exchange Buildings, is dotted with sculpture, ranging from Aimé-Jules Dalou's suckling mother, *La Maternité*, part of a drinking fountain of 1877–9, to Michael Black's luxuriantly whiskered Paul Julius Reuter, a granite herm bust erected in 1976 to mark the 125th anniversary of Reuters.

When it was opened by Queen Victoria in 1844 the Exchange was still an essential business forum, but its importance declined with the opening of specialist exchanges later in the 19th century, and in 1939 it became offices for the Guardian Royal Exchange Assurance Company. In 1986–91 the company commissioned substantial alterations by the Fitzroy Robinson Partnership that involved the replacement of Barry's roof in order to add an extra storey. In 2001 the entire building was refurbished for luxury shops, bars and restaurants (see p. 144).

Additional Places to Visit

O a **Moorgate alleys**

Linking Tokenhouse Yard (p. 159) to Moorgate, King's Arms Yard is one of a maze of alleys: go boldly through the archway at no. 12 Tokenhouse Yard to reach Whalebone Court and Copthall Close, encountering some fine 19th- and 20th-century commercial buildings, round to the Institute of Chartered Accountants (pp. 159–61) in Moorgate Place, by Great Swan Alley. This was the site of an unsuccessful insurrection by the Fifth Monarchist enthusiast Thomas Venner in 1661. He led a band, rumoured (according to Pepys) to be 500 men, but actually only fifty, to St Paul's Cathedral to demand the keys, but they were repelled by the Lord Mayor's forces and retreated to Kenwood in north London. They then attacked again but were forced to retreat to the Helmet Tavern on Threadneedle Street and the Blue Anchor on Coleman Street, where they were defeated. Venner was executed on 16 January 1661.

O b **Angel Court**

One of the oddities of the City environment is the occasional attempt to segregate walkers from motorists by the provision of highwalks or 'ped-ways'. This fashionable device was popular in the 1960s and the City made extensive plans for it, most thoroughly on the Barbican estate (pp. 215–17). Many City buildings made provision for high-level walkways and possible connecting bridges, and a late remnant can be seen at Angel Court in Throgmorton Street, in the purple marble building by Fitzroy Robinson and Partners, from 1974–80. But walkers and workers have tended to cling stubbornly to the street, in spite of the traffic, so apart from welcome bridges over Lower and Upper Thames Street there is now not much sign of this idealistically Corbusian plan.

O c **Adams Court, Fountain Court; White Lion Court, Sun Court**

Just south of the City of London Club (p. 165), Adams Court is a refuge from the City which leads to Fountain Court overlooking the City of London Club's lawn: access is from Threadneedle Street or Old Broad Street. The best City alleys are south of Cornhill (pp. 316–17) but it is worth going across Threadneedle Street via Finch Lane, to the north side of Cornhill, into White Lion Court with its fine 1767 house, and Sun Court for the curious brick building in the angle of the square with a Gothic window opposite a florid coat of arms. This is the extension to nos 66–67 Cornhill by Chatfield Clarke, at the back of the genuinely medieval Merchant Taylors' Hall (pp. 169–70).

O d No. 1 Bishopsgate

You cannot now see Crosby Hall, which stood in Bishopsgate near Great St Helen's, unless you go to Chelsea, whence its Great Hall was transported and rebuilt (p. 238); there is also a façade from the 17th-century Paul Pindar mansion from Bishopsgate in the Victoria & Albert Museum. But later buildings have been splendidly restored, including at the south end of the street, no. 1, an imposingly lavish office building with high-sprung arches, palazzo windows and Dutch-style dormer windows, whose refurbishment was highly commended in the City Heritage Awards in 1986.

O e Cardinal Newman; Thomas Gray

John Henry Newman (1801–90), the great theologian, thinker, and author of *The Dream of Gerontius* (1865, set to music by Elgar in 1900), was born at no. 60 Threadneedle Street, marked by a City blue plaque. He was beatified by the Pope in 2010. The poet Thomas Gray (1716–71) has a memorial by F. W. Pomeroy (1856–1924) with a portrait on the site of his birthplace at nos 39–41 Cornhill, inscribed with his most famous line, 'The curfew tolls the knell of parting day', from 'Elegy Written in a Country Churchyard' (1751).

O f Royal Exchange Buildings

As well as the public art of the Royal Exchange (pp. 172–3), in the middle of Cornhill, on the south side of the building, is the prominent statue from 1993–4 by James Butler (b. 1931) of James Henry Greathead (1844–96), engineer of the City and South London Railway, who developed shields that made underground tunnelling possible. He stands, rather hidden by his wide-brimmed hat, poring over a plan, with his coat on his arm. This statue and two smaller nearby structures have their origin in the extension of the Docklands Light Railway to Bank Station: venting structures had to be installed in nearby streets, so the City Planning Officer negotiated the installation of this statue, as well as a small funerary temple at the junction of Queen Victoria Street and Bucklersbury, and a decorated obelisk where King William Street meets Lombard Street.

5 Smithfield & The Barbican

This large area occupying the north-west limits of the City has a character unlike any other district of the Square Mile. It falls almost entirely outside the Roman city, was very much a suburb of medieval London and largely escaped the destruction of the Great Fire. Its two halves are also utterly unlike each other, Smithfield to the west having made another miraculous escape from fire in the 1940 Blitz, while the Barbican was burnt to a cinder. The result is a sharp contrast between these two halves. Smithfield has its great Norman priory church of St Bartholomew-the-Great, its charming patch of 17th-century streets, the Georgian and Victorian citadel of Barts hospital and the brick and crystal palace of its Victorian meat market. But the Barbican is just as striking – a single-minded essay in mid-20th-century social engineering expressed in the architecture of the Modernist sublime, the saw-toothed profile of its 122-m (400-ft) towers rearing up to startle the unwary visitor.

Smithfield today still retains a greater spaciousness than any other part of the City. The odd-shaped open space of West Smithfield is a relic of its origins as the 'smooth field' outside the City walls, a desolate marsh shelving westwards to the valley of the Fleet river, which today runs in a sewer under Farringdon Street. Only the fragments of City wall at the area's southern edges and the place names of Newgate, Cripplegate and Aldersgate Street show that the Romans were here. After their departure nothing much happened in the area until the Middle Ages. By the 11th century, ribbon development was creeping north up Aldersgate Street, but the centre of activity was in Smithfield itself, lying at the southern end of St John Street, the main route in from the north. Livestock were being driven down that wide street to the market that had been established at Smithfield by the 10th century. The 12th-century chronicler Fitzstephen called Smithfield a 'celebrated rendezvous of fine horses to be sold, and in another quarter are placed vendibles of the peasant, swine with their deep flanks, and cows and oxen of immense bulk'. Though the live-animal market left 150 years ago, Smithfield is still awash with meaty vendibles, especially at dawn.

The other great early medieval event for Smithfield was the founding of the priory and hospital of St Bartholomew, by one Rahere, a reputed one-time minstrel at the court of Henry I, around 1123. Although St Bartholomew was once just one of several monastic houses hereabouts, it is now unique not just locally but in London for the amount of Norman fabric surviving in the church, a solemn, atmospheric space of massive cylindrical columns. Although the rest of the priory has disappeared under

Opposite
Inside the Grand Avenue of Smithfield Market today, showing stalls updated to modern standards of hygiene.

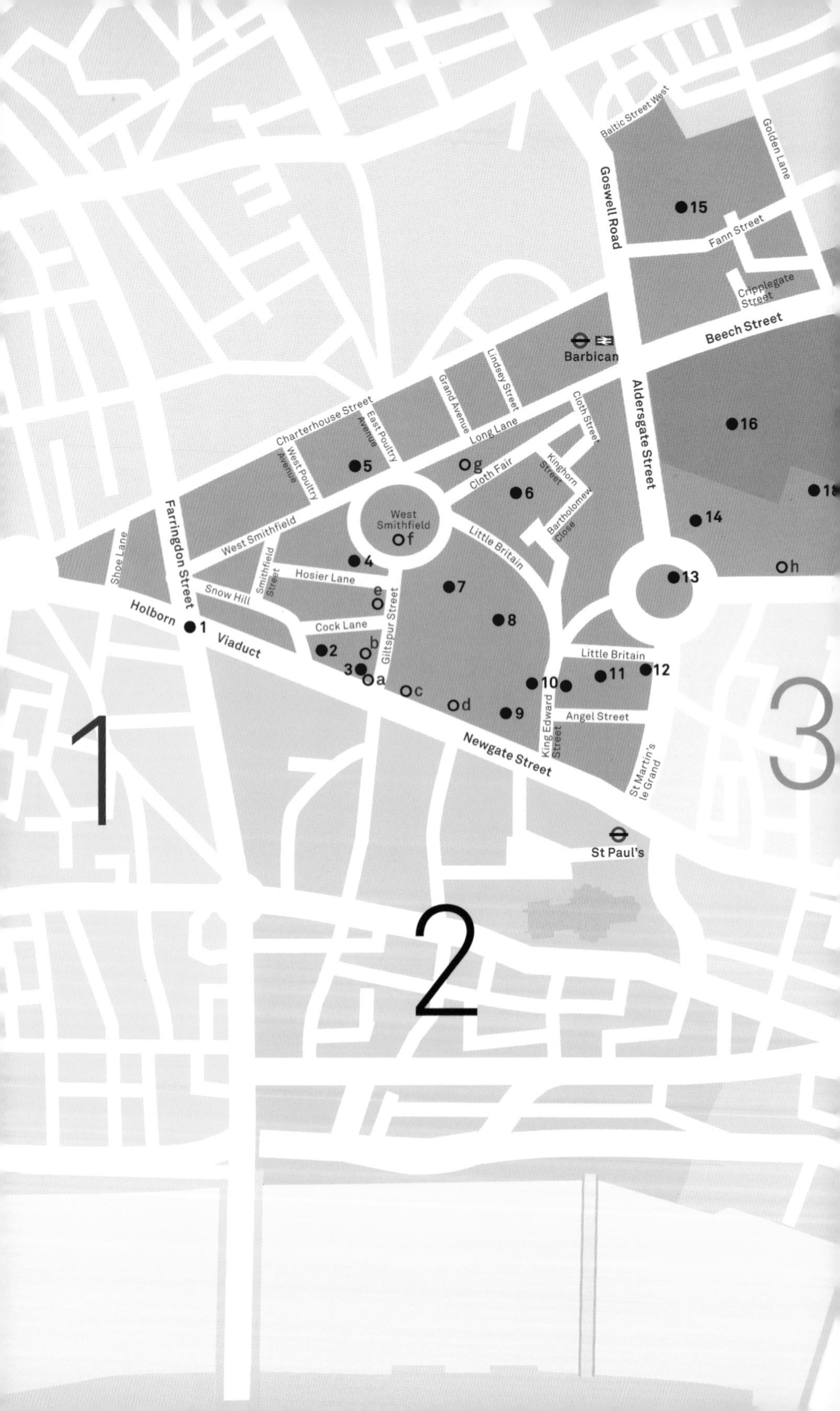

Baltic Street West
Golden Lane
Goswell Road
15
Fann Street
Cripplegate Street
Beech Street
Barbican
Aldersgate Street
16
Lindsey Street
Grand Avenue
Cloth Street
Long Lane
Charterhouse Street
East Poultry Avenue
West Poultry Avenue
5
g
Cloth Fair
Kinghorn Street
6
Bartholomew Close
14
West Smithfield
f
Little Britain
West Smithfield
Shoe Lane
Farringdon Street
Smithfield Street
4
Hosier Lane
Snow Hill
e
Giltspur Street
7
13
h
Holborn
1
Viaduct
Cock Lane
8
b
2
3
a
c
d
9
10
11
12
Little Britain
Angel Street
King Edward Street
Newgate Street
St Martin's le Grand
St Paul's
1
2
3

ll Street
Milton Street
Milton Court
Ropemaker Street
Moor Lane
Moorfields
New Union Street
Moorgate
Moorgate
Avenue
Fore Street
ore Street
Wall
● 21
○ k
● 25

KEY TO AREA 5

● 1 Holborn Viaduct
● 2 Snow Hill Police Station
● 3 St Sepulchre
● 4 Haberdashers' Hall
● 5 Smithfield Market
● 6 St Bartholomew-the-Great
● 7 St Bartholomew-the-Less
● 8 St Bartholomew's Hospital
● 9 Christ Church Newgate Street
● 10 General Post Office Buildings
● 11 Postman's Park & Watts Memorial
● 12 St Botolph Aldersgate
● 13 Museum of London
● 14 Ironmongers' Hall
● 15 Golden Lane Estate
● 16 Barbican Estate
● 17 Barbican Centre
● 18 St Giles Cripplegate
● 19 Guildhall School of Music & Drama
● 20 Whitbread's Brewery
● 21 Milton Gate
● 22 Salters' Hall
● 23 Alban Gate
● 24 St Alphage London Wall
● 25 Fox's Umbrellas

○ a Newgate
○ b Watchhouse; Snow Lane Court
○ c Giltspur Street Compter
○ d Greyfriars Monastery
○ e The Golden Boy of Pye Corner
○ f Smithfield Rotunda Gardens
○ g Cloth Fair
○ h Barber Surgeons' Herb Garden
○ i Barbican Waterside
○ j Cripplegate; Fore Street
○ k The Minotaur

N

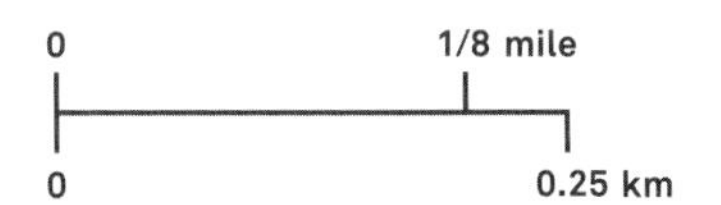

later development, and the hospital has been rebuilt several times, on its north side the church adjoins a grid of narrow streets from the late 16th-century development put up by the Rich family after they acquired the priory from Henry VIII. While many of the narrow, three-storey buildings in Long Lane and Middle Street, Cloth Fair and Newbury Street, Kinghorn Street and tiny paved East Passage date from the 19th century, they maintain the scale of the original development. But no. 74 Long Lane is an authentic timber-framed house of *c.* 1700, its white-painted front jettied out like a Tudor building, but coated in mathematical tiles, a rarity in London, designed to look like brick. Round in Cloth Fair, nos 41–42, completed in 1614, is grander, a brick house with a pair of square bays topped by pert gables. The poet and architectural warrior John Betjeman lived next door at no. 43 for many years.

The Victorian Smithfield Market buildings photographed during the First World War.

Smithfield was not always so civilized. From the 12th century it played host to Bartholomew Fair, an annual cloth merchants' fair that soon became notorious for partying and 'low entertainments': it lasted until 1855 when the City Corporation decided, after 700 years' reflection, that it had to be suppressed for encouraging debauchery and disorder. To the east, the Barbican area reached its peak of salubrity in the 17th century with a number of grand stone-fronted mansions on Aldersgate Street, such as Thanet House. Still further east, the medieval archery grounds around Moorgate had given way by the 17th century to a park with formal walks. The Great Fire entirely spared the Barbican area, protected by its isolation north of the City wall, and most of Smithfield except its southern fringes. The point where the Fire burned out is marked high up on the corner of Giltspur Street and Cock Lane by the Golden Boy of Pye Corner, a 17th-century gilded statue of a boy, accompanied by an inscription: 'This Boy is in Memmory Put up for the late FIRE of LONDON Occasion'd by the Sin of Gluttony 1666'.

The current form of Smithfield is due to Victorian philanthropy on a grand scale. Having fallen into disrepair, the hospital was rebuilt in the 18th century, with the fine classical courtyard that survives, but by the mid-19th century the squalor of the neighbouring market was giving cause for concern. Pip in *Great Expectations* finds it a 'shameful place…all asmear with filth and fat and blood and foam'. A decade later the City Corporation made the extension of the Metropolitan Railway from Farringdon to Moorgate the occasion to impose a new grid of wide streets on Smithfield, with spacious new glass-roofed meat-market buildings ranged above an underground goods station between West Smithfield and Charterhouse Street. The new Holborn Viaduct over the Fleet valley made the journey between City and West End less taxing for horse-drawn traffic. As well as the market buildings, the open space of West Smithfield is ringed by Victorian and Edwardian office and warehouse buildings, the latter now mostly offices and flats. Those on the north side of Charterhouse Street include several great sheer-fronted cold stores, the Central now, bizarrely, housing a small power station. On a smaller scale, Victorian offices and shops stretch up Snow Hill and along

Bartholomew Fair, depicted here around 1710, took place every August at Smithfield from 1133 to 1855. It became notorious for rowdy entertainments.

Smithfield, or 'smooth field', seen here in Pugin and Rowlandson's view of 1811, was an open livestock market for nearly a thousand years until the 1850s.

Newgate Street. Between the market and the hospital a great ramp still spirals down to the former goods station beneath.

From the 17th century to the Second World War the story of the Barbican is one of slow social decline as the street pattern became ever more dense with small courts of houses and cloth warehouses replacing the old mansions. All this came to a spectacular end on the night of 29 December 1940, the so-called Second Great Fire of London, when 64,000 incendiary bombs rained down on the City, burning a swathe from St Paul's to Islington. Smithfield escaped with minor scarring, but the Barbican was reduced to a sea of brick and ash and a few solitary survivors: Cripplegate Institute of the 1890s (it fared less well in a heavy-handed office conversion of the 1980s), Ironmongers' Hall and the Chiswell Street brewery. Plans for London's rebuilding were being hatched even as the Blitz flared up again in 1944, but while the planners planned the Barbican lay ruined, overrun with wild flowers and weeds for more than a decade. Eventually, in the early 1950s, a series of interrelated plans was designed to rebuild this wilderness, in the words of the housing minister Duncan Sandys, into 'a genuine residential neighbourhood incorporating shops, open spaces and other amenities, even if it means forgoing a more remunerative return on the land'. First came the Golden Lane estate to the north, in 1952–62, then the London Wall dual carriageway along the south side, known originally by the appropriately Roman designation of Route XI, and with the Barbican estate and arts centre as the filling in between. Route XI and the Barbican shared a new vision, inspired by Le Corbusier's Ville Radieuse, of a two-layer city with a new 'ground level' for pedestrians on elevated walkways ('ped-ways') and wide decks with shops and the main entrances to buildings, with traffic banished to the original street level below. The new London Wall was to be flanked by six curtain-walled towers set at a slight angle to the road and by a series of lower slab blocks, creating a zigzag pattern. The raised decks fed into the Barbican, first planned in 1956, and in 1959 a decision was made to extend the system of pedestrian ways across the whole City – amounting to nearly 50 km (30 miles) – so that new buildings would have their receptions raised, and the few historic buildings allowed to remain would have had an odd, sunken appearance.

Happily this idea was abandoned in the property slump of the early 1970s, but it is a pity that the coherence of the London Wall scheme itself has been lost through rebuilding of at least half the 1950s slabs and towers with a ragbag of flashier buildings since the 1980s, especially the mighty hulk of Alban Gate that squats across the whole road. A few delicate little pedestrian bridges still cross Aldersgate Street and London Wall and survive around Upper and Lower Thames Street, but the decks north of London Wall are mostly rather desolate spaces, the shops boarded up. Since then the Barbican and Golden Lane have been listed, so architectural innovation has been restricted of late to the east of the area: the green glass fortress of Denys Lasdun's Milton Gate, and the far less subtle thrusting bulk of

Thanet House was refronted, possibly by Inigo Jones, around 1641. It was in Aldersgate Stree which, it was said, 'resembleth an Italian stree more than any in London...'.

Opposite
The form of Frobisher Crescent in the Barbican estate, opened in 1969, harks back to a Georgia crescent of houses on the site bombed during the Blitz.

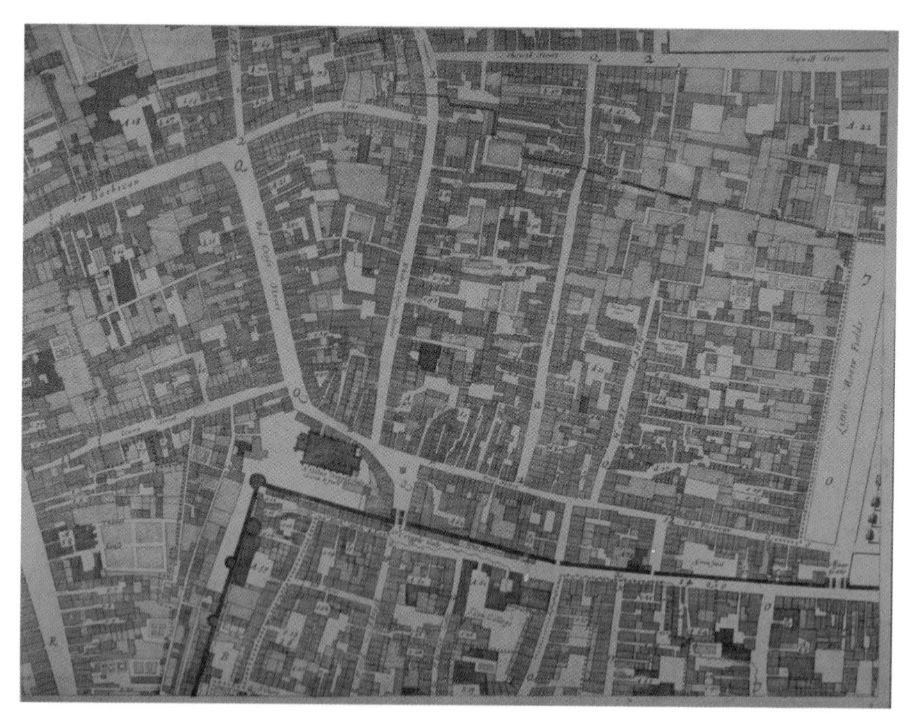

The Barbican area as it was in 1676. Today, little survives from this time apart from St Giles Cripplegate and parts of the City walls; Smithfield, to the west, fared better.

A promotional poster of 1970 for the Barbican estate, which aimed to make the City a residential area once more. Today around half of the City's inhabitants live in the Barbican.

An architects' model of the Barbican estate, as projected in 1962. The staggered blocks of the London Wall development, then already under construction, are seen at the left.

City Point on Ropemaker Street – a radical recasting in 2000, also in shiny green glass, of the 1960s traditional-Modernist BP headquarters.

Smithfield has had a quieter time since the war. Its merciful escape from the Blitz means that building since has mostly been small-scale infill or conversion. An interesting 'in keeping' building is Founders' Hall of 1984–6, by J. Sampson Lloyd of Green Lloyd architects, along the back of St Bartholomew-the-Great. It is the acceptable face of Postmodernism, with gables and jetties in brick and tile that allude to – but neither mock nor ape – the Tudor buildings originally here. Although the meat market, uniquely among London's wholesale markets, has survived on its original site, the area threw off its grimy image in the 1990s with the arrival of designers and architects and the conversion of warehouses, for example in Little Britain, to 'loft' apartments. A proliferation of new restaurants and bars has also neatly gainsaid those who predicted that the Barbican would never be a success as a residential development because of the lack of these facilities. Smithfield and adjacent Clerkenwell are now thriving areas with their own characters; Smithfield is not quite like the rest of the City and attempts to make it so should be resisted.

1 HOLBORN VIADUCT

EC1 • William Heywood 1863–9

London, unlike Paris, is a city of steep hills, criss-crossed by rivers such as the Fleet (now culverted under Farringdon Street), and as the city grew vast in the 19th century this caused problems for public transport – horse-drawn buses found the slopes difficult. So the municipal authorities built streets raised on bridges and viaducts to even out the slopes. Holborn Viaduct, built in 1863–9 by the City surveyor William Heywood, was designed to take traffic across the valley of the Fleet into the West End. Although the visible part is the handsome iron bridge supported on massive granite piers over Farringdon Street, the whole edifice is nearly 430 m (1,400 ft) long – vaults were hidden beneath the flanking buildings. Two of the original four office blocks, with a stone staircase linking the two levels, survive on the south side, and a third was recently rebuilt in replica, with a new lift, at the north-west, as part of the adjoining redevelopment of Atlantic House, an arresting design of red sandstone, metal and glass by Rolfe Judd (2001). Four bronze statues of Science and Fine Art, Commerce and Agriculture adorn the parapet. As an up-to-the-minute example of Victorian engineering, the viaduct contained conduits for water, gas and telegraph pipes as well as a sewer.

The engineering novelty that was Holborn Viaduct attracted a fashionable crowd of well-dressed visitors, seen here in 1870 taking a rest on a pile of masonry.

2 SNOW HILL POLICE STATION

5 Snow Hill EC1 • Sydney Perks 1925–6

The City of London Police is unique in many ways, including the architecture of its police stations. This little building may not have the significance or street presence of the headquarters building in Wood Street (see pp. 119–20), but it has its own charm – an unexpected quality for a police station. Designed by the City surveyor who was then nearing retirement, the

Snow Hill's original narrow frontage is notably sleek and luxurious for a police station, tricked out in stone and bronze.

Most police stations in London, even modern ones, feature this, the traditional 'blue lamp'.

delicately faceted bronzed bow that rises up the front has a hint of 1920s French early Deco and would look quite at home in Regent Street or Bond Street. A blue plaque recalls the Saracen's Head, an inn and coachyard that stood on the site until 1868, reputedly from the 12th century and said, implausibly, to have been frequented by John Bunyan.

3 ST SEPULCHRE

Holborn Viaduct EC1 • 15th century; Joshua Marshall 1667–71; Arthur Billing 1879–80

A quick glance at smoke-blackened St Sepulchre, with its enormous pinnacled tower and three-storey porch, suggests it might be a huge Gothic parish church, but it is actually a strange mixture of styles. The 15th-century church was burnt out in the Great Fire but the rebuilding afterwards was respectful, replacing the lost tracery with Gothic forms of the day. These were replaced again in 1790 with round-headed windows, which remain at the east end and the north chapel. However, as fashions changed once more, tracery was put back into many of the windows in the 1870s. Inside though, despite the Gothic tracery, the feeling is unmistakably of the late 17th-century repair, probably by Joshua Marshall, with a broad aisled nave on Doric columns, all painted white. The effect is enhanced by the array of 17th-century furnishings including pulpit, lectern, reredos and, most imposing of all, the organ and case: St Sepulchre is home to the Royal School of Church Music. Sir Henry Wood learned to play the organ here – the wreath that adorns his bust during the annual Proms concert series in the Royal Albert Hall normally resides on his bust in the Musicians' Chapel off the north aisle, where his ashes are buried. A 1960s stained-glass window here commemorates the singer Dame Nellie Melba, depicting her with the pudding named after her. Less sweet is the story told by the handbell on display in the nave, rung by the sexton outside Newgate Prison (site of the Central Criminal Court, opposite) on the eve of an execution to remind the prisoner to repent before he met his maker. The church bells up in the tower are the 'bells of Old Bailey' mentioned in 'Oranges and Lemons', that most sinister of nursery rhymes: the tenor bell of St Sepulchre tolled the prisoner on his way to execution at Tyburn (Marble Arch). Adjoining the churchyard on Giltspur Street is a 1960s replica of the 1790s watchhouse, destroyed in the Blitz, which was built to guard against body-snatchers.

St Sepulchre's three-storey porch is one of the few parts of the 15th-century church to have survived the Great Fire. The rest is Gothic as reimagined by architects in the 17th and 19th centuries.

4 HABERDASHERS' HALL

18 West Smithfield EC1 • Sir Michael Hopkins 2002

This is unusual: a newly built livery hall on a new site. In the mid-1990s the Haberdashers' Company decided to make the most of its valuable old site near Guildhall by redeveloping its dilapidated 1950s hall to benefit its educational charities, most famously Haberdashers' Aske's School. The old site became part of the Norman Foster-designed development at no. 100 Wood Street (1997–2000, see p. 109), and the company moved to Smithfield. The frontage of the new site is the former Vestey meat-company offices, now shops and flats, an imposing listed Edwardian range of red brick trimmed with stone, through which glimpses of the Haberdashers' new courtyard may be had. This is a calm, almost Japanese space, with plain double-height colonnades of handmade bricks and steep roofs covered in lead tiles set at 45 degrees. This diamond pattern is repeated inside in the floor tiles, and in the livery hall's American oak ceiling, tensioned with fine stainless steel, suggestive of a medieval roof. Further historical depth is created with reused fittings in some of the committee rooms, including 18th-century panelling. It is a beautifully detailed and deceptively simple design, a world away from the same architect's assertive Portcullis House for the MPs at Westminster.

The courtyard of Haberdashers' Hall may be glimpsed through entrance gateways on West Smithfield. The roof tiles are lead, each shaped by hand.

The hall of the new Haberdashers' Hall is both sparely modern and, with its steel tensioning wires, reminiscent of a medieval roof.

The striking copper-clad roof of the new poultry market built after the old building burnt down in 1958 was the largest elliptical concrete dome in Europe at the time.

5 SMITHFIELD MARKET

West Smithfield EC1 • Sir Horace Jones 1866–7, 1879–95; T. P. Bennett & Son 1962–3; HLM 1992–5

Smithfield is a sight not to be missed: the last of the great London produce markets still on the site it has occupied for a thousand years, it defines the character of the entire area. This is a working market, mostly aimed at the wholesale trade, so the time to see it in action is early in the morning, although the sheer quantity of raw flesh swinging on hooks as the carcasses are delivered in Charterhouse Street can be daunting. From 2 a.m. to the early morning it is open for small retail sales to the public. The present vast buildings strung along the south side of Charterhouse Street, and extending south of West Smithfield, date from the period after 1855 when the livestock market and its attendant slaughter were moved out to the new Caledonian Market near King's Cross. The earliest is the grandest: the portion to the east put up in 1866–7 to the designs of Sir Horace Jones, the City surveyor (architect of Tower Bridge many years later). It was built on top of the Metropolitan Railway and the architecture has something of the station about it, the long, low redbrick walls enriched with blind arcading that seems to go on forever; the glass canopies, from HLM's restoration of the early 1990s, add to the railway flavour. The main attraction is Grand Avenue, a crossing 'transept' the full height of the building topped by a timber, cast-iron and glass roof; the rather garish purple

Opposite
The challenging colouring of the ironwork in Grand Avenue dates from its restoration in the early 1990s.

and green colour scheme dates from the 1990s restoration. The avenue gives access east and west to the central Buyers' Walk aisle flanked by stalls of meat traders, some of which have been here since the 19th century, with their offices above. The whole building is 192 m (630 ft) long. With the exception of Grand Avenue the interior is largely a reconstruction by HLM to enable the market to meet new EU hygiene regulations and remain on its site. Before this, the early morning at Smithfield was frenetic, with meat deliveries made direct to individual open stalls. Now they are all handled from entrances with motorized conveyors, and the stalls are enclosed and temperature-controlled. A new floor of lettable office space was also invisibly sliced in at second-floor level.

The next building to the west is a surprise, and not to everyone's taste. This is the Poultry Market of 1962–3 by T. P. Bennett, replacing Jones's Poultry Market of the 1870s, which burnt down in 1958. The walls of rather forbidding dark-grey brick are pierced by wide honeycomb bays of attractive hexagonal glass bricks, under simple shallow gables with copper roofs. Inside, the building is dominated by a vast shallow-domed roof – an elliptical paraboloid, to be precise – with a thin concrete shell pierced to let in more light, devised by engineers Ove Arup. The stalls have appealing original 1960s lettered fascias. There is still a pub in the basement, the Cock Tavern, replacing the original burnt in 1958, serving early morning pints of beer. To get an idea of what Smithfield was like before the 1990s modernization, take a look through the gates of the General Market Building adjoining, added also to Jones's designs in 1879–83. This building narrowly escaped demolition in 2008 and is still the subject of redevelopment plans to the designs of John McAslan, believed to involve suspending an office block above the retained building. The General Market is linked via a covered walkway at first-floor level to the so-called Red House, another market building with an impressive sheer blank brick face to Snow Hill. Opposite is a triangular lavatory building with charming columns of red and white ventilators rising up at the corners.

This timber-framed house was built in 1595 on top of what was once the entrance to the south aisle of the nave of St Bartholomew's. The gateway now gives access to a garden.

6 ST BARTHOLOMEW-THE-GREAT

West Smithfield EC1 • Rahere 12th century; Aston Webb 1886–98; Seely & Paget 1950–52

It is easy to miss St Bartholomew-the-Great on a stroll around Smithfield. Despite its name, this exquisite remnant of a great Norman priory church is tucked away from view behind the shopfronts of Little Britain, given away only by a restored 13th-century arched stone doorway, with a late Tudor house on top, that was once an entrance to the church's south aisle. Once through this arch, the path through the garden leading to the surviving part of the church follows the line of the lost south aisle. The church today consists of just the choir, crossing, a tiny bit of nave, apse and Lady Chapel of the much-altered Augustinian priory church (founded by Rahere, the courtier-turned-priest

Opposite
The solemn interior of St Bartholomew-the-Great, with its solid Norman columns, was once just the choir of the great priory church founded by a courtier-turned-priest named Rahere.

who also founded the neighbouring hospital in the early 12th century), plus the east side of the cloister rebuilt in the 14th century – now the café. The rest of the priory lay to the south and east under Bartholomew Close. The long-lost nave was early English Gothic, not added until the 13th century. It was pulled down during the Dissolution of the monasteries in the 1540s, leaving the choir as a parish church. The Lady Chapel at the east end of the apse was then turned into a two-storey house, later used as a factory, making fringing for soft furnishings. A school was built into the north aisle gallery in the late 16th century – the red brick used for it and the schoolmaster's house can still be seen from the churchyard. The cloisters were turned into houses and later subdivided for stables, a cowshed and smithy in the 18th century.

Much of what remains was restored and repaired at the end of the 19th century by Aston Webb, better known as architect of the Victoria & Albert Museum, undoing some of these ungodly depredations – he created the transepts and reopened the end of the choir into the Lady Chapel, reinstating the curving ambulatory. Today the Lady Chapel feels utterly different from the rest of the church, all clarity, light and plainness (with the exception of the terrible altar painting in the style of Murillo) while the choir is mysterious, dark and solid. Despite Webb's restorations the character of the choir is authentically Norman, deriving from the great piers with scallop capitals and the slender columns in the gallery above. The crossing under the lost tower (the present brick tower at the west end dates from the 1620s) dates from the mid-12th century, its arches the earliest pointed ones in London. Rahere himself resides in effigy in the north aisle, under a great crocketed canopy, with two attendant bedesmen; he had been dead more than 250 years when this was put up in the early 15th century. Overlooking it on the other side of the aisle is an oriel window, built so that the prior of the time (*c.* 1517) could be within the church without leaving his adjoining lodgings.

St Bartholomew's atmosphere of ancient grandeur, and the fact that it is the only parish church in London with substantial Norman remains, make it a prized film location, most famously as the church where Hugh Grant jilted Duckface at the altar in *Four Weddings and a Funeral.*

St Bartholomew-the-Less, built as a hospital chapel, and seen here in 1814, when the unu octagonal nave was succumbing to dry rot.

The startling octagonal nave, as rebuilt with delicate plaster rib vaults in the 1820s, is a striking contrast both to the exterior, and to the solidity and solemnity of St Bartholomew-the-Great.

7 ST BARTHOLOMEW-THE-LESS

St Bartholomew's Hospital, West Smithfield EC1 • George Dance the Younger 1789–91; Thomas Hardwick 1823–5; P. C. Hardwick 1862–3

This church is even less visible from West Smithfield than St Bartholomew-the-Great. Only in winter do the trees thin enough for the top of the tower to peep over, tucked as it is just inside the hospital's Henry VIII Gatehouse. It began life as a chapel to the hospital in the 12th century, though the only portion that predates its becoming a parish church after the Dissolution of the monasteries is the crusty 15th-century west tower, which is fancier inside than out, and is the oldest part of the hospital. Though there are 16th-century monuments in the vestry, off the tower, visitors are usually distracted by the unexpected sight of the nave: light, bright and octagonal, like a Methodist tabernacle. It was rebuilt like this by George Dance in the 1780s and again in the 1820s (after dry rot set in) by Thomas Hardwick, who added an iron roof and the delicate riot of plaster rib vaults. His grandson P. C. Hardwick added the more vigorous High Victorian tracery in the high lunettes, and the alabaster pulpit and vaguely Ruskinian sanctuary. Viewed from the outside, from the east end at least, the church appears an untidy assemblage of geometric shapes that do not quite fit together, all surrounded by the trappings of a working hospital – iron escape stairs, ambulances and patients in hospital gowns.

8 ST BARTHOLOMEW'S HOSPITAL

West Smithfield EC1 • James Gibbs 1730–68, and others

Unlike his priory church of St Bartholomew-the-Great, the hospital founded by Rahere after his return from Rome has since disappeared, and the reason is simple. Whereas the way we worship God might be just about recognizable to our medieval forebears, the way we practise medicine would not, and for hospitals patient care rightly takes precedence over architectural conservation. Barts as an institution, however, is still here and, like the neighbouring meat market, has remained on the same site for nearly a thousand years, a continuity unmatched by any hospital in England. Originally the hospital was just one building in the priory complex founded by Rahere in 1123, but it continued to grow and by 1420 the two institutions were separate, although still funded by the priory. After the Dissolution the hospital was refounded by Henry VIII, who handed it over to the City. His statue sits in a niche in the Baroque gatehouse

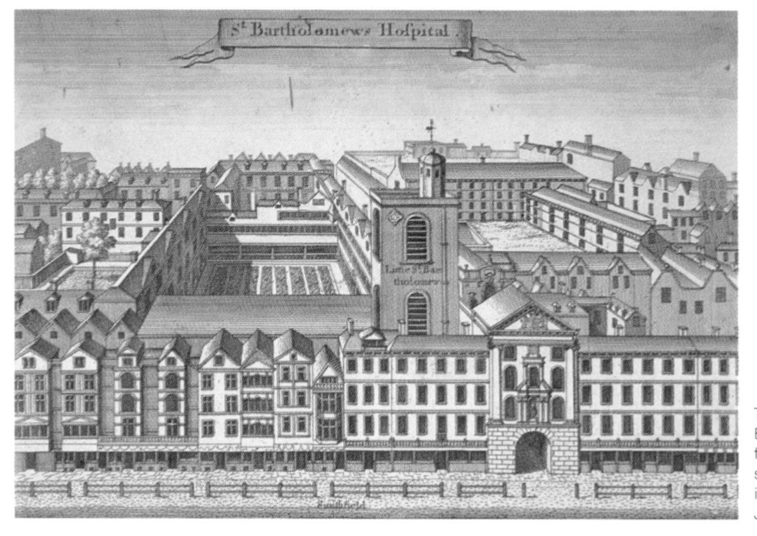

The hospital of St Bartholomew, also founded by Rahere, is seen in 1723 just before its major rebuilding by James Gibbs.

The Henry VIII Gatehouse on West Smithfield of 1702 is the oldest surviving portion of the hospital apart from St Bartholomew-the-Less.

of 1702 overlooking Smithfield, the oldest building on the site apart from St Bartholomew-the-Less.

The historic core of medical buildings is now the main courtyard, rebuilt in 1730–68 by James Gibbs, architect of St Martin-in-the-Fields, who was a governor of the hospital and gave his services for free. A High Tory Catholic who trained in Rome, his architecture was described by Sir John Summerson as Wren's architectural ideas brought to fulfilment. Three of his four buildings here survive. The grandest and least altered is the North Block, through which the courtyard is entered via an arch. This was the administration block for the hospital, with boardroom and clerk's house, and the governors certainly did themselves proud. The darkly impressive green and gold grand staircase at the east end is enrobed in huge history paintings by William Hogarth, who was born in Bartholomew Close. He got the work after hearing that an Italian was in line for the commission and offering to do it for nothing (thanks to him are recorded in the governors' minutes). Hogarth wanted to prove that 'the great style of history painting' had a future, but he never again produced work like this. The scenes are biblico-medical, showing Christ healing at the pool of Bethesda and the Good Samaritan tending to the travellers' wounds. The whole is rather artlessly

This view of hospital buildings along Giltspur Street offers a compendium of the different ways that Victorian and Edwardian architects interpreted the style established by James Gibbs in his original 1730s buildings.

enthusiastic, with the landscape background by the Covent Garden scene painter George Lambert. The governors' Great Hall is magnificent, a double-height room across the first floor, 30 m (100 ft) and nine windows long. Gibbs designed the plasterwork ceiling of foliage, rosettes and guilloches, and the walls are lined with purple-painted boards recording the names of donors, like a newly opened museum extension today.

The blocks on either side are slightly plainer, as befits their role as ward buildings, and are unconnected at the corners (a fire-prevention measure). Palladian in style, they have typical Gibbs window surrounds of alternate rusticated and plain quoins. The courtyard would have had a warmer glow when first built in Bath stone; it was refaced in the 19th century by harder-wearing but chillier Portland stone.

Expansion after Gibbs was less coherent as the new building spreading down Giltspur Street and Little Britain had to fill in awkward existing sites. However, the blocks along Giltspur Street (pathology, the old museum, outpatients) make for an impressive wall of Portland stone, a pleasingly varied display of Victorian and Edwardian interpretations of the Gibbsian manner. The south block was replaced in 1934–7 by the George V Building by Lanchester, Lucas & Lodge, steel-framed behind its respectful neo-Georgian stone front, and behind it is their Surgical Block (1929–30), now also about to be replaced.

Barts was slated for closure in the 1990s, but after a vociferous public campaign it was reprieved in 1998, joining with the Royal London in Whitechapel and becoming a specialist cardiac and cancer-care centre. The West Wing was carefully redeveloped as a Breast Cancer Centre in 2004: the serene design by Greenhill Jenner is enhanced inside by a £250,000 art commission on the theme 'anywhere but here' suggested by the patients, with Cornelia Parker's hanging silver teapots in the first-floor reception and mood-enhancing coloured light around the windows on the Georgian staircase. The new cancer centre on the south-east side, replacing the 1920s nurses' home, is self-effacingly unornamented, faced in Portland stone, with simple paired windows.

Barts is a working hospital still, and this redevelopment of the interwar medical block and nurses' home by HOK architects means it can provide specialist cancer and cardiac care on its historic site.

9 CHRIST CHURCH NEWGATE STREET

EC1 • Sir Christopher Wren and Robert Hooke 1677–87; Seely & Paget 1960, 1981

Although this is yet another Wren church reduced to its tower – albeit one of the best in London – following bomb damage, it is special in other ways. Instead of sweeping away the damaged walls – substantial parts of the north and west walls survived, along with a little of the south wall – the architects Seely & Paget kept them in their 1960 restoration, providing a reminder of what these churches looked like in the immediate aftermath of the Blitz. Shamefully the remains of the east wall were lost to road widening in the 1970s, though its line was reinstated as a dwarf wall during the building of the Merrill Lynch headquarters next door. In the 1980s Seely & Paget built an office into the south-west wall which imitates a Georgian vestry that once stood there. The sense of the building's ghostly form also survives in the clever garden made inside in 1989, sheltered by the ruined north wall. Pergolas were placed where the nave piers once stood, so it is still possible to walk down the aisle, imagining the broad space, composite columns and magnificent plasterwork. The conceit of the garden as building memorial is repeated on the other side of Christ Church's tower, though vestigially: it now mainly serves as an outdoor area for Merrill Lynch employees. Tall trees mark the 91-m (300-ft) nave of the

The nave of Christ Church, burnt out in 1940, is today marked by pergolas where the columns once stood, and terminates in the tower, now a private house.

Robert Randoll made this lightning sketch in 1896 of Christ Church's unusually wide nave, with galleries steeply raked to accommodate the boys of nearby Christ's Hospital School.

15th-century Franciscan Greyfriars church, then by far the largest church in London after old St Paul's, packed with magnificent tombs including those of four queens. After the Dissolution the west end became a warehouse – the tombs sold or broken up – and only the east end was kept on and rebuilt as a parish church. After the Great Fire, Wren (or more likely his assistant Robert Hooke) reduced this building even further when he rebuilt on the 14th-century medieval footings (adding buttresses just in case), but it was still a large church, a basilica intended to accommodate the schoolboys of Christ's Hospital School as well as the parishioners. The wonderful steeple was added above the louvred bell tower in 1703–4: each stage is a virtuoso display, with a free-standing colonnade, twelve urns and delicate square pierced spire. In 2006 Boyarsky Murphy ingeniously converted the whole tower to a house in super-minimalist style (clean white walls, glass and steel).

Henry Tanner's GPO North Range was hollowed out in the late 1980s to build a steel-framed bank headquarters inside, with an unusually large run of retained façades for the time.

10 GENERAL POST OFFICE BUILDINGS

King Edward Street EC1 • Sir Henry Tanner 1889–95, 1907–11; Fitzroy Robinson Partnership 1987–90; Swanke Hayden Connell 1996–2001

These grandiose late Victorian and Edwardian buildings facing each other across King Edward Street, reminiscent of Whitehall, are the former headquarters of the General Post Office which first moved from Lombard Street to St Martin's le Grand, in the next street, in 1829. It was there that Anthony Trollope began his career – according to his autobiography, he spent quite a lot of his time playing cards and smoking. The buildings spread west during the 19th century and these two big blocks are the survivors: the apotheosis of the post office as an imperial enterprise, effecting communication around the empire on which the sun never set. The former North Range, adjoining Postman's Park, is the earlier, comfortably Italianate with Michelangelo-esque carving and, more prosaically, carved heads of Postmasters General in some of the keystones. After the GPO left in 1984

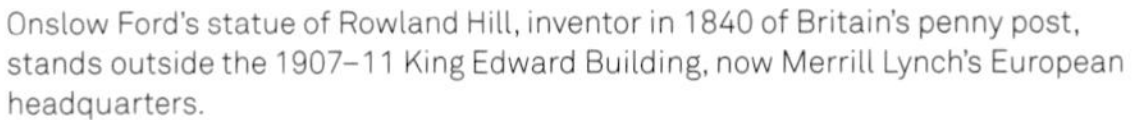
Onslow Ford's statue of Rowland Hill, inventor in 1840 of Britain's penny post, stands outside the 1907–11 King Edward Building, now Merrill Lynch's European headquarters.

The keystone over the GPO North Range building depicts Henry Cecil Raikes, who was Postmaster General at the time the building was constructed.

it was hollowed out by Fitzroy Robinson, who put in a steel-framed headquarters for Nomura behind the Portland stone.

The King Edward Building opposite, also by Tanner, is restrained, even dull, for an Edwardian Baroque frontage, but it was up-to-the-minute inside, held up by a wide-span concrete frame on the Hennebique system, used more obviously in the utilitarian sorting office that lay behind. This system, in which the concrete was poured *in situ*, was cheaper to erect and allowed much wider uninterrupted spans than steel framing. Outside Onslow Ford's 1881 bronze sculpture of Rowland Hill, inventor of the penny post, looks out calmly over the traffic. The sorting office was demolished in the late 1990s when David Walker and Swanke Hayden Connell built European headquarters for Merrill Lynch on the site in a serenely unassertive manner, with grid-like frontages in Portland stone or red brick. The main post office building was retained, its hall sadly bereft of the post-office counters, and converted to a reception hall. Remains of the City wall, including a Roman section and a medieval bastion, are preserved in the lobby of the Giltspur Street entrance of the new building.

Robert Schnebbelie's view from 1840 of the London Wall bastion that still exists near St Giles Cripplegate within the Barbican. It captures the way that portions of the medieval and Roman wall survived, often because they were incorporated into later buildings.

ROMAN LONDON

The City of London is a Roman city, even if the modern City has burst those boundaries in places. Its physical remains *in situ* are sparse – just enough to startle the visitor who comes across a 2,000-year-old wall among the glass and steel. There was no London to speak of before the invasion ordered by the emperor Claudius in AD 43. A shingly, watery region of low rolling hills, it was there for the taking: its natural state accounts for the Roman name Londinium, from the Celtic 'lond' meaning wild.

The Roman settlement that began in AD 50–60 grew up north of a crossing – maybe a bridge, probably a ford – about 50 m (165 ft) east of the present London Bridge. It had spread east and west along the main thoroughfares before the Iceni tribe under Boudicca came marauding down from Norfolk and burnt it all down around AD 60 – a distinctive layer of orange-red ash visible during archaeological digs is a telltale sign of this.

The Romans soon recovered, though, and by the end of the 1st century AD they had put up a forum where Gracechurch Street now meets Fenchurch Street. It was the biggest north of the Alps, with a town hall-cum-courthouse basilica on its north side longer than Wren's St Paul's. Waterfront terraces were created along Upper and Lower Thames Street, then the north side of the river, with docks, shops and warehouses which at their peak stretched 160 m (525 ft). Government offices, with gardens and pools, were erected where Cannon Street Station is now: so robust were their cement foundations that they resisted explosives in the 1860s when the station was built. An elliptical amphitheatre existed where the present Guildhall Yard is – only found in 1988, it is now displayed in the basement of Guildhall Art Gallery. A square fort was built at the far north-west reaches of the city, and substantial fragments are still visible near the Museum of London: by St Giles Cripplegate, in Noble Street and in St Alphage Gardens off London Wall.

The Roman amphitheatre discovered during the excavations to build the new Guildhall Art Gallery in 1988 has been conserved and brought to life with an evocative son-et-lumière in the new gallery's basement.

The streets of late 1st-century Roman London would have been tightly packed with single-storey timber-framed thatched houses. Only the public buildings and the very fanciest private houses, sited overlooking the river, would have been of stone or even mud brick, the very best with black-and-white mosaic flooring to the public rooms. Heating via hypocaust did not arrive until the 2nd century, and glazing was even rarer – unfortunately for the Mediterranean invaders.

Then came London's first Great Fire of *c.* AD 120, a devastation quite as great as that of 1666. Rebuilding this time saw more stone used for houses, the grandest of which featured wall paintings, but London was no longer such a great military centre and its population peaked at around 60,000 in the mid-2nd century. The last great enterprise was the one we know best – the building of the wall, up to 4 m (13 ft) high, created to define the 133 hectares of the City. It took 1,300 barges of Kentish ragstone brought from near Maidstone to build it *c.* AD 190–225. The largest surviving chunk is prominently on view beside Tower Hill Tube station. Late Roman London was characterized by an enthusiasm for obscure Eastern cults, exemplified by the Temple of Mithras unearthed in Walbrook in 1954, then reconstructed, but now part of a major redevelopment. Treasures from the temple are on show, with some of the thirty mosaic pavements raised in the City, at the Museum of London, as well as in the British Museum and the Bank of England Museum. Following the long sunset of their decline, the Romans withdrew from London about AD 410. Some of the larger villas appear to have been occupied into the later 5th century but by 600 the City was empty, effectively abandoned until Alfred the Great recolonized it in the 9th century.

Postman's Park, seen here in 1928, is so called because it was a popular relaxing spot for the postmen who worked out of the adjoining General Post Office buildings.

11 POSTMAN'S PARK AND WATTS MEMORIAL

Aldersgate Street and King Edward Street EC1 • Ernest George 1880–90

Winding from King Edward Street to Aldersgate, this spacious park was created in the 1880s from the churchyard of St Botolph and the burial grounds of Christ Church Newgate Street, whose ruin is opposite, and St Leonard Foster Lane, a church not rebuilt after the Fire. Its name reflects its popularity with workers in the one-time General Post Office headquarters adjoining it. The park surface is higher than the street level because overcrowding meant bodies were laid on the surface and then covered in earth.

The park would be worth a visit for the fine trees alone, but the greater draw is the Memorial to Heroic Self-Sacrifice, a uniquely grandiose Victorian name for a touching and unassuming structure – a covered wooden loggia on the north side of the garden containing fifty-four ceramic plaques. It was created at the suggestion of the painter G. F. Watts, who felt that ordinary people who had lost their lives in extraordinary acts of heroism were insufficiently well recorded. Having collected newspaper cuttings on self-sacrifice for years, his original plan was for something far grander – a 'Campo Santo' with covered way and marble wall recording names and deeds in Hyde Park – but material support was slow in coming. As Watts said, 'If I had proposed a race course round Hyde Park, there would have been plenty of sympathisers'. But by 1898 Postman's Park had been agreed as the location for a more modest scheme designed by Ernest George, with a long bench and space on the back for

The Watts Memorial was the idea of the artist G. F. Watts and was built in the form of a Japanese loggia housing seating and a wall of ceramic plaques.

rectangular tablets. Ceramic was chosen as the material for the plaques because the potter William de Morgan was a friend of Watts and pottery was cheaper than bronze or marble. Royal Doulton later produced them after Watts had died and de Morgan had given up potting. Though the style varies, they all have a Walter Crane-like charm in their hand lettering and simple decorative panels either side, in blue or green on an off-white background. Although space was available for 120 tablets, only fifty-three had been added by the time Watts's widow died in 1938. However, in 2009 a new tablet in the same style was added – the first for seventy-eight years – commemorating Leigh Pitt, a print worker who drowned in East London while saving a boy who had fallen into a canal. The memorial enjoyed a surge of interest after featuring in the film *Closer*.

The plaques commemorate civilians who lost their lives saving others.

Following pages
St Botolph is one of the few churches of the late 18th century in the City, and surprising, too, for the richness of colouring in the Georgian interior.

The 15th-century St Botol[illegible] seen here in an engraving of about 1740, survived th[illegible] Great Fire, only to be rebui[illegible] twice in the 18th century. Portions of the medieval foundations survived thes[illegible] rebuildings.

12 ST BOTOLPH ALDERSGATE

Aldersgate Street EC1 • Nathaniel Wright 1789–91

St Botolph is unusual in the City as a church of the late 18th century. Its modest, boxy exterior of painted stucco and warehouse-style stock brick belies its broad and magnificent interior. A 15th-century church on the site survived the Fire to be partly rebuilt in 1754, but most of what we see today was done to the designs of Nathaniel Wright in 1789–91, with the tower and north and south walls on the medieval foundations. Medieval memorials also survive inside, the most striking a rustic very late Gothic canopied altar tomb for one Ann Packington, who died in 1563. The interior is overwhelmingly opulent Georgian in atmosphere, spacious and elegant with coffered apses either end. There are galleries on Corinthian and Ionic columns, round-headed windows and ceiling lunettes, based on George Dance the Younger's All Hallows London Wall of twenty years earlier, much of it given an agreeably tobacco-stained look with marbling on the columns. Victorian fittings (font and pews) add further richness to the Georgian pulpit and organ, as does the striking Baroque painted window by James Pearson depicting the Agony in the Garden, also in tobacco tones, at the east end. The little curving staircases beside the organ led to schoolrooms upstairs off the galleries. St Botolph's churchyard is now Postman's Park.

13 MUSEUM OF LONDON ➲

London Wall EC2 • Powell & Moya 1968–76

Built as part of the Barbican redevelopment, the Museum of London was designed to display collections – some brought from Guildhall, some from the London Museum at Kensington Palace

The Museum of London retains a bridge from the 1950s 'ped-way' system designed to channel pedestrian traffic around the City at first-floor level.

– that illustrate the evolving history of London. The building is far more rewarding inside than out. It is slightly reticent from the outside, wrapping round the corner from Aldersgate Street into London Wall and spilling over into a garden inside the black-brick bastion in the middle of the roundabout. The upper part of the main building has long strips of Corbusian white tile and window, supported on pilotis over another black brick base; the Aldersgate Street frontage, containing offices, is taller and awkwardly angular. The galleries around a serene inner courtyard garden are mainly laid out on two levels of the main building on London Wall. Each level provides a 'walk' through London's history – on the upper floor from prehistoric times to the Great Fire, and from then to the present day below.

In 2010 the Museum reopened with a redisplay of its lower galleries, designed by Wilkinson Eyre, softening the

The Pleasure Gardens section of the Museum's Galleries of Modern London, which opened in 2010. The displays offer the chance to explore London's cultural history, as well as its major events.

linear progression of the old story (deeply unfashionable in these relativistic times), which offered the visitor little choice about diverging from the prescribed route, and also increasing the gallery space by 25 per cent. To counteract the perennial Barbican problem of finding your way about (or even into) its buildings, the revamped Museum now has a window at ground (road) level – the gold Lord Mayor's Coach inside makes an arresting sight.

14 IRONMONGERS' HALL

Shaftesbury Place, off Aldersgate Street EC1 • Sydney Tatchell 1922–5

Ironmongers' Hall is hard to find, squeezed in behind the Museum of London and all but invisible from the street. This is no coincidence. The City Corporation wanted to get rid of it entirely to make way for the Museum in 1966, but the livery company successfully resisted this. This means that the surprise and pleasure of suddenly coming across this Hollywood-Tudor fantasy amid the concrete and lavatory tiles is all the more acute. And it is a fantasy, less than half a century older than the Museum.

The Ironmongers had been in Fenchurch Street since the 15th century when their 18th-century livery hall was hit in the forgotten Blitz of 1917. This new building by Sydney Tatchell

Ironmongers' Hall, built in 1922–5, survived the Blitz only to be hemmed in by the City Corporation in the 1960s when it built the Museum of London.

Ironmongers' Hall is a spectacularly lavish but old-fashioned exercise in neo-Tudor, all hiding a modern steel-frame structure that no doubt contributed to its ability to survive the Blitz.

was amazingly old-fashioned for the time, but beautifully made. The peaceful, surprisingly spacious interior has a startlingly authentic patina with Jacobean-style plaster ceilings and oak panelling fixed with dowels; even the floors have a convincing unevenness. This is all the more surprising as the builders used all the latest technical tricks – the floors under the flags are reinforced concrete and the roof of the great banqueting hall is held up by steel trusses above the barrel vault of fine plaster – one reason that, unlike all its neighbours, it survived the inferno of the 1940 Blitz.

15 GOLDEN LANE ESTATE

EC1 • Chamberlin, Powell & Bon 1952–62

Golden Lane is the Barbican's prettier, petite older sister, built in 1952–62 by the same architects for the same clients – the initial phase in the comprehensive rebuilding of the Cripplegate area devastated in the Blitz. The architectural firm was created in a Musketeers'-style all-for-one pact among the young Peter Chamberlin, Geoffry Powell and Christoph Bon, who agreed that if any of them won the competition to design the estate, the first stage in the City Corporation scheme to arrest and reverse the City's depopulation, they would join together to carry out the job. Powell won. The estate as completed consists of 554 flats in loosely flowing courtyards of low-rise blocks pivoting round Great Arthur House, at 16 storeys very tall for the time (1957) and reflecting an increasing belief that building tall and thin was less oppressive than medium-height and bulky, while

Crescent House on Goswell Road was the last part of the Golden Lane estate to be built, in 1962, and is architecturally much closer to the same architects' Barbican estate, seen in the background.

Edwin Smith's photograph of the Golden Lane estate, seen through a ruined arch on Fann Street before the Barbican was built, captures its 'phoenix from the ashes' quality.

still achieving 200 people per acre, the standard density set down by the 1943 County of London Plan. At the top is a swooping curving aileron roof that houses water tanks and a lift mechanism. Sadly closed now is the roof garden with sitting area, pergola and reflecting pool, and a magnificent view of London. The tower's curtain walling features bright yellow panels, with blue and red on the low-rise blocks. The jolly colours are what differentiates Golden Lane first of all from the Barbican, along with the use of brick facing rather than raw concrete, the lightness of components (window frames, staircases) and the fact that it is all accessed from ground level – though sunken gardens built in the basements of bomb-damaged buildings between Basterfield, Bayer and Bowater Houses add to the visual interest. Crescent House, the building on Goswell Road, was the last block built, its rougher surfaces and sterner colouring looking forward to the Barbican.

Golden Lane's success as public housing is due to good design, good maintenance (typical of City Corporation public housing) and unusual communal facilities: as well as a community hall there is a leisure centre with swimming pool, tennis courts (originally a bowling green) and sports hall. Socially Golden Lane was always remarkably mixed, aimed at both locals and City workers, and it maintains that mix, even after thirty years during which tenants have had the legal 'right to buy'. One reason is that there was more emphasis on flats for single people and couples rather than large families, which helps explain why today it is preferred by those 'in the know', cool young architects and designers – plus the flats are cheaper than in the Barbican. On the south side of the estate in Fann Street and more typical of the period is the vaguely Scandinavian Jewin Welsh chapel of 1956–61 by Caröe & Partners, with a copper roof and Gothic-style west window.

Opposite
Great Arthur House dominates Golden Lane, though it is dwarfed by the neighbouring Barbican's towers. Its golden glass panels and butterfly-winged roof must have been thrilling in the austerity London of 1957, when it was completed.

The distinctive saw-tooth profiles of the three Barbican towers which dominate the northern half of the City of London.

16 BARBICAN ESTATE

EC2 • Chamberlin, Powell & Bon 1956–81; T. P. Bennett 2009

The Barbican has won an award as London's ugliest building, yet it is the most fashionable place to live in the City. This is primarily because there is nothing else like it. Over the twenty-five years it took to build, the City Corporation never wavered in its commitment to complete what had first been dreamed up in the 1950s: repopulating an area of the City and giving its residents what was to be the largest arts complex in Europe. The Barbican was the central portion of the City's larger scheme for the bomb-destroyed Barbican area, sandwiched between the Golden Lane estate and the replanned London Wall, to which it is linked by high-level 'ped-ways'. Designed by the same firm of architects as Golden Lane, it is also driven by the idea of a traffic-free housing estate of low blocks punctuated by towers, combined with social facilities. The plan is once again based on courtyards open in various ways – at the corners or along one whole side – and towers, long stand-alone blocks and Frobisher Crescent (a ghostly reminder of The Crescent, a Georgian street on the site that was lost in the Blitz). But the Barbican differs from Golden Lane in two key aspects of both aesthetics and planning.

By the time the Barbican's designs were finalized, architects had developed a taste for a rawer use of concrete, inspired by Alison and Peter Smithson's pioneering 'Brutalism'. Architecturally, it is much more muscular and assertive than Golden Lane, a celebration of the expressive possibilities of concrete, both in the plastic sense of the varied surface finishes inside and out – bush-hammered, granite-faced – and structurally, with the ends of the concrete beams used for visual effect beneath the balconies. But it is not all concrete – there is a lot of warm dark-red engineering brick and tile, and colour creeps in here and there.

The key difference in the planning is the use of a raised pedestrian level that is conceived of as 'ground level', though it is not. Herein lies the famous problem of 'getting lost in the

Opposite
A general view of the Barbican estate takes in its variety of forms and textures. The three triangular towers are the highest residential buildings in the City.

The City of London School for Girls was the first building on the Barbican estate to be completed.

Frobisher Crescent shows the more delicate side of the Barbican estate with slatted extern window screens and white-painted canopies featuring the ubiquitous semi-circular motif.

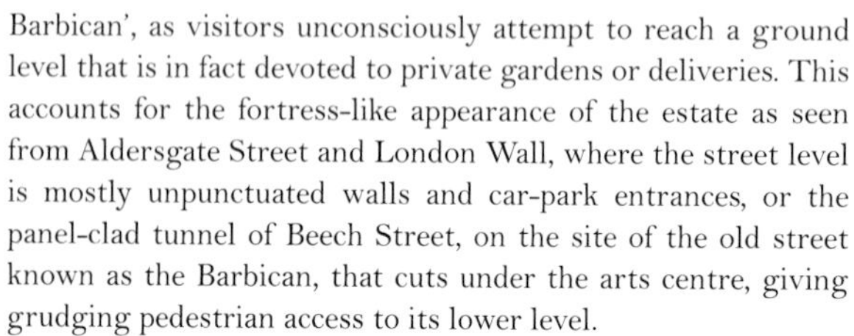

Barbican', as visitors unconsciously attempt to reach a ground level that is in fact devoted to private gardens or deliveries. This accounts for the fortress-like appearance of the estate as seen from Aldersgate Street and London Wall, where the street level is mostly unpunctuated walls and car-park entrances, or the panel-clad tunnel of Beech Street, on the site of the old street known as the Barbican, that cuts under the arts centre, giving grudging pedestrian access to its lower level.

After planning and replanning to incorporate two schools, work on the 40-acre (15.2-hectare) estate got under way in 1963, and by the early 1970s there were 2,113 flats housing 6,500 people. Running through the middle is an L-shaped lake, which goes under the City of London School for Girls: to its south is St Giles Cripplegate, to its east the Guildhall School of Music & Drama, and to its north the Barbican Centre. The estate is thrilling in its vertiginous heights, bridges, soaring cylindrical columns (sometimes planted in the water like elephants' legs), all softened by the curves of barrel vaults, sills and canopies and mitigated by lush vegetation and cascades. The variety of layouts is ingenious: 140 different plans offer everything from studios to huge multifloor penthouses as well as a secret terrace of houses. Recognizable Barbican features are the galley kitchens, white-tiled bathrooms and full walls of hardwood-framed windows. The three towers of 42 or 43 storeys, triangular in plan and saw-toothed in profile, were the tallest residential buildings in Europe at the time. Space Age lift lobbies have controls in a central pod. Parapets are electrically heated to prevent icing up.

The Barbican is proof that high-rises and concrete are not the driving force in the creation of slums, as is often lazily asserted in relaying the sorry story of postwar public housing in Britain. The difference is that the Barbican was thoughtfully designed, built of robust materials and properly maintained. As a result it has attracted residents who can afford to contribute to the estate's well-being, both literally and metaphorically.

The historic Barbican area, filled with warehouses and offices, was destroyed in a firestorm at the end of 1940. Only St Giles Cripplegate, seen back left, survives of these buildings.

A view of Andrewes House in the Barbican estate when it was new, showing the ground level devoted to cars, and flats with balcony-gardens above.

The giant white blocks mark the Barbican Art Gallery within the arts centre, contrasting with the more delicate lines of the residential flats. Glass-clad City Point looms behind.

17 BARBICAN CENTRE

Silk Street EC2 • Chamberlin, Powell & Bon 1968–82

The Barbican Centre was the last portion of the Barbican estate to open, taking a prodigious fourteen years to complete – the City of London's Court of Common Council spent its longest sitting on record deciding whether or not to proceed with the project, and their caution might have been justified. Originally budgeted for £16.7 million, it cost £156 million. The idea of including an arts centre emerged early on in the Barbican scheme but it had grown threefold by the time it opened, housing the Royal Shakespeare Company (who left in 2002), the London Symphony Orchestra, cinemas, two art galleries and a City Corporation lending library. The radical idealism of the architects' vision occasionally gave rise to some unusual ideas: the proposals for the cinema, for example, originally included placing the screen on the auditorium ceiling and having the first few rows of the audience lying on their backs.

The Barbican Centre sits at the heart of the estate, marked out as different from the residential buildings all around by its cladding of white tiles and the massive cube-like forms that house the gallery spaces. But it is an iceberg of a building, most of it hidden underground. Opening off the ground-level terrace overlooking the water garden, the foyer is a free-flowing space, giving access to the 2,000-seat concert hall, 1,200-seat theatre, 300-seat cinema, conference and lecture theatres, with conference and exhibition space above, and the soaring indoor jungle of the conservatory at the top. The piazza in front of Frobisher Crescent is the roof of the concert hall.

The many uses of concrete are explored here in the low coffered ceilings of the lift lobbies and library on the west side and the soaring walls of the main foyer and concert hall, augmented by a rich palette of other materials – bronze doors and brass rails, wood and orange carpeting. The concert hall, although its

Opposite
The high-level walkway that crosses the lake provides some of the most spectacular views of the estate.

The experience for performers and audiences in the Barbican Hall was transformed in 1994 and 2001 by the acoustician Larry Kierkegaard, who added canopies over the stage.

ceiling is punctuated by giant concrete crossbeams and recent metallic acoustic 'wings', derives a contrasting serenity and delicacy from its reeded wood panelling. The theatre is more startling, especially the zigzag profile of the balconies jutting out over the stalls. The shapes – in the deep coffered ceilings of the foyer – are generous and rounded. Not all of it works – the spaces of the foyer can be disorientating, switching suddenly from low and cave-like to tall and soaring, the floor tipping away disconcertingly. But it also gives the lie to the idea that Brutalism – Modernist architecture that makes an honest display of concrete's raw power – is necessarily brutal: the finish of the concrete walls has a warm woolly texture.

The woolly texture of the concrete in the Barbican's main foyer takes its cue from rusticated masonry used in classical architecture.

18 ST GILES CRIPPLEGATE

Fore Street EC2 • 16th century

St Giles Cripplegate comes as a surprise as you wander about the Barbican: a large late Gothic church marooned in a sea of brick and concrete, it is bereft of any contextual churchyard or even street. But then the church is lucky to be here at all, surviving first the firestorm of December 1940 and then the Barbican springing up around it. Preservation was hardly guaranteed, and the lack of context was the accepted way of presenting conserved buildings at the time. The church's Saxon origins are long gone and it owes its current form to a rebuild after a fire in the 1540s. The top of the tower, in startling red brick, was added in the 1680s, while the east end is an interesting – and untypical for 1960 – recreation of its medieval form, removing 18th-century alterations. The church is surprisingly atmospheric inside for a building that had been reduced to a shell. The slender clustered piers bear the signs of their long, rough life with dignity, and some 16th- and 17th-century memorials survive. John Milton is buried here and his monument, by John Bacon the Elder of 1793, features a serpent and apple, an allusion to *Paradise Lost.* Reused fittings from less fortunate churches – the organ was put together using 17th- and 18th-century pieces from St Luke Old Street and St Andrew Holborn – give it an appropriate patina. Outside is a clutch of 19th-century rounded coffin-shaped tombstones, apparently intended as seating. From here is the best view of the remains of the Roman and medieval fort. The late 19th-century gas lamps in the 'churchyard' came from Tower Bridge.

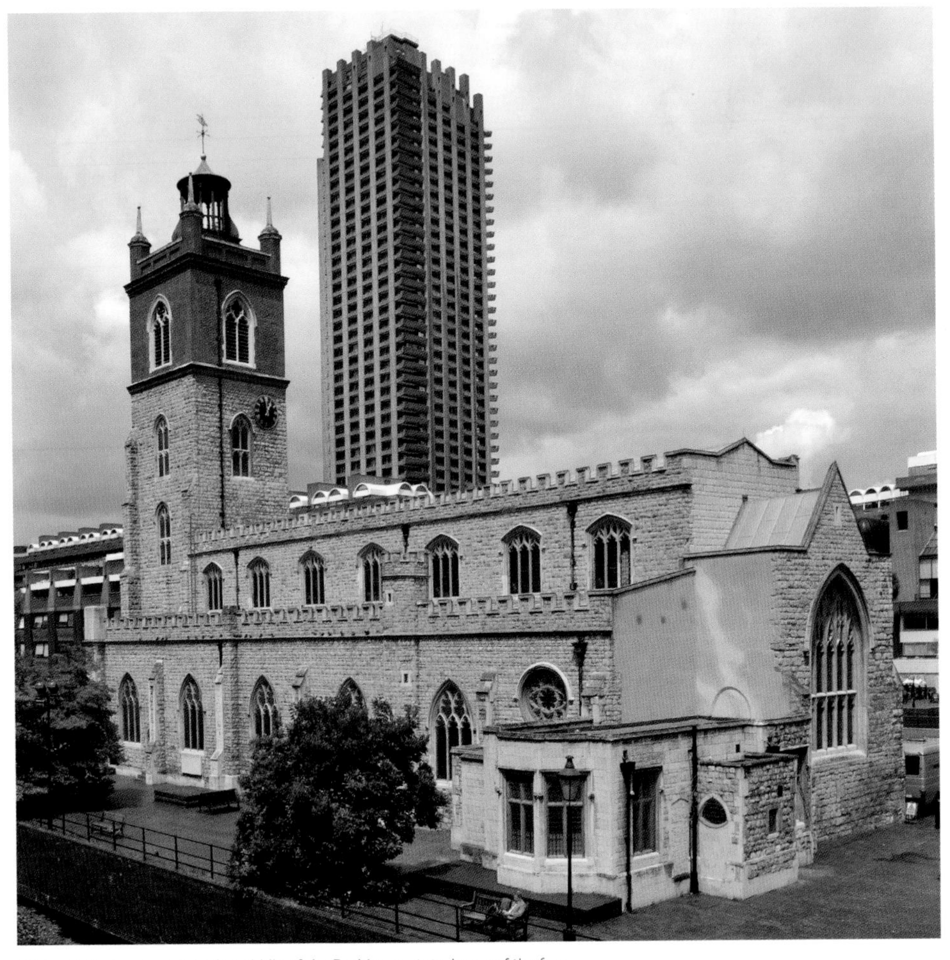

St Giles Cripplegate, now in the middle of the Barbican estate, is one of the few churches to have survived both the Great Fire in 1666 and the Luftwaffe in 1940.

Alan Gilbert conducts the New York Philharmonic, now an International Associate of the Barbican, in the Centre's concert hall (© Chris Lee).

ARTS AND CULTURE IN THE CITY

For a single square mile, the City punches above its very considerable weight as a provider of arts and culture; the City of London Corporation is surpassed only by the Government and the BBC as an investor in cultural life. Since the days of bread and circuses in the Roman amphitheatre, the arts have thrived in the City through the guilds and livery companies, and a theatre was established by the Burbages in 1596 near Blackfriars. Over the postwar years this support has grown hugely, and the City Corporation now considers support and patronage of the arts a fundamental part of its mission, alongside the promotion of the City as a world leader in business and financial services.

A diverse range of arts organizations and activities are supported by the City Corporation: the world-famous London Symphony Orchestra, dating back over a century, moved to the Barbican Centre when it opened in 1982, and the Guildhall School of Music & Drama was also a key part of that utopian estate when it was being designed. The three organizations – Barbican, LSO and Guildhall School – now work together in an 'alliance for creative excellence', sharing ideas and resources and reaching out beyond the City to East London. While the Barbican's two galleries host a range of adventurous art from Le Corbusier to Japanese fashion, with contemporary artists commissioned for the Curve Gallery, the more restrained splendours of the City Corporation's art collection can be appreciated at the Guildhall Art Gallery.

The arts in the City are not aimed only at adults with deep pockets – family events at the Barbican introduce dance and classical music to new young audiences.

The libraries and archives service of the City includes the London Metropolitan Archives, which houses historic images. Shared between the City Corporation and the Greater London Authority is the Museum of London, based on London Wall. The famous Mermaid Theatre started by Bernard Miles by the river is now a conference centre, and the Royal Shakespeare Company, resident at the Barbican for some years, now performs elsewhere, but the fine Barbican Theatre now hosts a range of innovative international work.

There is an increasing emphasis on making the City's arts and heritage more accessible to a new generation. The City Corporation's support extends to the London Schools Symphony Orchestra and the Centre for Young Musicians, which now forms part of the Guildhall School. Wide-ranging education and outreach activities take place in the City fringes and beyond. The annual City of London Festival, fifty years old in 2012, uses churches and livery halls as the venues for its concerts and also mounts an extensive free programme around the City, ranging as far as the open spaces of Hampstead Heath. The Corporation supports the Spitalfields Festival, many City churches offer regular free concerts and organ recitals, and St Paul's Cathedral boasts an outstanding choir. Public art such as Antony Gormley's figure in Shoe Lane and well-designed public spaces around Carter Lane and elsewhere are beginning to animate the streets and complement the increasing retail and leisure facilities of the City.

The City's main venue for major contemporary exhibitions is the Barbican Art Gallery, seen here in 2010 playing host to 'Future Beauty', the Japanese fashion exhibition.

The Guildhall School of Music & Drama (left above) was the first cultural building in the Barbican to be completed, in 1977. The project boxes on the frontage house practice rooms and offices. The school is due to be augmented in 2013 by a new building nearby (shown in the computer-generated rendering above) by David Walker and RHWL/Arts Team, financially enabl by the slimline 36-storey tower of flats.

19 GUILDHALL SCHOOL OF MUSIC & DRAMA

Silk Street EC2 • Chamberlin, Powell & Bon 1977, David Walker and RHWL 2011–13

At the heart of the Barbican estate next to the arts centre is this not-so-simple shoebox of a building occupied by the Guildhall School of Music & Drama. Though its materials are typical of the Barbican – bush-hammered concrete, dark engineering brick, woodblock floors and wood-strip ceilings (in the words of the architect Christoph Bon, it is 'a building without sugar icing') – its grander forms mark it out as a public building. The school began life in a converted warehouse in Aldermanbury, beside Guildhall, in 1880, as the first municipal music college in Britain. It soon outgrew the space and in 1887 joined the City of London Schools for Girls and Boys in John Carpenter Street, by the Embankment; its handsome new buildings (the façades survive) by the City surveyor, Horace Jones, were equipped with soundproofed practice rooms. By the 1970s the school had nearly 600 full-time students, so the move to the Barbican was timely. When it opened in 1977 it was the first cultural venture to be completed in the Barbican. A theatre and concert hall form the core, ringed by offices and practice rooms – these are expressed externally as brick boxes within the concrete frame, which look like upended tuning forks. Barbican-style curves appear in the barrel-vaulted canopies over the library, tying it in with the residential blocks. Narrow windows in canted corners overlook the students' terrace and water gardens. The school is scheduled to benefit in 2013 from a glassy new building by David Walker and RHWL/Arts Team on the site of Milton Court (1966), which was an ultra-Corbusian public services block at the north-east corner of the Barbican estate incorporating a fire station and municipal offices: the new facilities will include an extra concert hall and two small theatres, all enabled by a slimline 36-storey residential tower on top.

The frontage of the brewery to Chiswell Street is now being redeveloped.

20 WHITBREAD'S BREWERY

Chiswell Street EC1

The buildings of the former Whitbread brewery along both sides of Chiswell Street are the rump of a beer-making complex that by the end of the 19th century covered six acres. It is still an impressive sight. The historic core is right on the street – the redbrick Partners' House, built about 1700, is where the brewer Samuel Whitbread moved when he took over a derelict brewery around 1748. By the time of his death in 1796 it was the largest brewery in London, producing more than 200,000 barrels a year. As a contemporary put it, 'The sight of a London brewhouse exhibits a magnificence unspeakable'. The site occupies the whole block from Milton Street to Silk Street, stretching back along wide, shallow South Yard, entered through an arch. The most impressive building is the Porter Tun Room, built in the 1780s and with the widest kingpost roof at the time after Westminster Hall. Up to the minute in technology, Whitbread installed a Boulton and Watt steam engine that powered everything from stirrers and crushers to beer and water pumps. It was in use for more than a century until it was decommissioned and sent off to Australia, where it can still be seen working in the

Powerhouse Museum, Sydney. Other survivors in South Yard are the elegant Sugar Rooms of 1792 and huge three-storey brick-vaulted stables for 300 horses from the 1860s. Brewing stopped at the site in 1976 and the buildings became a venue for conferences and dinners. A long narrow courtyard of Victorian buildings on the other side of Chiswell Street, entered though gates, is the remains of the depot where the beer was casked – converted, appropriately enough, into student accommodation in the 1990s. The entire complex survived the horror night of bombing on 29 December 1940 with only minor damage, protected by Whitbread's own fire service, and brewing restarted only four days after the raid.

21 MILTON GATE

Chiswell Street EC1 • Sir Denys Lasdun, Peter Softley & Associates 1987–91

It is to the credit of this deep-green building that it is not obvious when it was built – it could have been any time in the past forty years. It is also hard to identify as a work (the last completed in his lifetime) by Denys Lasdun, architect of the concrete machine that is the National Theatre, as Milton Gate is an essay in the possibilities of frameless glass. Only the various towers and 'turrets', the giant vestigial oriels and the big pitched aluminium roof hint at Postmodernism. The glass cladding is also unusual. This was one of the first triple-skinned ventilated façade buildings – the cavity space minimized the cost of air-conditioning, making it green in more than the literal sense.

The sheer, shiny green-glas walls of the Milton Gate off building were triple-glazed very high-tech and eco-friendly for the late 1980s.

Salters' Hall, though unusual for a livery hall in its outfit of concrete, steel and smoked glass, sits comfortably alongside London Wall and the Barbican.

22 SALTERS' HALL

Fore Street EC2 • Sir Basil Spence 1968–76

The City is peppered with rather wan 1950s livery halls put up quickly after the Blitz in a starved classical style whose thinness owes a lot to the rationing of building materials at the time. Salters' Hall is quite different, a robustly modern interpretation of what a livery hall might be, built at a time when hope, money and architectural innovation had returned to the City. The Salters' previous hall, lost to the Blitz in 1941, was their fifth hall in 400 years, on two different sites. Designed by Basil Spence in 1968, this new hall on a new site set back from London Wall shares with Spence's reviled Home Office at 50 Queen Anne's Gate a massive high-level projection. Here this contains the staircase and the double-height livery hall itself, the inside humanized by David Hicks's interior designs with reeded ash wall panelling and floor-to-ceiling windows at the end; the adjoining Court Room is darker, rosewood-lined. These rooms

The travertine-lined entrance hall of Salters' Hall by David Hicks is remarkably spare and plain for a livery hall.

sit over four floors of commercial glass and concrete office space, but the ground-floor level, partly open, is made more decorative by rich wrought-iron gates dated 1887 from the old 1820s Salters' Hall. A sunken garden on the south side is the site of the churchyard of the first St Alphage London Wall, which was built into the tall section of the real London wall, the Roman wall (the garden on the south side of the wall is public, see p. 230, and was the site of the church itself). This wall, part of the 2nd-century Roman fort, is topped with medieval flint and other masonry from the church walls and finally brickwork battlements of the 15th century.

23 ALBAN GATE

London Wall EC2 • Terry Farrell Partnership 1988–92

Very much of its period is this great monolith on London Wall. At the time that it was built Alban Gate's brash style was novel, and certainly helped define and shape the architecture of the 1990s – it is just debatable whether that was a good thing. What is certain is that Alban Gate, squatting heavily over London Wall, killed off the 1950s vision of what that street might be. Once one of the slab blocks was gone, London Wall became like a toothless smile. Alban Gate is in fact two skyscrapers that angle rather awkwardly together as each tries to align with a different route – one over London Wall and the other, hovering slightly uncertainly beside it, replacing Lee House, one of the 1950s slabs. Architects in Britain were excited in the mid-1980s by the colourful Postmodernism of Michael Graves in the USA – his Portland Public Services building in Oregon and La Jolla hotel

Alban Gate put paid to the 1950s Le Corbusian vision for London Wall and introduced the brash shapes and colours of Postmodernism to the City.

complex in California – that made classicism a simple colourful game, here expressed in big segmental arches and oriels. While it blocks the view down London Wall, Alban Gate maintains the dual-level approach of the 1950s, and it is hard not to be impressed walking through at podium level by the huge diagonal struts, shiny grey and pink granite and monumental columns. This route also gives a great view of the tower of Wren's St Alban and the other architectural delights of Wood Street. Behind adjoining Monkwell Square to the north is a terrace of houses, a smaller, less shiny interpretation of this style in red brick and stone.

24 ST ALPHAGE LONDON WALL
EC2

While many churches ruined in the world wars have received reverential treatment as part of a garden scheme, poor scruffy St Alphage is squeezed against the podium of the 1950s London Wall, almost tipping onto the pavement. The best view is from the pedestrian walkway above the north side of London Wall. For such scant remains it has a very complicated history: beginning as a priory church, possibly in the 10th century, it was refounded in 1331 as Elsing Spital, a hospital for the blind run by Augustinian canons. Their priory church became the parish church of St Alphage when the original St Alphage London Wall was demolished at the end of the 16th century. The building then suffered a 300-year cycle of neglect and repair, surviving the Great Fire to be largely rebuilt in the 18th century, only to succumb to German bombing in the First World War. Its 18th-century tower survived until 1959 when, standing in the way of progress, it was reduced to its surviving core of 14th-century tower and north transept.

The 1770s frontage of St Alphage, once the pri church of Elsing Spital, seen in a drawing of around 1830, was demolished in 1923 after be bombed in the First World War. Only a stump of the 14th-century tower survives, marooned beside modern London Wall.

St Alphage garden just west of the old tower is the site of the original St Alphage, replaced as parish church by the priory church after the Reformation. It is separated from what was once the churchyard and is now the garden of Salters' Hall by an unusually fine stretch of City wall, rising up through Roman, medieval and Tudor layers.

Fox's frontage is effectively nearly all glass as the black panels are Vitrolite, a type of glass into which colour is fused during manufacture.

25 FOX'S UMBRELLAS

118 London Wall EC2

At its east end London Wall opens out on the north side with a group of 18th- and 19th-century houses, soothing after the architectural clamour. The star attraction here is a beautifully preserved shopfront and fittings of 1937, created for Fox Umbrellas, who have been, as they say, 'Keeping You Dry Since 1868'. In the early days the building housed a hair salon and tailor, also owned by Fox, and it was common for customers to come, leave their umbrella to be repaired and have their hair cut while they were waiting. Despite their Victorian roots, Fox's sleek black shopfront was up-to-the-minute moderne in 1937, with a neon sign and, like Simpson's of Piccadilly (now Waterstone's), curving glass, a trick to avoid distracting reflections. The shiny black panels are Vitrolite, a glass cladding manufactured in Britain by Pilkington, in which the colour was fused into the body. Inside, glamorous mirrored steps (incongruously flanked by mahogany-framed advertising mirrors – 'Experienced Workmen Only' – kept from earlier days) lead up to the offices, where other Victorian fittings survive out of view. Umbrellas were made in the basement until twenty years ago. Though it is no longer owned by Fox, which is now in Croydon, the shop still sells their umbrellas. It is decked out in more obviously Art Deco walnut shelves, drawers, a clock and glass display cabinets for ties and other gentlemen's necessities.

Although the mirrored steps adjoining Fox's umbrella shop date from the swish 1930s refitting, the mirrors on the wall survive from its Victorian incarnation.

Additional Places to Visit

O a Newgate

The western entrance to the City was demolished in 1777, and is marked by a blue plaque on the Central Criminal Court and an information panel on the railings of St Sepulchre (pp. 187–8), on the corner of Giltspur Street. In the same railings is preserved London's very first drinking fountain, installed on Holborn Hill in 1859, inaugurated by the daughter of the Archbishop of Canterbury. It was moved here when the viaduct was built, and is looking rather forlorn. We are instructed to 'replace the cup', but the two vessels are now firmly chained.

O b Watchhouse; Snow Lane Court

In Giltspur Street, past St Sepulchre, is a 1962 reconstruction of the original watchhouse of 1791, designed to prevent bodies being stolen from St Bartholomew's Hospital nearby. Behind is the small and hidden Snow Lane Court, with its old school buildings, now converted.

O c Giltspur Street Compter

In the pub basement, under the flamboyant Victoriana of the Viaduct Tavern at no. 126 Newgate Street, are the grisly remains of some prison cells. Once thought to be part of Newgate Prison, they are more likely part of the Giltspur Street Compter, demolished in 1855. No attempt has been made to glamorize them.

O d Greyfriars Monastery

The site of the medieval monastery established in 1224 was north of Newgate Street: a blue plaque on the former General Post Office marks the area. The neighbouring modern office block has been carefully built around the site (it won the City Heritage Award in 2002) and houses some remains of the Roman wall. Greyfriars Passage leads to the beautiful open garden of Christ Church Newgate Street (pp. 198–9), with climbing plants and trellises where the church pillars once stood.

O e The Golden Boy of Pye Corner

Going north up Giltspur Street towards Smithfield, a late 17th-century gilded statue of a chubby child is mounted in the wall at the corner of Cock Lane; it was originally on the Fortune of War pub, demolished in 1910 (see introduction, p. 180 and p. 351). It marks the western extent of the Great Fire, and the inscription recalls arguments about the origins of the disaster, counter-acting the blame heaped on Catholics on the Monument.

O f **Smithfield Rotunda Gardens**

At the hub of Smithfield, this round open space is surrounded by the ramp to the old goods station beneath (see introduction, p. 182), and at its centre is the 'Peace' drinking fountain of 1871–3, now missing its original large Gothic canopy. It includes a competition-winning stone bench designed by students and made by apprentice masons. Much earlier it was a gruesome place of public execution, where many died, including William Wallace 'Braveheart' (1270–1305). He has a noble plaque on the wall of Barts opposite, where flowers are often left.

O g **Cloth Fair**

To the left of St Bartholomew-the-Great is the small street where the poet John Betjeman (1906–84) lived (blue plaque and painted window in no. 43 Cloth Court) next to two very fine 17th-century houses (nos 41 and 42); their restoration won a City Heritage Award in 2000.

O h **Barber Surgeons' Herb Garden**

North of London Wall, just to the right of the Museum of London, are well-preserved fragments of the Roman and medieval wall, and a delightful herb garden behind Barber Surgeons' Hall. The access down the car park slope (across London Wall from Noble Street) is unappealing, but well worth it to go across the grass and see the finest bastion of the Roman wall, part of the Wood Street fort, by the Barbican lake.

O i **Barbican Waterside**

Among the many public spaces of the Barbican Centre (pp. 219–20), the waterside terrace by the lake provides rest and refreshment far from traffic: access is from inside the Centre via Silk Street, or from Wood Street and Alban Gate via the highwalk to Gilbert Bridge.

O j **Cripplegate; Fore Street**

The site of the City gate next to the Roman fort is marked in Wood Street, north of London Wall. Round the corner in Fore Street, next to Salters' Hall, a stone tablet marks the spot where the first bomb hit the area in the Second World War at 12.15 a.m. on 25 August 1940; bombing eventually led to the devastation of the whole area.

O k **The Minotaur**

Up in the highwalk gardens by the soon-to-be replaced St Alphage House, near the remains of St Alphage London Wall (p. 230), is the threatening sculpture of *The Minotaur* (1968–9) by Michael Ayrton (1921–75).

MILLIE'S
M&S
Stansted Express
Bus station
Underground
Way out
Way out

6 Liverpool Street Station & The 'Gherkin'

Back in the 1960s Ian Nairn wrote memorably of the transition from City to East End experienced in a short walk along Sun Street Passage, between Liverpool Street and Broad Street stations – in just two hundred yards, the 'affluent flurry of the City' gave way to 'the sad emptiness of south Shoreditch'. Close by was 'the wrecked grandeur of Spitalfields'. Sun Street Passage still exists (though Broad Street Station went in the 1980s for the development of Broadgate, which then became the City's riposte to the rise of Docklands as a business location). But the acute contrast between affluence and squalor so evident even fifty years ago is no longer apparent – Shoreditch and Spitalfields have become fashionable quarters (and the latter a major office location). The borderline between City and East End has become blurred. Even today, however, the line of the ancient City wall, from Bishopsgate to Aldgate, has some significance as a boundary, with Middlesex Street (otherwise known as Petticoat Lane) clearly on the very edge of the Square Mile. The north-eastern sector of the City was, until the Reformation, dominated by monastic foundations: Holy Trinity Priory at Aldgate, the nunnery of St Helen's and the house of the Poor Clares (or Minoresses) in the Minories, a little to the south, just beyond Aldgate. The hospitals of St Mary of Bethlehem (Bedlam) and St Mary Spital were sited further north, the latter just outside the walls. The monasteries and hospitals have vanished but the church of St Helen's survives, along with the medieval parish churches of St Ethelburga and St Andrew Undershaft and the rare 1630s church of St Katharine Cree, in an area that escaped the ravages of the Great Fire of 1666.

East of Bishopsgate, offices still give way to warehouses and wholesale businesses and, beyond Aldgate, Whitechapel High Street is one of the fulcrums of the new multicultural capital. This was once the focus of Jewish London and within the City the historic synagogue of Bevis Marks – Britain's oldest – still survives. But the relentless tide of commercial development has pushed eastwards. The great warehouse complex of Cutlers' Gardens was part demolished, part converted, for offices in the late 1970s and early 1980s. At the end of Houndsditch the new Heron Tower marks the start of a new phase of high-rise development in a 'cluster' that will include high-profile office towers on Bishopsgate and Leadenhall Street. The stage was set for the City's new generation of tall buildings by Norman Foster's 'Gherkin' at no. 30 St Mary Axe, a distinctive building that has become a global symbol of London and which the public came to like. The 'Gherkin' is where it is because of the 1992 IRA bomb that largely destroyed the late Victorian Baltic Exchange on the site. The City

Opposite
The redevelopment of Liverpool Street Station that was completed in 1991 restored and extended the western train shed to create a new concourse.

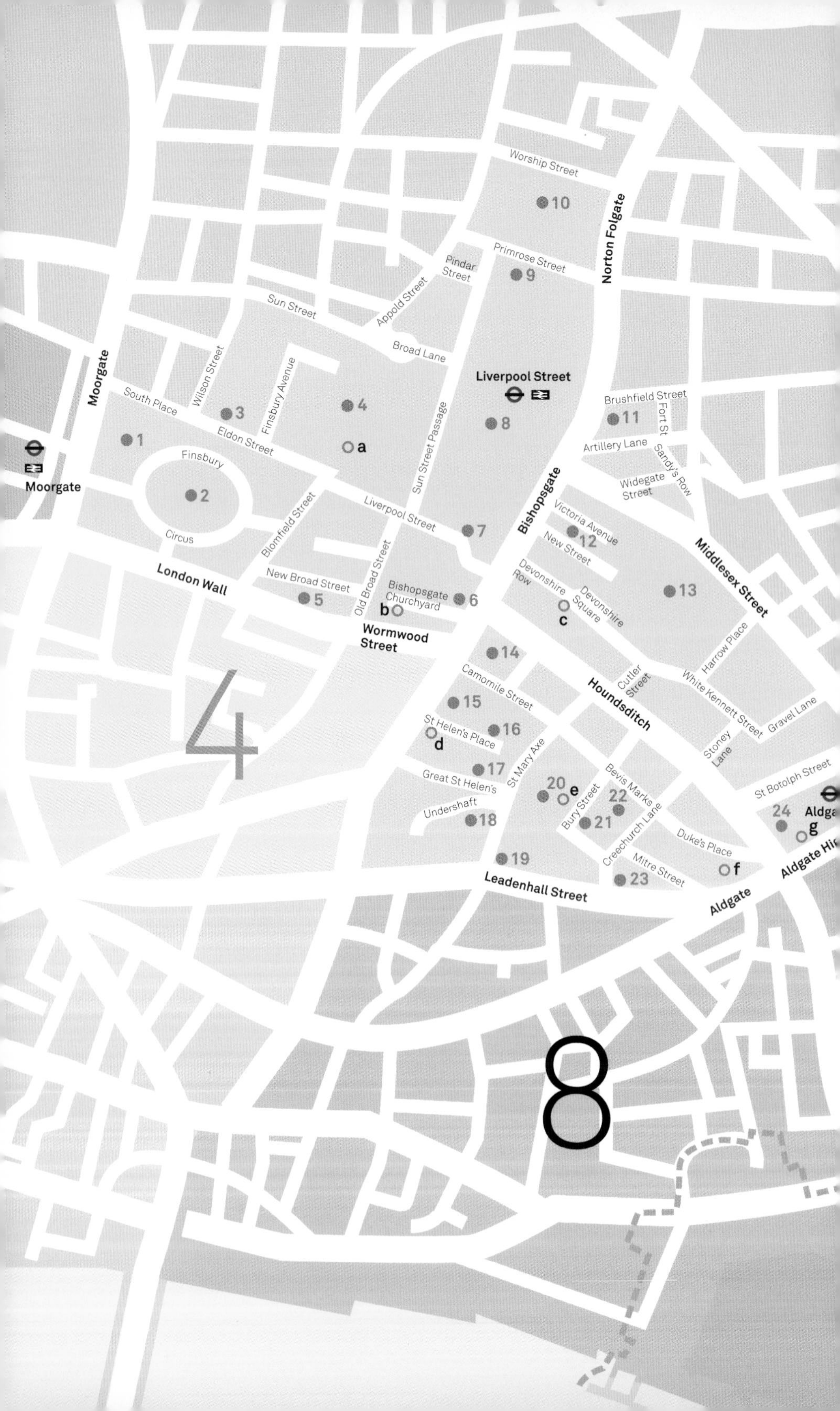

Worship Street
10
Norton Folgate
Primrose Street
9
Pindar Street
Appold Street
Sun Street
Broad Lane
Liverpool Street
Moorgate
South Place
Wilson Street
Finsbury Avenue
3
4
1
Eldon Street
a
Sun Street Passage
8
Brushfield Street
11
Fort St
Artillery Lane
Sandy's Row
Widegate Street
Moorgate
Finsbury
2
Circus
Blomfield Street
Liverpool Street
7
Bishopsgate
Victoria Avenue
12
New Street
Middlesex Street
London Wall
New Broad Street
Old Broad Street
Bishopsgate Churchyard
5
b
6
Devonshire Row
Devonshire Square
c
13
Wormwood Street
14
Camomile Street
Houndsditch
Cutler Street
Harrow Place
White Kennett Street
Gravel Lane
4
15
St Helen's Place
16
d
17
St Mary Axe
Stoney Lane
St Botolph Street
Great St Helen's
20
e
Bevis Marks
22
Bury Street
21
Undershaft
18
Creechurch Lane
Duke's Place
24
Aldgate
g
19
Mitre Street
f
23
Leadenhall Street
Aldgate
Aldgate High
8

KEY TO AREA 6

- 1 Britannic House
- 2 Finsbury Circus
- 3 St Mary Moorfields
- 4 Broadgate
- 5 All Hallows London Wall
- 6 St Botolph Bishopsgate
- 7 Andaz Hotel
- 8 Liverpool Street Station
- 9 Exchange House
- 10 Broadgate Tower
- 11 Bishopsgate Institute
- 12 Bishopsgate Police Station
- 13 Cutlers' Gardens
- 14 Heron Tower
- 15 St Ethelburga
- 16 Leathersellers' Hall
- 17 St Helen Bishopsgate
- 18 Aviva Tower and Plaza
- 19 St Andrew Undershaft
- 20 No. 30 St Mary Axe
- 21 Holland House
- 22 Spanish and Portuguese Synagogue
- 23 St Katharine Cree
- 24 St Botolph Aldgate

- a Broadgate sculpture
- b Victorian Turkish Baths
- c Devonshire Row; Jubilee Gardens; Petticoat Square
- d St Helen's Place
- e Roman Girl's Grave
- f Charity Boy and Girl
- g Sanctuary, Aldgate High Street

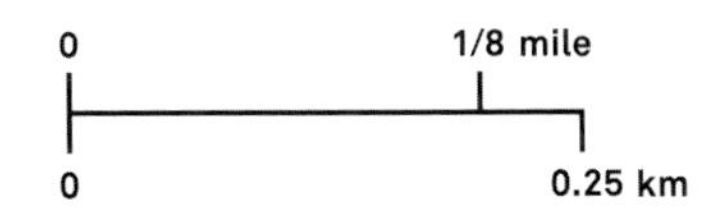

bombings of 1992 and 1993 caused death, injury and massive damage to property, including many historic buildings, but also generated the 'ring of steel' – as a result, through traffic in the City was significantly reduced and the potential for the creation of a more pedestrian-friendly environment was realized.

Liverpool Street Station is a massive presence in this part of the City, used by over a million travellers every week and a good example of how a historic station can be adapted to present-day needs. The advent of Crossrail, with a new station here designed by Wilkinson Eyre, will reinforce the importance of Liverpool Street as a transport hub. Broad Street Station, which stood just to the west, was, in Betjeman's words, 'the saddest of all London stations' before it finally closed in 1985 to make way for Broadgate. Since then Broadgate has grown into a complex of sixteen buildings where more than 30,000 people work. The Broadgate Tower at its northern edge acts as a marker at the entry point to the City, which, here as elsewhere, seems poised to leap across its historic limits – most of Broadgate was not within the City before the boundary changes of the 1990s. Finsbury Square, clearly prime office territory, remains within the London Borough of Islington, while Finsbury Circus is firmly within the City. Surrounded by big office buildings faced with Portland stone, it has a sober character of its own, though it is hard to imagine it as the residential enclave it once was. The garden at the centre is – or was – perhaps the most delightful in the City, but is (temporarily) a construction site for Crossrail.

Bishopsgate, extending north from the junction of Cornhill and Leadenhall Street, has a solidly commercial character at first, though road widening in the 1970s removed a number of buildings on the eastern side between Threadneedle Street and Leadenhall Street – the worst loss was Barings Bank, a major work by Richard Norman Shaw, with interiors by Lutyens. East of Bishopsgate, the old courts and alleys that survived the Second World War have vanished, leaving only Great St Helen's as a remnant around the church of St Helen. Crosby Square has vanished totally, largely destroyed for the Standard Chartered Bank (designed by Fitzroy Robinson Partnership) in the early 1980s – the latter has now itself gone, demolished to make way for the 'Pinnacle', a 288-m (945-ft) office tower designed by Kohn Pedersen Fox and currently due for completion in 2013. Crosby Square was the site of Crosby Hall, part of Crosby Place, the great mansion built for the City merchant Sir John Crosby in 1466–75. The magnificent hall survived various owners – Sir Walter Raleigh briefly lived in part of it, and subsequently it was a library and a restaurant – until 1908, when it was demolished for commercial development. Fortunately, the London County Council and City Corporation intervened and the structure was carefully dismantled and stored until, in the 1920s, it was re-erected close to Chelsea Old Church – where, remarkably, it once more forms part of a private residence. Too much of Bishopsgate is now dominated by mundane commercial development, much of it in the heavy masonry-faced Postmodern manner once favoured by City planners. (The Commercial Union Tower on

Barings Bank, seen here in a photograph of c. 1890, was a major work by the great Victoria architect Richard Norman Shaw but was demolished in the 1970s for the widening of Bishopsgate, a major architectural loss.

The 15th-century Crosby Hall was a rare surviv of a great medieval merchant's house at the heart of the City. The great hall of John Crosby's house was dismantled for redevelopment in 19 and rebuilt in Chelsea, where it forms part of ar opulent private residence.

Bethlehem Hospital ('Bedlam') was originally located on the site of what became Liverpool Street Station. In 1675 it moved to new buildings in Moorfields, shown here. In 1815 it relocated to Lambeth, to premises that now house the Imperial War Museum.

Liverpool Street Station in the 1950s, when it was a confused, if romantic, place.

Leadenhall Street – latterly called the Aviva Tower and recently renamed no. 1 St Helen's – with its Manhattan-style plaza, was a radical 1960s intrusion into the historic fabric of the area but now seems refreshingly direct and rational.)

Beyond the junction with London Wall, the character of Bishopsgate changes rapidly. The west side is dominated by the bulk of the Andaz (formerly Great Eastern) hotel and the even more elephantine block, nearly 275 m (900 ft) long, designed by Skidmore, Owings & Merrill in transatlantic Postmodern style as part of Broadgate and constructed over the eastern platforms of Liverpool Street Station. The eastern side has an altogether more modest scale. The Bishopsgate Institute is the most significant feature, founded by the energetic Victorian incumbent of St Botolph Bishopsgate, William Rogers, as a place where City workers could read books and attend evening lectures and classes. The former fire station, Gothic in style and designed by George Vulliamy in 1884–5, has been converted to offices with a branch of Tesco on the ground floor. Dirty Dick's pub is an unremarkable Victorian building but commemorates Nathaniel Bentley, a City merchant whose fiancée died on the eve of their wedding: shutting himself away, he lived the rest of his life in abject squalor in his premises on Leadenhall Street. An astute Victorian publican took up the legend and turned what had been the Old Jerusalem tavern into a shrine to 'Dirty Dick', complete with 'cobweb festoons dangling from the black rafters'. Devonshire Square – there was once a garden here belonging to the Dukes of Devonshire – is now a mere fragment, with a few Georgian houses surviving amid a mix of later development including a large new office building on the south side.

The City ends, somewhat untidily, at Aldgate, where the elegant church of St Botolph sits hemmed in by roads. There has been much redevelopment in this area in recent years – Grimshaw's St Botolph's is the best of the new office buildings, a contrast to the Postmodernist vulgarity of the 1980s Beaufort House by RHWL – and more is promised, including a major mixed-use scheme on the bus station site close to Aldgate Station. Even here, however, there are fragments of the old City. Aldgate High Street retained a number of timber-framed houses into the 20th century and the Hoop & Grapes still remains, reopened as a pub in 2007 after restoration – it is 17th-century in origin and may predate the Fire.

Grimshaw's St Botolph's is the most striking ne office development in the area around Aldgate on the eastern fringe of the City.

The 1880s fire station on Bishopsgate is a good example of Victorian public architecture, now converted to offices with a supermarket where the fire engines were formerly housed.

Opposite
Norman Foster's no. 30 St Mary Axe, known as the 'Gherkin', is seen here framed by Richard Rogers's 1980s Lloyd's Building and, on the right, Terence Heysham's Lloyd's Building of 1958, now demolished.

Paul Ponsonby

1 BRITANNIC HOUSE

Finsbury Circus EC2 • Sir Edwin Lutyens 1921–5; W. Nimmo & Partners with Inskip & Jenkins 1987–9; Gaunt Francis 2008–10

After the First World War, Edwin Lutyens turn increasingly to commercial work. Britannic House is, along with the former Midland Ban at Poultry, the finest of his works in this field.

In the years after the First World War, with commissions for new country houses few and far between, Lutyens turned to commercial work, acting as consultant, for example, to the Midland Bank (for whom he designed a magnificent head office on Poultry). Britannic House was built for the Anglo-Persian Oil Company (later BP) on a site that extends around the corner from Finsbury Circus on to Moorgate (where it incorporates an entrance to the Underground station). The building is a masterly composition, topped on the Finsbury Circus elevation by a monumental two-storey Corinthian order – a truly Roman gesture. It is also rich in outstanding craftsmanship, including excellent stone carving, with figurative sculpture by Derwent Wood. Lutyens's hand is equally apparent inside, with a particularly memorable entrance sequence and splendid main staircase of grey Brescia marble, demonstrating the architect's mastery of spatial effects. The chairman's office is a nobly vaulted space. It was retained, along with the principal circulation spaces, when the building was internally remodelled in 1987–9 by W. Nimmo & Partners with Inskip & Jenkins and again in 2008–10 by Gaunt Francis. The project gave this fine building a new lease of life.

2 FINSBURY CIRCUS

EC2 • George Dance the Younger 1802; William Mountague 1815–17

Among the features of the gardens at Finsbu Circus are the bandstand and the drinking fountain of 1902, the latter said to be based c the wellhead at William Morris's Red House ir Bexleyheath.

The public garden at the centre of Finsbury Circus, beautifully maintained and complete with drinking fountain, bowling green and clubhouse, was one of the delights of this part of the City. Currently it is a massive hole in the ground, part of the construction works for Crossrail's Liverpool Street Station – but the garden will be fully restored, it is promised, when the project is finished, and City workers will again be able to eat their sandwiches there on fine summer days. Finsbury Circus was the City's only significant Georgian square, laid out in 1815–17 by the City Surveyor William Mountague to a plan of 1802 by his predecessor George Dance the Younger following the demolition of Robert Hooke's magnificent Bethlehem Hospital (which was relocated to Southwark). The early 19th-century houses, many of them formerly occupied by doctors' surgeries, were progressively demolished for commercial development in the first decades of the 20th century. The London Institution, with its fine library and programme of lectures open to all, occupied an imposing building by William Brooks on the north side from 1815 until 1912; subsumed into London University, it was demolished in 1936.

The clearance of the Circus's original buildings provided sites for the construction of large, up-to-date office buildings conveniently close to Liverpool Street Station and Moorgate

Park House on Finsbury Circus was completed in 1921 to designs by Gordon & Gunton, a typical commercial palazzo of the era. A radical internal reconstruction, completed in 2008, provided 26,000 sq. m of new office space around a central atrium, with the most important internal features retained.

Underground station. The finest of them is Lutyens's Britannic House, completed in 1925. Other new buildings reflected the predominant commercial style of the period – a late version of Edwardian Baroque executed in Portland stone on steel frames. The first was Salisbury House, in the south-west corner of the Circus, designed by Davis & Emmanuel and completed in 1901. The character of Finsbury Circus (a conservation area) has been maintained, although there has been much redevelopment behind retained façades – Park House, a 1920s block by Gordon & Gunton, now features a dramatic new full-height atrium behind a bombastic classical frontage. New buildings, including the Bank of Tokyo, designed by GMW Partnership, and River Plate House (by Kenzie Lovell Partnership), are among the best examples of 1980s commercial Postmodernist architecture in the City, stone faced and taking their cue stylistically from their neighbours.

The atrium in Park House, Finsbury Circus.

George Sherrin's new church, completed in 1903, reworked the classical style of its predecessor to produce an interior at once grand and intimate, a calm place on the edge of Broadgate.

3 ST MARY MOORFIELDS

4–5 Eldon Street EC2 • George Sherrin 1899–1903

The only Roman Catholic church in the City – and only within the City since the boundary changes of 1994 – St Mary Moorfields hardly looks like a church from the street: the entrance, flanked by shops and marked by a fine sculpture of the Virgin and Child, is through a block that could easily house offices but is actually the clergy house. The history of the parish extends back to the late 17th century – a chapel in Ropemakers' Alley was burned down in the 1780 Gordon Riots. St Mary's replaced a large classical church in Moorfields (Finsbury Square), demolished in 1899–1900 for commercial development. The architect of the new St Mary's, George Sherrin, worked mostly in the commercial field, designing a number of buildings in the City, but had completed the dome of the London Oratory church following the death of its architect, Herbert Gribble. Sherrin's choice of a Renaissance style doubtless reflected a desire to preserve memories of the former church (though it was equally in tune with the City churches of Wren). The interior, set below street level, with a nave aisled on one side only and a shallow sanctuary, has a simple gravitas and a great deal of atmosphere, with candle-lit shrines and an ethos of prayer – appreciated not only by Catholics as a place to be still and reflect. Sherrin reused the high altar from the former church, along with the six marble columns that framed it, providing an impressive internal focus – the reordering carried out since the Second Vatican Council is suitably sensitive. The marble font is also a relic of the old church.

4 BROADGATE ➔

EC2 • Arup Associates 1985–7

Following the abandonment of plans to redevelop Liverpool Street Station, British Rail went into partnership with developer Rosehaugh Stanhope to develop the site of Broad Street Station, closed in 1985, and the adjacent goods yard, long used for car parking. The driving force behind the project was the need to provide accommodation for international banks and other financial businesses attracted to London by the deregulation of the financial sector under the Thatcher government. Large, flexible

The Broadgate development was constructed to a 'fast-track' programme in 1985–8 on former railway land, with buildings tailored to the needs of large financial institutions.

dealing floors were a key element in the development package, with 'fast-track' construction allowing completion of all the buildings within two years. Following the success of its no. 1 Finsbury Avenue project, Arup Associates under Peter Foggo was appointed as architect for a series of eight-storey blocks disposed around a central square. Externally the buildings feature perforated screens of pink granite masking the glazed façades. The central square was developed around the Broadgate Arena, a travertine-faced amphitheatre containing shops and restaurants, which has become a highly popular place for City workers to relax both in summer and in winter, when it houses an ice-skating rink clearly inspired by that at New York's Rockefeller Center.

The strength of Broadgate lies less in its architecture – efficient if a little monotonous – than in its public spaces and the way it has created new pedestrian routes, including connections to Liverpool Street Station. Public art was taken seriously from the beginning – Richard Serra's *Fulcrum* (1987) marks the point of entry from Liverpool Street. Later phases of the Broadgate estate were designed by the practice of Skidmore, Owings & Merrill and include Exchange House, the Broadgate Tower and the blocks along Bishopsgate, which cover the eastern platforms of Liverpool Street Station and are among the more flamboyant examples of American Postmodern styling to be seen in London.

All Hallows, built hard against the City wall, provides an elegant contrast to the large-scale commercial development of later centuries.

5 ALL HALLOWS LONDON WALL

EC2 • George Dance the Younger 1765–7

Dance the Younger's masterpiece, Newgate Prison, completed in 1778 (and damaged in the Gordon Riots of 1780), was demolished in 1902 and replaced by the Central Criminal Court in Old Bailey. All Hallows was his first London building, designed when Dance was just twenty-four. It is a pioneering example of radical neo-classicism, possibly influenced by French models (but certainly reflecting Dance's study of Roman architecture) and much admired by the young John Soane, who studied under Dance. It replaced a medieval church located directly against the City wall – a fragment can be seen in the churchyard. Externally, All Hallows is extremely restrained, its austerity relieved by the modest west tower and cupola. Its interior, elevated on a crypt, is wonderfully elegant and dramatic in its intensity – a single volume (no aisles), lit by three semi-circular windows in the south wall and with the sanctuary in an eastern apse. The coffered vault, springing directly from Ionic columns, and the apse feature delightful plasterwork inspired by antique examples. The church was too radical for some tastes but was enough to secure Dance the post of Clerk of City Works, in succession to his father, in 1768. Newgate followed. The Victorians did little damage to a building that was out of tune with the taste of the period, but All Hallows did suffer significant damage from wartime bombs. It was well repaired but no longer served as a parish church. Today it houses an art gallery and the offices of a number of charities while remaining a consecrated building.

Opposite
Richard Serra's monumental *Fulcrum* sculpture, the largest of a number of art works located within the development, forms a marker at the southern entrance to Broadgate.

REISS

The interior of St Botolph Bishopsgate is a rich mix of Georgian and Victorian work. J. F. Bentley, the architect of Westminster Cathedral, remodelled the east end and designed a number of fittings

6 ST BOTOLPH BISHOPSGATE

EC2 • James Gould 1725–8; J. F. Bentley 1890–94

An imposing and dignified Georgian building, now outfacing the Heron Tower across the road, St Botolph's survived the Blitz and IRA bombs and retains a solemnly impressive interior with a rich mix of Georgian and Victorian fittings. The present church replaced a medieval predecessor – described as standing 'in a fair churchyard adjoining the town ditch' – deemed to be beyond repair. The rebuilding, to a design by James Gould, was carried out by a group of masons including Gould's son-in-law,

George Dance the Elder. The church is traditionally aligned, so that the altar is placed immediately behind the Bishopsgate (east) front, with its imposing tower. Inside, the galleries remain – the glazed dome, lighting the nave, dates from 1821. The pulpit is contemporary with the building, but many of the furnishings date from restorations of the later 19th century. The church was fortunate in having the services of J. F. Bentley in one of the relatively few Anglican commissions carried out by this great Roman Catholic architect. Bentley was brought in to repair and remodel the church by the Rev. William Rogers, an energetic High Churchman who was incumbent from 1863 until his death in 1896 (Bentley designed the memorial tablet to Rogers). The chancel was enriched with marble panels and oak stalls, with a lectern in Italian Renaissance style, and the pews in the body of the church were replaced by new open benches. Further work in the church was done by Bentley's son Osmond. Rogers was also responsible for the landscaping of the old graveyard, south of the church, as a public garden – the first of many City churchyards to be rescued from dereliction and turned into public amenities. Behind the church is the former schoolhouse of the 1860s, designed in keeping with its neighbour. Two Coade stone statues of charity children dating from 1821 were brought here from the previous parish school.

The Great Eastern Hotel photographed in 1976, prior to the redevelopment of Liverpool Street Station.

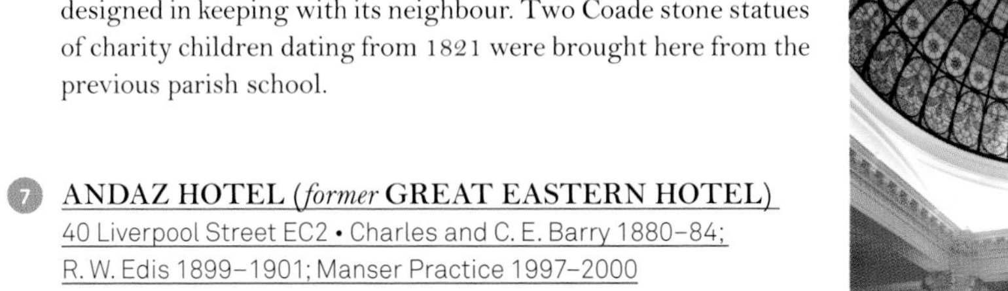

7 ANDAZ HOTEL (*former* GREAT EASTERN HOTEL)

40 Liverpool Street EC2 • Charles and C. E. Barry 1880–84; R. W. Edis 1899–1901; Manser Practice 1997–2000

The Great Eastern Hotel (now rechristened the Andaz and run by the Hyatt chain as a 'boutique hotel') was constructed by the Great Eastern Railway as part of the Liverpool Street Station development. The second phase of the hotel, along Bishopsgate, was added after the station was extended eastwards in the 1890s. One of the last of London's great railway hotels, the Great Eastern was also, until quite recently, the City's only substantial hotel – those at Cannon Street and Holborn Viaduct were both casualties of the Blitz. Both the Barrys' and Edis's work at the Great Eastern is in a French Renaissance manner. The interiors are suitably opulent and include a fine dining room with a glazed dome and the Hamilton Hall, run under separate management as a pub. The most magical (and most unlikely) is the Masonic temple on the first floor, dating from 1912, richly decorated in a heavy classical manner with much mahogany and marble. A £70 million reconstruction completed in 2000 increased the number of guest rooms by 40 per cent, rebuilding the top two floors and finally addressing the lack of connection between the two phases of building by inserting a dramatic new full-height atrium at first-floor level. Sir Terence Conran was part of the consortium behind the project and his design practice was responsible for a comprehensive revamp of the interiors.

The hotel's magnificent dining room dates from the 1880s and was splendidly restored in the reconstruction project completed in 2000.

Following pages
The remarkable Masonic temple at the Andaz (formerly Great Eastern) Hotel was designed by the architects Brown & Barrow and completed in 1912. Richly decorated in marble and mahogany, it contains twin thrones for use in Masonic ceremonies.

TACE

8 LIVERPOOL STREET STATION

EC2 • Edward Wilson 1873–5; W. N. Ashbee 1890–93; British Rail Architects' Department 1985–91

The original London terminus of the Eastern Counties (later Great Eastern) Railway was at Shoreditch, but in 1873–5 the new City terminus at Liverpool Street was constructed, designed by the company's chief engineer, Edward Wilson. The rapid growth in traffic led to the construction of further platforms to the east in 1890–93. The resulting station, its two halves poorly connected, was never convenient for travellers, but John Betjeman described it as 'the most picturesque and interesting of the London termini'. In the 1970s the station was threatened with total demolition and replacement by a new station beneath a raft of offices – Betjeman led opposition to the proposals. A compromise scheme, linked to the Broadgate project on the site of Broad Street Station, saw the eastern platforms demolished for an 'air-rights' office development along Bishopsgate, with replacement platforms below. In the 1980s the spectacular, distinctively Gothic 1870s western train shed was retained and restored – and, in fact, extended to the south in keeping with the original – as part of a project by the British Rail Architects' Department which gave the station a spacious new concourse, conveniently accessed from the Underground and from street level via escalators. Twin brick towers in neo-Victorian mode mark the entrance from Liverpool Street, with a second entrance on Bishopsgate. Shops are provided in a gallery, formed in white-coated steel and glass in a manner typical of the 1980s, which extends at upper level around the concourse and connects to the bus station. London's third busiest rail terminal, Liverpool Street represents a successful compromise between the forces of commerce and modernization and the imperative to preserve the best of the railway heritage. It may have lost something of its picturesque muddle, but it is now one of London's more agreeable stations, and a worthy point of entry to the City.

As part of the restoration project, the decorative iron capitals of the columns in the western shed were restored and brightly painted.

The redevelopment project extended the western shed and created a very large new passenger concourse at the southern end, giving Liverpool Street the sense of space and light it previously lacked.

The western train shed at Liverpool Street, completed in 1875, is one of the most spectacular of London's railway structures and was retained and restored in the redevelopment of the station completed in 1991.

The opening of the Metropolitan Railway connected the City to the major rail termini and was the beginning of a new phase in London's history.

RAILWAYS IN THE CITY

The City could not function without railways, underground and overground. The first of the City passenger termini to open was Fenchurch Street in 1841 (rebuilt in the 1850s), followed by Broad Street, Cannon Street and Blackfriars in the boom years of the 1860s, and Holborn Viaduct and Liverpool Street in the 1870s. All developed as major commuter stations – within thirty years of its opening Broad Street, serving a network of routes across north and east London, handled 60 million passengers a year. Liverpool Street became, and remains, the busiest of the City termini, serving huge tracts of suburbia in north-east London and the nearer parts of Essex as well as providing mainline services to East Anglia. Railways did not only carry passengers – equally if not more significant was their traffic in freight. In general, goods yards were restricted to the edge of the City – the Great Eastern Railway constructed a huge depot at Bishopsgate, on the site of its original passenger terminus – but a substantial goods depot was developed at Broad Street. A vast subterranean goods station was built in 1862–5 to serve the new Smithfield Market – trains could access it from the Great Western via the Metropolitan Railway.

This map of 1870 shows the connections between the London, Chatham and Dover network and the Midland and Great Northern lines – also the site of a proposed new fruit and vegetable market at Smithfield.

For all their significance, the railways had a limited visual impact on the City – of the City termini, only Liverpool Street retains something of its original appearance, and there was never a station to rival Paddington or St Pancras. The crudest intrusion of the railway builders was the bridge spanning Ludgate Hill, which carried trains into Holborn Viaduct, but it was removed in 1990 – Thameslink trains now run below Ludgate Hill, serving the new City Thameslink Station, which replaced Holborn Viaduct. A new Blackfriars Station on the bridge, spanning the Thames, is due to open in 2012.

The Crossrail station at Liverpool Street (shown here in a computer-generated image) will form part of a new transport hub with the mainline station and Underground. Crossrail is set to have as dramatic an impact on the City as the coming of the Underground had more than a century ago.

The first underground railway in the world, the Metropolitan, opened between Paddington and Farringdon in 1863 and was extended into the City, with a station at Moorgate, two years later, reaching Aldgate in 1876. By 1884 the Metropolitan was linked to the District Railway, which ran along the southern edge of the City, and the Circle line was created. The advent of the 'Tube' – the deep underground lines, driven by electricity and created by tunnelling through the London clay (rather than the cut and cover method used by the Metropolitan) – linked the City efficiently to more distant suburbs. The City and South London Railway (later incorporated into the Northern line) opened from Stockwell to King William Street in 1890, with trains consisting of just three carriages (almost windowless and known as 'padded cells'). The C&SLR extended to Bank and Moorgate in 1900, with the Central London Railway (Central line) reaching Bank the same year. The Underground system remains vital to the City but is working at full capacity, and the prospect of Crossrail opening in 2017, with stations at Farringdon and Liverpool Street, has been enthusiastically supported by the City Corporation.

Exchange House is the most remarkable of the buildings in the later phases of development at Broadgate, an 'over the tracks' development that looks back to the functional tradition of railway engineering.

9 EXCHANGE HOUSE

Exchange Square EC2 • Skidmore, Owings & Merrill 1987–91

The famous American practice SOM established a London operation in the 1980s. They produced the masterplan for Canary Wharf and were responsible for all the later phases of Broadgate, including the massive block of offices along Bishopsgate, constructed over the eastern side of Liverpool Street Station and a prime example of Postmodernist styling – 'tyrannical' was the verdict of *The Buildings of England*. Exchange House is a very different beast – firmly in the functionalist tradition that generated the firm's finest work in the USA. The offices, eleven storeys of them, are contained within a massive steel frame that looks like – and is, in effect – a bridge, constructed across the tracks into Liverpool Street, so that conventional foundations were out of the question. The effect is highly dramatic and only slightly undermined by the use of straight steel sections, giving the frame a somewhat crude look at close hand. The ground floor of the building is a void, save for a glazed pavilion housing escalators and lifts serving the offices, so that there is a view straight through from Appold Street into Exchange Square. The square is sunk to provide a clear view into the restored western shed of the station. A prominent feature is the huge bronze sculpture, weighing five tons, of the Broadgate Venus by the Colombian artist Fernando Botero.

10 BROADGATE TOWER

EC2 • Skidmore, Owings & Merrill 2004–8

In common with other later phases of Broadgate following on from the development of the Broad Street Station site in the 1980s, the Broadgate Tower, with the adjacent Bishopsgate block, is an 'air-rights' development, constructed over the railway. The two buildings sit on a concrete raft over the tracks into Liverpool Street Station (which remained in use throughout the 'fast-track' construction process). The 35-storey tower, 165 m (540 ft) tall, provides a vertical endpoint to Broadgate – a glazed galleria links it to the 13-storey no. 201 Bishopsgate. Like Exchange House, the tower is a building in the great tradition of SOM's work in Chicago, with cross-bracing that recalls the iconic John Hancock Tower. Unusually for tall buildings in London, it won planning consent without facing significant objections, yet in some respects it would be a better building if it were half as tall again. A number of the earlier buildings in Broadgate face possible replacement in the next decade, but it is unlikely that high-rise development will be possible anywhere else on the estate.

The Broadgate Tower, designed by Skidmore, Owings & Merrill, forms the latest phase of the Broadgate development and is a high-rise marker on the edge of the City.

11 BISHOPSGATE INSTITUTE ➲

Bishopsgate EC2 • C. Harrison Townsend 1892–4

Born in Birkenhead, Townsend moved to London in the 1880s and became a highly successful practitioner of the so-called 'Free Style', mixing Arts and Crafts and Art Nouveau influences. The Bishopsgate Institute was the first of his three major London public buildings (the others were the Whitechapel Art Gallery and the Horniman Museum in Forest Hill, both completed in 1901). He won the commission for the Institute in competition in 1892. The brief was for a free public library and lecture hall for City workers, and the prime mover behind the project was the Rector of St Botolph Bishopsgate, the Rev. William Rogers, a social reformer who funded it from the assets of defunct parochial charities. The Institute remains a lively presence on the edge of the City – exercise classes and yoga complement more cerebral offerings. The interiors are relatively plain, with a glazed dome lighting the well-stocked library. The most significant feature is the street façade, tall and narrow, wedged in between adjacent buildings. Faced in terracotta, it is richly decorated with a frieze depicting the Tree of Life, a favourite Arts and Crafts theme. This highly radical building was relaunched after being refurbished in July 2011.

The Bishopsgate Institute, by the architect C. Harrison Townsend, is strongly Art Nouveau in feel. It was a pioneering project in terms of popular education.

Municipal Modernistic: the Bishopsgate Police Station adapted contemporary architectural fashion to the needs of the City Police.

12 BISHOPSGATE POLICE STATION

Bishopsgate EC2 • Vine & Vine 1935–8

The practice of Vine & Vine appears to have had something of a speciality in police stations. This one replaced a Victorian building by Sir Horace Jones. It was a major project – the relatively modest street front belies a structure that provided sleeping accommodation for seventy officers, with an infirmary on the top floor. The interest of the building lies in its Modernistic styling, breaking away from the neo-Georgian widely favoured for such buildings and featuring banded metal windows (now unfortunately replaced) with a granite-faced ground floor.

13 CUTLERS' GARDENS

E1

Located on the eastern fringe of the City, the Cutler Street warehouses were constructed, from 1769 onwards, by the East India Company, principally to house imports of tea brought in via the Port of London. 'A priceless treasure house', Cutler Street also handled wines, spirits, tobacco, carpets and (allegedly) opium. The Old Bengal Warehouse on New Street was the first to be completed, in 1771, to designs by the Company's surveyor, Richard Jupp. Later blocks, around a series of secure

From 1976 onwards, Cutlers' Gardens was transformed into a self-contained office quarter – in some respects the forerunner of Broadgate. Most of the buildings were retained but were internally gutted.

enclosed courtyards bordered by Cutler Street, Harrow Place and Middlesex Street, were designed over the next fifty years by Henry Holland and Samuel Pepys Cockerell. The resulting complex was an outstanding example of what became known as 'the functional tradition'. It remained in use by the Port of London Authority into the 1970s, finally closing in 1976. Proposals to redevelop the area as offices, with Richard Seifert as architect (1978–82), faced fierce opposition from conservationists and the outcome was what appears, in hindsight, a rather poor compromise, with parts of the site cleared – the large warehouse extending along Middlesex Street was demolished – and other buildings rebuilt behind the façades, with the loss of original interiors that would today be treasured and sash windows replaced by plate glass. The last phase of the project (1984–5) was given to Quinlan Terry, who took a more sensitive approach, retaining many internal elements.

14 HERON TOWER

110 Bishopsgate EC2 • Kohn Pedersen Fox 2000–11

Given planning consent after a hard-fought public inquiry and in the face of opposition from English Heritage, the 46-storey, 230-m (755-ft) high Heron Tower is currently (2012) the City's

bagelmania
STARBUCKS
COFFEE
EAT

tallest building, finally overtopping Seifert's Tower 42. The site, on the corner of Houndsditch, formerly housed a group of banal 1970s office blocks. The Tower is innovative in many respects. Designed for multiple occupation, it is conceived as a series of office 'villages', each extending over three floors around a central atrium. With all services, including lavatories, stairs and double-deck high-speed lifts, placed along the south side of the tower – baffling solar gain into the offices – the office floors are largely column-free, thanks to an external steel structure. Located outside protected view corridors, the Tower forms part of a cluster of high buildings in this part of the City. In contrast to other London high-rises, it is freely accessible to the public, with the top three floors housing a bar and restaurant. Restaurant and retail space is also provided at street level, where a new piazza has been created. Eschewing any attempt at sculptural effect, this is a highly rational building, elegantly detailed.

Structural cross-bracing gives the Heron Tower a forcefully functional appearance like SOM's John Hancock Tower in Chicago.

15 ST ETHELBURGA

78 Bishopsgate EC2 • 15th century; Purcell Miller Tritton 2002

St Ethelburga's was one of the few City churches to survive the Great Fire. A simple little building, largely of 15th-century date (though much restored), its nave and chancel were under one roof, with a narrow south aisle. The weather-boarded 18th-century bellcote was a distinctive feature of the street frontage. Fittings by Sir Ninian Comper (1912) added to the almost rustic charm of the interior. Much of this was destroyed – the west front was totally demolished – in April 1993 by an IRA bomb that caused massive devastation in this quarter of the City. Initially it was assumed that the church was beyond repair: it had not even been insured and there were no funds for rebuilding. In 1995, however, an architectural competition for reconstruction produced a winning scheme that proposed the enclosing of the ruins within a glazed container housing parish offices for St Helen Bishopsgate. The decision by the Bishop of London that the church would be rebuilt as a Centre for Reconciliation and Peace led to the abandonment of this scheme and the appointment of Purcell Miller Tritton to produce proposals for a more conservative rebuilding, completed in 2002. From the street St Ethelburga's now looks much as it always did, with the cupola rebuilt in replica. The interior, covered by a lightweight steel roof structure, is kept clear of fittings so that it can be used for lectures, concerts and other events. Simply paved in stone, it is a dignified, reflective space. Remnants of the original east window by C. E. Kempe (1878) have been incorporated in a new window by Helen Whittaker depicting St Ethelburga. To the east of the church, a quiet garden was created in 2004 – it contains a replica Bedouin tent, designed by Keith Critchlow as a space in which people of all faiths can meet.

The medieval church of St Ethelburga Bishopsgate was grievously damaged by a terrorist bomb in 1993 and appeared to be beyond repair. However, it has been carefully rebuilt and is appropriately in use as a centre dedicated to the cause of peace and reconciliation.

Opposite
The Heron Tower forms a strong vertical element on Bishopsgate and is the first of a group of new tall buildings in this quarter of the City.

This interactive scale model by Pipers, in the City Marketing Suite, gives a dramatic impression of the way in which the eastern sector of the City is being transformed by tall buildings.

PLANNING AND CONTEMPORARY ARCHITECTURE

The destruction of so much of the City in the Second World War was tragic, yet ironically it opened the way for the redevelopment that re-equipped London as a world business capital. Much of the new development of the 1950s and 1960s was of routine quality at best, but there were exceptions – the Commercial Union Tower (later renamed the Aviva Tower and now no. 1 St Helen's), Richard Seifert's Drapers' Gardens tower (now demolished), and the extension to the Institute of Chartered Accountants by William Whitfield, for example. But the last twenty years have seen the City re-equipping itself once more, with new buildings replacing the now obsolete commercial structures of the postwar period.

Globalization has fuelled the ongoing rebuilding of the City – in more ways than one, with funding for new developments increasingly provided by foreign investors. The 1980s saw the twin challenges of deregulation of the financial markets, culminating in the 'Big Bang' of 1986, and the rise of London's Docklands as a new business centre, assisted by the absence of conventional planning restrictions. The City responded vigorously – Broadgate created a new office quarter on redundant railway land and has continued to develop. The scheme was notable less for its architecture than for its enlightened creation of new public spaces, always a rare commodity in the City. Another landmark was the selection of Richard Rogers to design the new Lloyd's Building, completed in 1986. Rogers and his sometime partner Norman Foster are now well represented in the City – Foster's 'Gherkin' is perhaps the

In this computer-generated image, the proposed 'Walkie-talkie' tower on Fenchurch Street is seen to the right of the 'Pinnacle', the latter set to become the City's tallest building when completed in 2013.

At street level, Kohn Pedersen Fox's 'Pinnacle' features a sweeping glazed skirt enclosing public space and retailing.

best-known modern building in London, while Rogers's practice is building another spectacular tower (the 'Cheesegrater') nearby on Leadenhall Street.

Appointed the City's chief planning officer in 1987, Peter Wynne Rees has presided over a dramatic process of transformation in the Square Mile – until recently, its modern architecture was seen as second-rate. Now architecturally minded tourists from all over the world come to see its new buildings. Among them are towers: the Broadgate Tower, the Heron Tower and the forthcoming high-rises by Rafael Viñoly, Rogers Stirk Harbour and Kohn Pedersen Fox, forming part of a 'cluster' of tall buildings grouped to protect historic views of St Paul's and the Tower. Not only are major British architects now building in the City – Rem Koolhaas's OMA is responsible for the new headquarters for Rothschild's Bank, while the New Change development east of St Paul's was designed by the leading French architect Jean Nouvel. A welcome phenomenon in the last decade has been the emergence of retail, hotel and residential projects alongside offices, promoting a new sense of animation and diversity in the City. All of this has been achieved in the context of a vigorous conservation programme – the days when listed buildings could be sacrificed to new development, as in the case of the no. 1 Poultry project, are gone. Historic landmarks such as Billingsgate and Leadenhall markets and the Royal Exchange have successful new uses. The coming decade may, indeed, be a time when new developments focus on infill and reuse rather than redevelopment.

Leathersellers' Hall has gone through a number of incarnations: the 1820s hall seen here was demolished in the 1870s for a replacement, which was itself destroyed in the Second World War.

Leonard Walker's stained glass, showing King Henry VI, was made for Leathersellers' Hall in 1937 but fortunately was not installed then and so escaped the Blitz. It formed a prominent feature of the hall completed in 1960, which is now being replaced.

16 LEATHERSELLERS' HALL

15 St Helen's Place EC3 • Henry Saul 1926; Louis de Soissons 1948–60

The Leathersellers' Company received its first royal charter in 1444 – the beautifully illuminated document can still be seen in the hall, the sixth on (or close to) this site to be occupied by the Leathersellers. The second hall was a conversion of part of the Benedictine nunnery of St Helen's, following its dissolution in 1538. It survived the Fire but was demolished in 1799, when the Company embarked on a radical redevelopment of its estate around St Helen's – the result was St Helen's Place, where the replacement hall was located. It burned down in 1819 and its replacement in turn was demolished in the 1870s; the fifth hall, designed by G. Andrew Wilson, opened in 1879. Wilson's lavish interiors were retained when St Helen's Place was comprehensively rebuilt in the 1920s as modern office chambers – the block fronting Bishopsgate was designed by Mewès & Davis as the London headquarters of the Hudson's Bay Company – but were totally destroyed by bombing in May 1941. The most recent hall was entered through a 1920s frontage by Henry Saul, but everything inside dated from the postwar rebuilding (1948–60) by Louis de Soissons (under partner Kenneth Peacock). This was one of the best of the postwar livery halls, with interiors fitted out in high-quality materials (including leather) – the livery hall was an impressively lofty cube, topped by a distinctly Soanian vault. In the adjacent corridor was a fine stained-glass window by Leonard Walker dating from 1937 but (fortuitously) never installed before the Second World War. The Company has embarked on ambitious plans for its estate, which has already involved the demolition of the hall. Eric Parry is designing its replacement.

St Helen's stands in a churchyard that forms an oasis in this part of the City. The church had to be heavily restored after damage by terrorist bombs in 1992 and 1993, and the restoration by Quinlan Terry undid much of the work of Victorian restorers.

17 ST HELEN BISHOPSGATE

Great St Helen's EC3

St Helen's is, despite the damage inflicted on it over the centuries, one of the most touching relics of pre-Fire London, all the more appealing for its proximity to some of the City's most dramatic modern towers. The unusual form of the church – twin naves, side by side – reflects its dual role as both a parish church (on the south side) and the chapel of a nunnery established in the 13th century. After the Reformation the whole building passed into parochial use, and the monastic cloister and other buildings to the north were demolished. Most of the surviving fabric dates from the 14th and 15th centuries, incorporating earlier remains, all much restored and worked over in subsequent centuries – the little bell turret crowning the west front was constructed in the 18th century.

In 1892–3 J. L. Pearson, one of the best of the Gothic Revivalists, carried out a thorough restoration, lowering the floors of the two naves to their original level and fitting up the south chancel with screens, choir stalls and other fittings in Tractarian style, with stained glass further enriching the interior. However, in recent decades St Helen's has developed a strongly evangelical tradition, with a style of worship at odds with the internal arrangements left by Pearson. The massive damage caused to the church by IRA bombs in 1992 and 1993 provided the opportunity for another radical reordering, aimed at creating 'an assembly hall for preaching', with Quinlan Terry as architect (1993–5).

His proposals were only approved after a hard-fought church consistory court hearing. There were objections to Terry's scheme, particularly to the raising of the floors to a uniform level throughout the building, altering the medieval arrangement which Pearson had reinstated. One of the most important features of St Helen's is its wealth of monuments, some now unhappily compromised by the new floor level, while surviving fittings have been randomly rearranged. The bare whitewashed interior is undoubtedly suited to the needs of its users and some of Terry's additions – the new west gallery, for example – are of merit. The new doorcase he added to the south transept is an excellent piece of stone carving, but looks insubstantial alongside the nearby pedimented door of 1633, a vigorous example of so-called Artisan Mannerism. St Helen's thrives, but has its special charm vanished?

Designed by the architects GMW, the Aviva Tower is one of the best buildings from the 1960s in the City, taking its cue from Mies van der Rohe's Seagram Building on Manhattan's Park Avenue.

18 AVIVA TOWER AND PLAZA

1 Undershaft, Leadenhall Street EC3 • GMW Partnership 1963–9

Built as the Commercial Union Tower and now no. 1 St Helen's, the Aviva Tower is one of the few 1960s buildings of special architectural quality in the City. Both the tower and the plaza to the south are clearly inspired by American precedents and the work of Mies van der Rohe in particular. As a public space, the plaza is hardly a success – many cross it, but few linger. Its principal function is to showcase the tower: a sleek, minimal 28-storey box clad in tinted glazing set in bronzed metal frames which was constructed 'top down', with floors hung from the central core – an innovative technique used for the contemporary Kleinwort Benson tower on Fenchurch Street (now demolished) which allowed the creation of column-free office floors. The double-height ground-floor lobby area is an impressive space, again American in inspiration. Services are located on top of the tower and in an enclosed zone halfway up. In April 1993 the building was severely damaged by the IRA bomb that also destroyed the Baltic Exchange on St Mary Axe – all the glass was blown out and interiors wrecked. A refurbishment by RHWL preserved its qualities. The adjacent P&O Building, also designed by GMW and standing on the west side of the plaza, has been demolished to make way for Rogers Stirk Harbour's new Leadenhall Tower (the 'Cheesegrater').

The medieval church of St Andrew Undershaft survived the Great Fire and the Second World War, only to be badly damaged by a terrorist bomb in 1992. It has been restored, though the splendid west window was destroyed.

19 ST ANDREW UNDERSHAFT

Leadenhall Street and St Mary Axe EC3 • 1520–32

St Andrew's takes its name from the shaft of a famous maypole that once stood nearby – destroyed in 1547 by Protestant reformers. It is one of the small group of medieval City churches that survived the Great Fire and subsequent rebuilding campaigns but suffered badly in the 20th century from wartime bombing and the terrorist attacks of the early 1990s. The worst loss at

Opposite
St Helen Bishopsgate, which originally served as both a monastic and parish church, has an outstanding collection of pre-Fire monuments, including this late 15th-century tomb chest commemorating Sir John Crosby and his wife.

St Andrew's was the fine 17th-century west window (the glass relocated from the east window by Victorian restorers) with its portraits of monarchs from Edward VI to William II, wrecked in 1992.

First mentioned in the early 12th century, the church itself was completely rebuilt in 1520–32 at the expense of two Lord Mayors and is a typical design of the period, more impressive inside than out (externally it is overpowered by nearby commercial buildings and makes little impression on the street). The interior is a simple rectangle of nave and aisles – no separate chancel – much in the manner of the great medieval churches of East Anglia, though on a smaller scale. The original fittings, which must have included a rood screen, were destroyed at the Reformation but the church received many enrichments over the next two centuries – a decorative scheme of the 1720s included an ornate setting for the chancel, with 'a rich crimson curtain, fringed with gold, painted in grand folds, and with hovering angels, etc'. Some remains of this scheme can be seen in the spandrels of the nave, but the rest was erased by censorious Victorian restorers bent on reasserting the medieval character of the building. Some fragments of medieval glass remain in the aisle windows. Monuments include one to the great historian of London, John Stow, who died in 1605. He is shown holding a quill pen – the pen is ceremonially replaced at a service held annually and attended by the Lord Mayor. Administered by St Helen Bishopsgate and no longer used for public worship, the church is rarely open to visitors except by special arrangement.

The highly distinctive form of Norman Foster's no. 30 St Mary Axe reflects the building's role as a pioneer of low-energy design – the atria spiralling up the building are part of a strategy for natural ventilation, reducing its energy load

20 NO. 30 ST MARY AXE

EC3 • Foster & Partners 1997–2004

Universally known as the 'Gherkin', no. 30 St Mary Axe has become a new symbol of London, recognized internationally alongside Big Ben and Tower Bridge. The site was formerly occupied by the late Victorian Baltic Exchange, wrecked by an IRA bomb in 1992. In 1996 Sir Norman Foster unveiled plans to build the Millennium Tower there – at 386 m (1,265 ft) this would have been the tallest building in Europe but was judged to be an over-development of the site. At 180 m (591 ft), the 'Gherkin' is slightly less tall than the nearby Tower 42. Given planning consent despite moves by conservationists to retain the remains of the Baltic Exchange, the building was developed by reinsurance giant SwissRe but sold in 2007 for a record £630 million.

Foster's building is known for its unusual form, but this is not arbitrary. The aim was to create a low-energy, environmentally benign structure that made optimum use of daylight and natural ventilation – one of Foster's inspirations was the visionary American architect Buckminster Fuller. Opening windows allow fresh air to be drawn into the building and circulated via a series of spiralling atria. The most spectacular internal feature is the top-floor restaurant and bar (open only to tenants and their guests), set under a fully glazed dome and with stunning views.

Opposite
The top-floor restaurant of no. 30 St Mary Axe is among the most spectacular modern spaces in London but is only rarely open to the public.

The tower takes up only part of the Baltic Exchange site – the remainder has been laid out as a new public square, with shops and restaurants occupying its base. The 'Gherkin' is significant as the building that changed public perception of tall buildings in London, opening the way for the further development of the cluster of office towers in the City's eastern sector.

H. P. Berlage's Holland House is the only work in Britain by the great Dutch architect and is faced in faience made in Delft. Norman Foster's 'Gherkin' can be seen here as a reflection.

21 HOLLAND HOUSE

32 Bury Street EC3 • H. P. Berlage 1914–16

One of London's most remarkable 20th-century buildings, this is a rare work outside the Netherlands by the great Dutch architect Hendrik Petrus Berlage (1856–1934) – his most famous work is the Beurs (commodities exchange) in Amsterdam. The construction of Norman Foster's no. 30 St Mary Axe tower (the 'Gherkin') on an adjacent site provides a striking juxtaposition of two very different Modernist visions. Foster frankly exposes the structure of his building; Berlage expresses the steel frame of Holland House but clads the façade in green faience blocks (specially made in Delft) on a black granite base – it was designed to be seen obliquely in a narrow street but Foster's new piazza provides a frontal view, perhaps reducing its impact.

The building, constructed during the First World War in which the Netherlands remained neutral, was commissioned by the Muller shipping magnates: a ship's prow carved in granite is a prominent feature of its exterior. Berlage, a committed socialist, fell out with his wealthy clients before the building was completed and the interior fit-out was entrusted to the leading Belgian designer Henri van de Velde. The entrance lobby and staircases feature decoration by the De Stijl artist Bart van der Leck and there are handsome timber-lined offices on the first floor. Only the replacement of the original windows mars the exterior of the building – Pevsner thought it 'very alien to the London of its date' but, urbane and contextual, it looks very much at home in the City.

The elevation of Holland House is designed to be seen in perspective along a narrow street – the construction of the 'Gherkin', with its open piazza, opened up a frontal view of the building.

22 SPANISH AND PORTUGUESE SYNAGOGUE

Bevis Marks EC3 • Joseph Avis 1699–1701

Seen from outside, the Bevis Marks Synagogue could be mistaken for a particularly modest Wren church or, more likely, a dissenting chapel of the period, given its location in a secluded courtyard away from the City streets. It is a simple brick box, with two rows of windows and no attempt at architectural elaboration. Its designer was probably the Quaker carpenter Joseph Avis, who had worked for Wren – Avis certainly superintended its construction. (His tender price was £2,650, but 'he returned to the wardens on the day of the opening such profit as he had made, refusing to take financial gain from the building of a House of God'.) The synagogue was built for a group of Spanish and Portuguese (Sephardic) Jews: with the Jewish community in

Opposite
The interiors of Holland House, overseen by Henri van de Velde, feature extensive use of mosaic, glazed brick and faience and are well preserved.

The Spanish and Portuguese Synagogue is set in a quiet courtyard, with an unassuming entrance from the street.

Bevis Marks is the oldest surviving synagogue in Britain. It retains a magnificent array of original fittings. The interior is arranged on the lines of contemporary Anglican churches.

London growing rapidly, their former base in Creechurch Lane, established in the 1650s, became too small for their needs. The significance of the synagogue as the flagship of Anglo-Jewry saved it from demolition in the 19th century, when the Sephardic community had dispersed across London. Externally austere, it possesses one of the finest interiors of its period in the City. Illuminated by the clear glass windows, its plan and fittings resemble those of contemporary City churches. The galleries (used by women) are supported on marbled Tuscan columns, with open benches – some brought from Creechurch Lane – in the body of the building. The ritual furnishings, including the bimah and ark, are of high quality, the latter closely resembling a reredos in a Wren church, richly carved and painted. The seven magnificent brass chandeliers are a memorable feature – the biggest of them was given by the congregation of the Sephardic synagogue in Amsterdam, the largest in Europe and a strong influence on the design of Bevis Marks. Repaired after damage from the 1993 IRA bomb, the synagogue has remained virtually unchanged over the last three centuries.

23 ST KATHARINE CREE

86 Leadenhall Street EC3 • 1628–31

Somewhat overpowered by the big commercial blocks along Leadenhall Street, this is one of the relatively few new churches dating from the reign of Charles I, a rarity not only for London but nationally. As Bishop of London, William Laud promoted the rebuilding of the dilapidated medieval church that stood on the site, of which only the tower was kept. The architecture (the name of the designer is not recorded) was an eccentric mix of Gothic and classical. The exterior was much altered during the 18th and 19th centuries, and postwar repairs were made, but inside Corinthian columns contrast with a roof vault and windows of distinctly medieval character. The great rose window at the east end, reputedly inspired by the one in Old St Paul's, is the most spectacular feature and contains some glass of *c.* 1630, though the majority of it, with figures of saints, was destroyed along with other fittings in the 1640s. Laud and his patron Charles I became the first martyrs of the Anglican Church – St Katharine Cree was cited by Laud's Puritan opponents as evidence of his 'popish' leanings. Laud consecrated the church in January 1631,

Consecrated by Archbishop William Laud, St Katharine Cree was seen as a reflection of his 'popish' tastes but was funded by City merchants. The glass in the east window includes elements surviving from the 1630s.

and since there was no form of service for consecrating churches in the Prayer Book, he created his own elaborate liturgy, to which the Puritans took exception – it was recalled in evidence against him at his trial in 1644. In fact, St Katharine Cree was not Laud's personal creation but was funded by City merchants who do not seem to have questioned its form. The roof bosses feature the arms of City livery companies and the font displays prominently the arms of Sir John Gayer of the Fishmongers' Company. The fine organ was played by both Purcell and Handel. St Katharine is one of the City churches that faced possible closure under the recommendations of the 1994 Templeman Report, but it has remained in use. At the time of writing, a project was being launched to develop St Katharine as a 'refectory church', adapting the interior to host conferences and 'commercial hospitality' while remaining a place of worship.

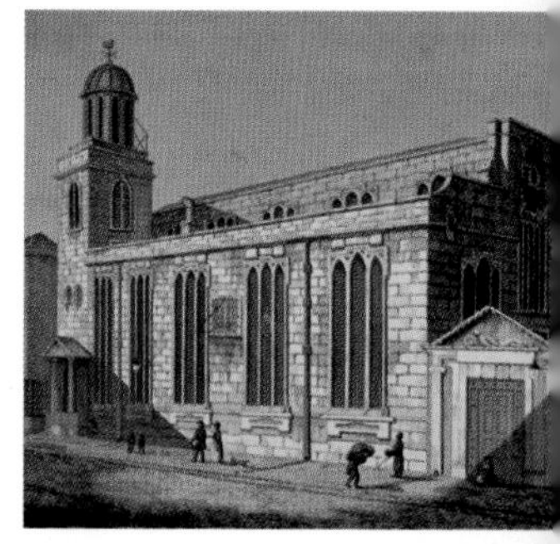

This engraving of 1813 shows the exterior of St Katharine Cree after alterations in the 18th century. The unusual aisle windows, Gothic in spirit if not in exact form, are the originals.

24 ST BOTOLPH ALDGATE

EC3 • George Dance the Elder 1741–4; J. F. Bentley 1888–95

On the very edge of the City and isolated by busy roads and insensitive new development, St Botolph's is a building of real charm, with an interior enhanced rather than compromised by Victorian restoration. The medieval church (probably Saxon in origin) was reported in 1727 to be 'well and sufficiently Repair'd, the floors, Pews & Seats in good Order'. By 1740, however, it was said to be in danger of collapse and designs for a replacement were commissioned from George Dance; the new church was realigned on a north-south axis. It is a solid, workmanlike structure, with a tower and spire that would not look out of place in a New England township. The interior retains its galleries, organ (1676, removed from the old church) and some interesting monuments – including one to Thomas, Lord Darcy, who was executed in 1537 for his part in the Pilgrimage of Grace. In 1888–95 a major refurbishment took place under the direction of J. F. Bentley, the architect of Westminster Cathedral. Bentley treated the Georgian building with tact, opening up the galleries with balustrade fronts, lowering the pews and creating a chancel in line with Victorian liturgical taste. Bentley's most dramatic intervention was the remodelling of the ceiling, with elaborate new plasterwork in a Gothic manner, complete with lines of angels, which blends surprisingly well with Dance's architecture. More recent additions include the attractive engraved glass screens (1988) enclosing the side chapel.

The interior of St Botolph Aldgate is seen here prior to the late Victorian restoration carried out by J. F. Bentley, who retained most of the original features.

Opposite
St Botolph's church is a charming survival among later development, and a tangle of roads, at Aldgate, on the edge of the City.

Additional Places to Visit

○ a **Broadgate sculpture**

Around the Broadgate arena (pp. 245–6) are several vigorous pieces of public art, of which Richard Serra's (b. 1939) huge steel *Fulcrum* (1987), at the south of Broadgate by the western entrance to Liverpool Street Station, is hard to miss (p. 247): five massive sheets of steel supporting each other. North into the arena on the right is *Leaping Hare on Crescent and Bell* (1988) by Barry Flanagan (1941–2009), and turning left into Finsbury Avenue (itself a piece of public art with its illuminated pavement) is the gloomy *Rush Hour* (1983–7) by George Segal (1924–2000), a small group reminiscent of T. S. Eliot's crowd that flows over London Bridge in *The Waste Land* (1922). Turning down Finsbury Avenue to Eldon Street there is the violent *Bellerophon Taming Pegasus* (1966) by Jacques Lipchitz (1891–1973), a dramatic physical conflict that is now set against a stone wall in a small square. There are some oases of peace to the north of the station, and where Pindar Plaza reaches Bishopsgate there is the cheerful *Eye-1* (1993) by Bruce McLean (b. 1944), with a dash of colour.

○ b **Victorian Turkish Baths**

One of the most surprising sights in the City, a colourful Turkish bathhouse suddenly pops up at no. 8 Bishopsgate Churchyard, off Bishopsgate to the west by St Botolph Bishopsgate (pp. 248–9), where there is also a garden with netball and tennis facilities, and a former primary school with figures of charity children. The baths were built in 1896 by architect Harold Elphick for bath owners Henry and James Forder Nevill. The ground-floor exterior is modelled on the shrine at the Church of the Holy Sepulchre in Jerusalem (the onion dome housed the baths' water tanks). A winding staircase leads downstairs to a tiled room produced by the Craven Dunhill Company. Mosaic, marble and tiled seats and stained-glass windows made this 'an arena in which health, pleasure, culture and curiosity could collide: a mystical world far from the restrictive Victorian society in which it could be found'.

○ c **Devonshire Row; Jubilee Gardens; Petticoat Square**

Off Bishopsgate opposite Liverpool Street Station, a typical busy narrow City street, rebuilt after railway construction and now pedestrianized, leads past the Bull Inn to Devonshire Square, with its fine buildings (nos 12 and 13 are perfect mid-Georgian houses) and sitting spaces, next to Cutlers' Gardens (pp. 258–9). This entire area has been revitalized with great skill. On Houndsditch near Cutler Street, Jubilee Gardens is a small landscaped area, refurbished in 2004; behind, on Middlesex Street, is Petticoat Square, near the famous market.

○ d **St Helen's Place**

This imposingly self-important close, with columns and iron gates, off Bishopsgate towards the south, gives way to an impressive façade of 1929 by Mewès & Davis. Nash had planned a residential square here in 1800, but this was never built: what we see today are 20th-century offices presented as French imperial grandeur. At no. 15 the Place houses the Leathersellers' Hall (p. 264), currently being reconstructed; the Place was also where the first Rothschild settled in London, before the family occupied their present premises in St Swithin's Lane (p. 303).

○ e **Roman Girl's Grave**

One of the discoveries when the 'Gherkin' was being built was the grave of a young Roman girl. This is commemorated with an inscription easy to miss on the east side of the surrounding low wall, opposite Holland House (p. 271): 'To the spirits of the dead the unknown young girl from Roman London lies buried here.' Enigmatic poetic inscriptions, lines from the Scottish poet Ian Hamilton Finlay's *Arcadian Dream Garden,* are set into stone benches around the iconic building.

○ f **Charity Boy and Girl**

These figures of 1710–11, in the usual genre of a boy and girl depicted with winning pathos, were originally on the front of the first Sir John Cass School and were placed here at the Foundation Primary School in Duke's Place in 1908.

○ g **Sanctuary, Aldgate High Street**

Sanctuary (1985), a sculpture by Naomi Blake of an oppressed figure crouching under a large plant-like overhang, can be found in the churchyard of St Botolph Aldgate (pp. 274–5). Though crushed by traffic, there is sanctuary of another kind at the pre-Fire building, now happily restored, of the Hoop & Grapes at 47 Aldgate High Street (see introduction, p. 240), and also at the Still and Star down Little Somerset Street, an isolated survival, always beautifully decorated with flowers. A blue plaque to the poet Geoffrey Chaucer (*c.* 1343–1400) awaits re-erection at no. 2 Aldgate High Street.

7 The Mansion House

The area around Mansion House encompasses extreme varieties of scale, with alleys and courtyards of medieval dimension in Bow Lane and St Swithin's Lane, and many much larger units, such as Bucklersbury House in Cannon Street (awaiting redevelopment at the time of writing), the result of postwar or later rebuilding on the same sites, although no tall towers are found here. There are livery halls of some of the most eminent Worshipful Companies, either by the riverside (Fishmongers and Vintners) or on the slopes above Upper Thames Street (the cluster of Skinners, Dyers and Tallow Chandlers). These slopes give the area much of its character, although there is a terrible bathos as one reaches Upper Thames Street and finds access to the river blocked both visually and psychologically by a wall of ugly buildings, despite the lure of the now almost-completed river walk.

The railway station at Cannon Street would have been one of London's finest had it survived intact with the exceptional curved train shed roof of 1865, taller than St Pancras, that was badly damaged in the Second World War and later removed, although the fine turreted towers, originally housing hydraulic equipment, were later restored. Bringing the trains in above the level of Cannon Street corresponds with the heights of the south London viaducts to which it connects via London Bridge Station. The interruption of scale caused by the gigantic works of Victorian engineering can be felt when looking south in Dowgate Hill, where the domestic scale of the pre-Victorian City prevails.

The line of Walbrook and Dowgate is formed by one of London's lost rivers, the Walbrook, around which many Roman finds have been made. The Walbrook mosaic, now in the Museum of London, created great excitement in 1868. Beneath the pavement was a well-preserved hypocaust heating system. More exciting still was the discovery of the Temple of Mithras in 1954 during the excavations for Bucklersbury House. The Mithraeum was built around AD 240 and belonged to a secret cult favoured by the military who usually built underground. The chief sculptural finds are also in the Museum of London, while the structure itself was preserved for viewing nearby. Odder still is the 'London Stone', close by at no. 111 Cannon Street, housed in a sort of pavement-level cage. Is it the 'Stone of Brutus', the legendary founder of Britain as an outpost of Rome? It seems to have acted as a measuring marker for distances from London before being walled into St Swithin's church, and was relocated after bombing. According to legend, the City's safety depends on the safety of the stone.

The Wren churches in this area are an instructive bunch and arguably the best of the crop. Considering the whole set as

Opposite
The Mansion House, designed by George Dance the Elder, Clerk of Works to the City, was built in 1739–52. It is the official residence of the Lord Mayor.

3

4

2

St Paul's
New Change
Cheapside
Bread Street
Bow Churchyard
Bow Lane
Queen Street
Poultry
Bank
Cornhill
Lombard Street
Birchin Lane
Watling Street
Cannon Street
Queen Victoria Street
Walbrook
Mansion House Place
Bond Court
St Swithin's Lane
Nicholas Lane
Clement's Lane
King William Street
Gracechurch Street
Abchurch Lane
Mansion House
Cannon Street
Cloak Lane
College Hill
Little Trinity Lane
Queen Street
College Street
Dowgate Hill
Cannon Street
Bush Lane
Suffolk Lane
Laurence Pountney Hill
Laurence Pountney Lane
Martin Lane
Arthur Street
Monument
Queenhithe
Queen Street Place
Upper Thames Street
Walbrook Wharf
Cousin Lane
Allhallows Lane
Angel Passage
Swan Lane
King William Street
Southwark Bridge
London Bridge

a 1 b 2 3 4 5 6 7 8 9 10 11 12 13 14 15 c d e f 16 17 18 19 20 21 22 23 24 25 26 27 g h i

KEY TO AREA 7

- ● 1 One New Change
- ● 2 St Mary-le-Bow
- ● 3 Bow Lane
- ● 4 Nos 64–66 Cheapside
- ● 5 St Mary Aldermary
- ● 6 No. 60 Queen Victoria Street
- ● 7 No. 1 Poultry
- ● 8 St Stephen Walbrook
- ● 9 Mansion House
- ● 10 Nos 1–6 Lombard St
- ● 11 St Mary Woolnoth
- ● 12 Nos 81–82 King William Street
- ● 13 St Mary Abchurch
- ● 14 No. 115 Cannon Street
- ● 15 St Swithin's Lane
- ● 16 Tallow Chandlers' Hall
- ● 17 Pellipar House
- ● 18 Skinners' Hall
- ● 19 Dyers' Hall
- ● 20 St Michael Paternoster Royal
- ● 21 College Street/College Hill
- ● 22 St James Garlickhithe
- ● 23 Vintners' Hall
- ● 24 Southwark Bridge
- ● 25 Watermark Place
- ● 26 London Bridge
- ● 27 Fishmongers' Hall

- ○ a Nail
- ○ b John Milton
- ○ c St Swithln's Church Garden
- ○ d The London Stone
- ○ e The City alleys
- ○ f Cleary Garden
- ○ g Whittington Gardens
- ○ h Laurence Pountney Hill
- ○ i Riverside Walk West

8

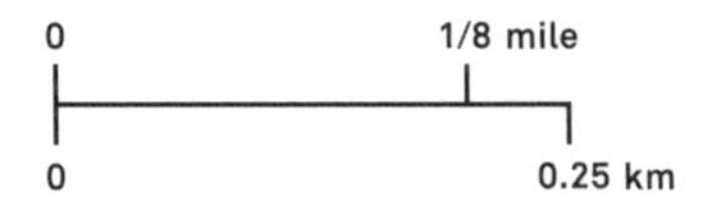

equivalent to Bach's *Goldberg Variations* (published in 1741), St Mary-le-Bow sets the theme with its entirely original concept of a classical spire and its confident adoption of ancient Roman precedent inside. The dome variation plays grandly at St Stephen Walbrook and then, in a different mood with a touch of improvisation, at St Mary Abchurch. The Gothic of St Mary Aldermary is a genre exercise, playing old tunes with new harmonies, while St James Garlickhithe is a sparkling square dance. Our interpretation of these buildings may keep to an understanding of the architect's intentions, as written in the score. Owing to the accidents of time, however, we are left with the interpretations of many different performing artists when we actually visit. Some have been lucky not to need drastic reconstruction – St Mary Abchurch seems miraculously like hearing the actual sounds of the 17th century on a recording. St Mary-le-Bow, by contrast, seems to have been rescored for Mantovani by Laurence King. There is also Hawksmoor's St Mary Woolnoth, the only church in the City by this architect who is now more admired by cognoscenti than Wren, whose faithful backroom assistant he was in life. It is instructive to move from Walbrook to Woolnoth considering the change in tone. Both are Baroque, but the effect is different. Some cast Hawksmoor as a proto-Beethoven, with an intensity of imagination and emotion that creates strength against which delicacy can be counterposed.

In 1886, the 'London Stone' was more decorously housed in Cannon Street than it is today.

By coincidence, the sightlines run clear from no. 1 Poultry by James Stirling and Michael Wilford to St Mary Woolnoth. Like several New Brutalists of the 1950s, Stirling felt that Hawksmoor was their generation's discovery – when Stirling died unexpectedly during routine surgery in 1992, his funeral service was held at St Mary's. The long-lasting planning dispute that led up to Stirling's selection for this job marked the worlds of conservation and urbanism in the 1980s. The underlying issue was the terms under which it was legal to demolish a listed building, in this case the original no. 1 Poultry by John Belcher. Where property is as valuable as it is in the City, any form of protection is bound to be disputed, but in this case the Planning Inspectorate, usually reliable guardians of the law, wavered under pressure to allow a second attempt when a Mies van der Rohe tower design was rejected. Stirling even prepared a version of his scheme that kept the listed building, a marriage that might have been as productive as that between Sir Albert Richardson and Michael Hopkins at Bracken House a few years later.

As always, the frontier of listing is moving to include more recent buildings. One New Change replaced the 1950s neo-Georgian New Change by Victor Heal, a prolific architect who has never been highly rated, yet despite its being turned down for listing by English Heritage, there were many who felt the building should be kept for the sake of its good-quality materials and workmanship. The amount of carbon dioxide emissions 'embodied' in any building is considerable, and in the USA retention of older fabric contributes to the energy rating of the new work. Victor Heal's building would probably have proved as adaptable as Bracken House has done, and saved a lot more

The Mansion House, shown in a lithograph of *c.* 1854, stands on a former marketplace at a historic junction.

Cannon Street Station towers over its neighbours in this engraving of 1867, shortly after completion.

Looking west from the Royal Exchange, with the Mansion House on the left and John Belcher's 'flatiron' building at no. 1 Poultry gracefully turning the corner.

carbon emissions in terms of the production of materials, transport and site work involved in Jean Nouvel's replacement.

One significant aspect of the no. 1 Poultry dispute was about the nature of the City and its spaces. In the 1950s the St Paul's precinct was the battleground between the formalists and the followers of picturesque. Mies van der Rohe's tower was out of fashion in 1984, but even more so the accompanying concept of a broad open plaza. The City, the other side argued, is not like that. It doesn't 'do' big public spaces – its life is carried on semi-invisibly, in places like Bow Lane where pedestrians can meet close up and news can travel. Stirling's building achieved a dramatic pedestrian cut-through, reinforcing the existing right of way, in order to create the currently desired effect of permeability and connectivity. Now pedestrianization and the curbing of car use seems an article of universal faith. The City Corporation has certainly put its money on improving design at street level, in a series of small interventions that add up to a considerable difference. The Mayor of London's congestion charge also protects the City (and a wider area) from the worst traffic excesses produced by drivers using it as a shortcut. It is a good beginning, and there should be more to come.

The City Corporation is also working to return retailing in a planned way, with Cheapside as its 'high street', a policy embodied in One New Change. Street names still carry some of the quarter's history as a food market, with Poultry meaning what it says (the ducks walked in from Essex wearing special canvas bags to protect their feet), while close by are Bread Street and Fish Street. Goldsmiths' wives in the pre-Fire period would sit before their shops dressed in jewellery as a living advertisement. Much of the City is still delightfully silent and deserted on weekends, but the tourists around St Paul's are now starting to be pulled eastwards. Keeping shops, cafés and bars open until late hours contributes to making places safer for everyone. Where there is no vision, the people perish, says the Book of Proverbs, but equally, where there are no people, the vision perishes.

Unloved in its youth but lamented at its passing, Victor Heal's Bank Chambers in New Change represented the prevailing architectural conservatism of the City in the 1950s.

Jean Nouvel's replacement building includes a cluster of shops and restaurants, deliberately changing the character of this part of the City, and a public roof-garden with striking views.

One New Change reflects the sky and other buildings in its canted planes of glass cladding.

1 ONE NEW CHANGE

EC4 • Jean Nouvel 2010

The French architect Jean Nouvel describes his building as a 'stealth bomber', a commentary on the restrictions on building around St Paul's as well as a clue to the faceted radar-proof forms of the external envelope, sheathed in ambiguously toned glass that can reflect a whole sky. It follows the City Corporation's policy of returning Cheapside to a high street, with retail shops below and a floor of restaurants above. Office floors high up are capped by a public roof terrace with spectacular views.

The best aspects of Nouvel's project are seen from the inside, with intersecting promenades crossing at an open atrium: reflective surfaces of silvery steel and black glass, laced with bright red, attempt to bring some commercial vulgarity into the good manners of the City. The *coup d'oeuil* is the framing of St Paul's between inclined cliffs of glass.

A deep cut into the depth of the building frames the view of the east end of St Paul's through the tactful gap left between the pavilions of the Cathedral School.

2 ST MARY-LE-BOW

Cheapside EC2 • Sir Christopher Wren 1670–80

To be born within the sound of Bow bells is the traditional test of a Cockney, appropriate when Cheapside was the principal street for food trades in the City but now a long-standing anachronism, although a Cockney Harvest Festival, with pearly kings

Opposite
The tower of St Mary-le-Bow can claim to be the ancestor of classical steeples all over the English-speaking world.

COSTA

and queens, is held every October. The church is, however, distinguished by its bell tower and steeple, the first to be completed by Wren in the post-Fire rebuilding and one of the most original and adventurous in its ascending stages and the successful scaling of the classical forms he had to invent for the purpose.

The suffix 'le-Bow' or 'de arcubus' is sometimes thought to refer to flying buttresses on the pre-Fire tower, reproduced in classical form by Wren, but may apply to the arches of the Norman crypt (now open to visitors as a café). Wren's plan, begun in 1670, is unusual, involving a journey from Cheapside through one of the grand rusticated archways beneath the tower, for which Wren had noted a precedent on his trip to Paris. These lead via a vestibule to the north-east corner of the church, where the grand scheme of the three-arched arcade (narrow-wide-narrow) rises into an elliptical barrel vault, based on the Basilica of Maxentius in Rome, illustrated in the Renaissance by Serlio, as Wren's son tells us. The east wall is a version of the triumphal arch motif with round and oval windows above. The interior was burnt out in the Blitz and restored, less sensitively (in the opinion of many) than some of the other City churches, by Laurence King (1956–64), with bright and rather jazzy windows by John Hayward. The one to the left of the high altar is interesting since it shows the towers of all the City churches damaged in the Blitz.

The needs of City workers and visitors are met by small streets such as Bow Lane where, free from cars, coffee bars and other useful services create a cosmopolitan feeling.

3 BOW LANE
EC4

It does not take long to discover where the evening *passeggiata* takes place in any Italian town – people strolling up and down slowly, pausing for talk and drink, and, above all, watching others doing the same. If the City has a *passeggiata*, it seems that Bow Lane and Watling Street are becoming the place. The combination of cafés, bars and luxury shops, housed in a pleasing variety of old shopfronts, plus the City's policy of levelling off the curbs to create pedestrian streets, has meant that Bow Lane, leading from Cheapside down to Cannon Street Station, lies in the right place to take a break from work or relax on the way home. The buildings have individual interest, including Williamson's Tavern, a 1930s rebuild in 'Quality Street' style, and the unquaint but historically interesting nos 6–8, with a rare 'reform Gothic' shopfront set behind slender cast-iron columns of 1871.

Williamson's Tavern in Groveland Court, off Bow Lane, photographed in 1905, with a light reflector projecting from the building on the right.

4 NOS 64–66 CHEAPSIDE
EC2 • M. E. & O. H. Collins 1930–33

The City architects Marcus Evelyn Collins and (presumably) his son Owen Hyman Collins knew how to make buildings fun, as demonstrated by their 1929 Carreras 'Black Cat' cigarette factory in Mornington Crescent, Camden. At nos 64–66 Cheapside, built

The façade of nos 64–66 Cheapside. The elevations of many City offices repay inspection, even if they are not by well-known architects.

for the British General Insurance Company, one of their many City buildings in various styles, they treat the classical orders with irreverence although the resulting elevation is pleasingly decorative. Their use of pilasters rising from scrolled leaf bases, and terminated without capitals, seems very similar to Maurice Webb's design for the Commercial Union Insurance, Cornhill (1929), as Simon Bradley points out in *The Buildings of England.*

These are not the only features, however. The north-facing elevation is notable for the wide extent of its glazing, which nonetheless is held within a classical frame of stone that does not lose its sense of the logic of loads transmitted downwards through the structure.

Inside St Mary Aldermary, Wren and his associates created their own decorative version of Gothic, anticipating the 'Strawberry Hill' style of the following century.

5 ST MARY ALDERMARY

Queen Victoria Street EC4 • Sir Christopher Wren 1679–82

In 1672 Henry Rogers, a Somerset squire, died and left a cash sum of £7,500 in the hands of his niece Ann Rogers, instructing her to give it to the rebuilding of a London church that needed it. After legal wrangles, she asserted her right to the money and settled on St Mary Aldermary, being able to provide all the necessary funds, for which she was rewarded with a haunch of venison by the parish. Wren's authorship has been disputed, but the work came from his close associates, John Oliver for the body of the church and William Dickinson for the tower, so there is no need to doubt his presence.

The building damaged in the Fire dated from 1511 and beyond, although the name of the church implies that it was one of the oldest in foundation. The present fan-vaulted interior might pass as being authentic Perpendicular, except that it is made of plaster and quite different in style from any original example. Furthermore, fan vaults were never used for parish churches. The columns of the nave arcades are passably Gothic but the scrolled ornament with coats of arms in the spandrels above them clearly is not. Six saucer domes hover between the fans like lace doilies, while the eastern bay over the altar has its own variant version of barrel vault, now richly coloured. The tower, completed in 1704, may have been a partial pre-Fire survival, but the bottle-shaped pinnacles are the thumbprint of Dickinson, found also on his designs for a central tower at Westminster Abbey.

Opposite
The exterior of St Mary Aldermary, although bu after the Great Fire, could almost pass as a late medieval work.

The remainder of the church interior is rather plain, having been insensitively restored in the 1870s at the time that Queen Victoria Street sliced its way past the south side, resulting in a complete external refacing. The leafy enclave round the corner in Bow Lane by the church tower belongs, however, to a different secret world.

6 NO. 60 QUEEN VICTORIA STREET

EC4 • Peter Foggo Associates 1990–2000

Stone has been the favourite material for City buildings since the time of Wren, but it is hard to justify as a medium for modern architecture. Metal is one of the alternatives, and it has rarely been used with such imagination and skill as in the work of Peter Foggo, an architect who contributed to the high reputation of Arup Associates before starting his own practice in 1989. He died in 1993, but this project carries his signature.

The elevations are formed by a grid of columns and beams, within which the glass is screened with pierced panels of patinated bronze. The critic Jeremy Melvin described the technique as 'structural façadist expressionism'. It reflects the decorative turn in high-tech pioneered by Foggo at Broadgate and achieves Postmodernist richness of expression without importing imagery from beyond the logic of construction.

Peter Foggo contributed major City buildings before his early death. At no. 60 Queen Victoria Street the challenge to modern architects of making a good corner treatment is successfully met.

7 NO. 1 POULTRY

EC2 • Sir James Stirling and Michael Wilford Associates 1986–98

In the 1980s opposing factions in British architecture lined up to argue over the future of this site, occupied by a listed 1870s Gothic office building by John Belcher but earmarked in the 1960s by developer Peter Palumbo for a tower by Mies van der Rohe. In listing, the quality of the replacement has no bearing on the arguments for or against the loss of an existing building, and an epic battle was joined in which every issue was blurred by media attention. The Conservative government bent the rules and allowed Palumbo to re-apply with another scheme.

For this purpose, his choice of James Stirling could have been a lot worse: although not one of his best buildings, it brings life to the Bank area with two-tone banded stone and opens up public space inside its colourful hollow drum.

James Stirling and Michael Wilford's no. 1 Poul brings a toy-like character to the architectural assembly around Bank. The Prince of Wales called it a 1930s wireless – an object that man people find attractive.

8 ST STEPHEN WALBROOK

EC4 • Sir Christopher Wren 1672–80

When Wren designed St Stephen's in 1672, it seems that the parish provided a more generous budget than usual, giving him the chance to experiment more fully on the theme of the still-emergent St Paul's – how to place a dome on a cruciform church crossing.

Opposite
At St Stephen Walbrook, Wren used his geomet skills to place a circle on a square, connected b eight equal arches.

The magnificent counterpoint of pillars, arches and dome in St Stephen Walbrook; the white paintwork suits the disciplined architecture of the church interior, contrasted with dark woodwork.

Bar one extra westward bay, the church could be square on plan, but the difference makes it an amalgam of longitudinal and central planning. A plan is needed to understand exactly what is going on, but the many geometric aspects of Wren's self-imposed problem are beautifully resolved at the point where the church widens into the dome. The slightly wider nave is matched by a wider bay, fourth in line from the west wall, so that when the dome sails over the corners, he can insert four diagonal arches of the same span as the four to north, south, east and west, making a regular rhythm of eight beneath the circular base of the dome, while bringing in light from pairs of clerestory windows where one might expect to find solid pendentives.

The fact that the dome is built of timber and plasterwork, not of stone, makes possible a device that could not be so simply done with the scale and materials involved at St Paul's. Nikolaus Pevsner called St Stephen's 'spatial polyphony', to which Ian Nairn responded, 'worthy not of Purcell, who never forgot his heart, but of J. S. Bach, who sometimes mislaid his'.

The church passed through several internal transformations, including bomb damage and structural undermining by the underground Walbrook stream. Work was funded in the 1980s by Peter Palumbo, arts patron and controversial developer, who led the repair project that included the insertion of a central stone altar by Henry Moore.

The Mansion House extends back from its Corinthian portico, reaching the north side of St Stephen Walbrook.

An elegant dinner at the Mansion House in 1795, with tables arranged as landscape gardens. The setting still provides a platform for important national occasions.

9 MANSION HOUSE

Walbrook EC4 • George Dance the Elder 1739–52

North-facing, and consequently mostly in shadow, the Mansion House makes the most of its pomp, with a full Corinthian portico raised over a ground-level basement storey, in the manner approved by the English Palladian revivalists. The architect was George Dance the Elder, Clerk of Works to the City from 1735. The idea of building an appropriate official residence for the Lord Mayor, Head of the City of London Corporation, had been considered after the Great Fire. The site, just north of St Stephen Walbrook and formerly a marketplace, stood at a historic road junction that, until this point, lacked any significant monuments.

The plan was an ingenious attempt to combine multiple functions in a small space, including provision for lavish ceremonial banquets and private apartments for the Lord Mayor and his family. The ground level was for service accommodation and from 1842 provided a more convenient entrance through the Walbrook Hall, in place of the front portico steps, which were soon trimmed back by the construction of Queen Victoria Street in 1867. Originally, visitors mounted these steps and passed through an internal first-floor courtyard to reach the main reception room, the Great Egyptian Hall, at the back. This is not literally Egyptian but based on an account by the Roman writer Vitruvius, interpreted by Palladio, of what he believed such a hall to be, framed internally by grand Corinthian columns with windows above the entablature. Dance originally provided a top-heavy upper storey to complete the effect, but this was modified in 1795 when George Dance the Younger substituted a neo-classical barrel vault.

The Old Ballroom, on the second floor, also had its ceiling lowered, but it is lightened by plaster trophies in the Rococo style that Dance the Elder introduced in the late 1740s to keep up to date. They depict the pleasures of music, dancing, drinking and dalliance, appropriate to the function of the room if a little frivolous for the dignity of the City.

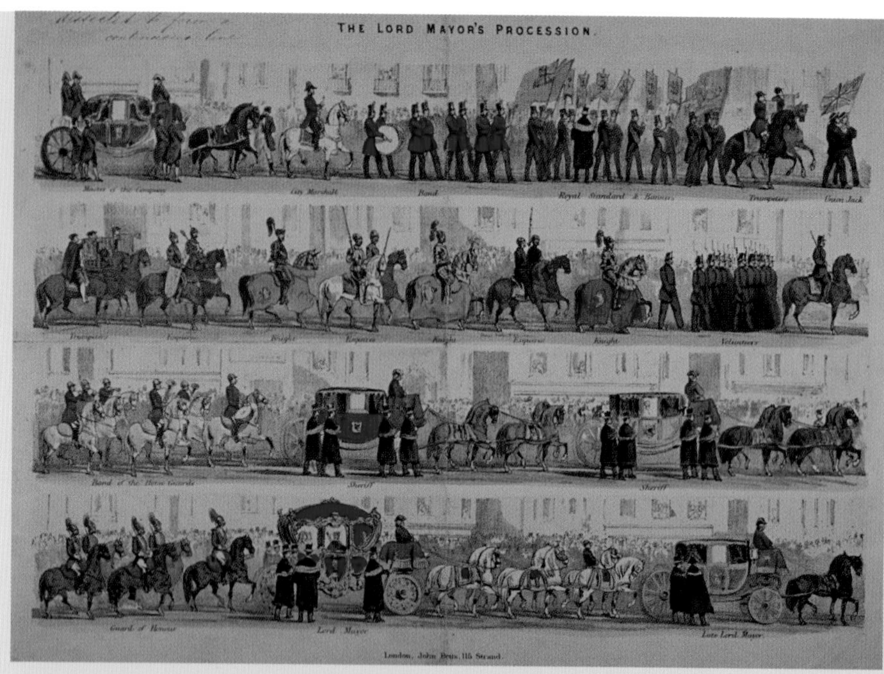

A lithograph of the annual Lord Mayor's Show procession in 1845, with knights in armour representing the historical element of the pageant.

THE LORD MAYOR

The City of London has its own local government, carried down from Saxon times. It was worth more than any king's while to challenge it, and in 1215 the Magna Carta signing was attended by the Lord Mayor, who agreed protection for its 'ancient liberties by land and by water'. The City's banking role was important in giving it a hold over monarchs who needed funds.

The office of Lord Mayor is held for twelve months, although Richard Whittington, a figure celebrated in largely fictitious English legend and pantomime, did – as the bells predicted – hold the position three times. The role is unsalaried and highly demanding. The focus is now on building relationships for British business and financial services in foreign countries. Between his foreign visits, the Lord Mayor and Lady Mayoress (there has only been one woman Lord Mayor to date, Dame Mary Donaldson, 1983–4) live at the Mansion House opposite the Bank of England. Turtle soup was a delicacy served there and at the Guildhall in former times, a symbol of lavish hospitality.

For the public, the most visible manifestation of the Mayoralty is the Lord Mayor's Show in early November, the continuation of an agreement with King John that the Lord Mayor should swear an oath of allegiance and 'show' himself to the people. The latter is done as he rides from the City to the Royal Courts of Justice in his 1753 gilded coach, appearing at the window and doffing his hat.

A sunny Thames on Lord Mayor's Day, 1746, painted by Canaletto, showing the livery companies' barges and the Lord Mayor's barge on their chief annual outing.

The former task is accomplished with chief judges as proxy for the sovereign.

Until 1856 the journey extended to Westminster Hall (where the judges then sat), and was taken by water in a splendid gold barge, recorded in a painting by Canaletto, and the return was by carriage. Popular and unpopular Lord Mayors alike were mobbed. Deprived of religious processions by the Reformation, the people of London found a substitute in this annual junket and it acquired a Baroque symbolic dimension, with men in antique-style armour and other fancy costumes for allegorical purposes, all organized by a Pageantmaster. In 1554 the presence of artificial giants, based on the mythical figures Gog and Magog, is first recorded. The figures were destroyed in the Great Fire but recarved in wood by Thomas Saunders for exhibition in the Guildhall in 1708. A new set was made in 1953 after the Blitz, but these were too heavy to go on parade, and in 2006 a new pair of wickerwork giants was created by Olivia Elton Barratt as Prime Warden of the Basketmakers' Company, with a volunteer team. They now front the procession. After 1856 allegory gave way to literal representation of history, military and the empire, including, in 1884, 'a Nile boat similar to those sent out to Lord Wolseley [for the rescue of General Gordon] exhibited properly manned'. Elephants were provided by Mr Sanger, a circus manager, in order that the Indian Raj (instituted in 1876) could be properly honoured.

Nos 1–6 Lombard Street is one of the more thoughtful Edwardian classical buildings in the City, rewarding a close look at the ground-level carving.

10 NOS 1–6 LOMBARD STREET

EC3 • Dunn & Watson 1905–8

For Sir Edwin Lutyens, writing in 1903, classical architecture was 'the high game'. The architects Dunn and Watson played their own variation in Lombard Street for the Scottish Provident Institution, making good use of the curved frontage of the site to introduce a grand order of Corinthian columns over a rusticated basement, with 'end stop' bays at each end.

As described thus far, this could be a standard boilerplate design by Sir Edwin Cooper, who conveniently demonstrated his version across the other side of the Bank interchange (see pp. 138–9). In their building, Dunn and Watson refuted the criticism made at the time and later that classicism's overthrow of the Arts and Crafts movement necessitated a loss of sensitivity. The carving of the doorways by Laurence Turner and of the Corinthian capitals were based on the first-hand experience of the Eastern Roman empire of one of the firm's assistants.

11 ST MARY WOOLNOTH

Lombard Street EC3 • Nicholas Hawksmoor 1716–27; William Butterfield 1875–6

Nicholas Hawksmoor's only City church, a rebuilding of a medieval church that was repaired in the 1670s, lurks behind the Bank junction, its west front offering a fistful of horizontal rustication wrapping round the columns across the full breadth of the lower stage. The tower is a stage front resolving into a pair of squat turrets over a screen of columns, ambiguous about whether they should be read as two units or one. The north side onto Lombard Street is equally remarkable, with blank niches, possibly intended for statues, like hollow cheeks sucked into the wall. Contrasts of scale, such as the heavy sills and the console brackets on which they sit, emphasize the lightness of the columns squeezed within the niches above, as does the miniature blind arch at the base of each niche. The plain south side was not visible until the creation of King William Street in 1829. Later the church escaped not entirely unscathed from the insertion on this side of an entrance to the underground.

The interior of St Mary's, normally open during the day, is an architectural treat to be taken slowly: first, the compression of the transverse space beneath the tower, then emergence beneath the organ gallery into a square box of light, with a smaller square inscribed within by the entablature supported on clusters of Corinthian columns. The slight projection of the entablature at the corners does something to tighten the sense

The blind niches on the north side of St Mary Woolnoth are one of Hawksmoor's great inventions.

The interior of St Mary Woolnoth in a pencil drawing by Robert Randoll, 1902.

of enclosure, one of the many ways through which one realizes how Hawksmoor carried the understanding of architecture's expression through form a stage beyond Wren. Above these, four big half-round clerestory windows on each side form a lantern. The altar is modestly placed beneath a flat arch on the east wall. The church was restored by William Butterfield in the 1870s, who took out the side galleries without any serious loss.

Curtis Green followed the compositional outline of the previous building on the same site at nos 81–82 King William Street, shown here in an etching of 1913 by William Monk.

12 NOS 81–82 KING WILLIAM STREET

EC4 • W. Curtis Green 1925–7

W. Curtis Green was skilled as a classical designer in the cool American manner that replaced Edwardian Baroque. The 1920s was his high period, with buildings facing each other in Piccadilly near the Ritz, using the architectural language, as C. H. Reilly wrote, 'in a fine simple way that the public could appreciate'.

The King William Street building was commissioned by the London Life Association. It makes the most of its broad south-west facing frontage, skilfully subdividing the elements of the composition with bold openings and delicate mouldings in which the distinction between those that are enriched with carving and those that are left plain is the key to understanding the hierarchy of the different parts of the building. The building is now empty and inaccessible, but originally contained 'a great entrance hall…with stone screens at either end and a great curved niche facing one as one arrived'.

Entering St Mary Abchurch, one of the most enjoyable City church interiors, is like stepping back into the period of this print from 1760.

13 ST MARY ABCHURCH

Abchurch Lane EC4 • Sir Christopher Wren 1681–6

Tucked away from the main streets with its own rather Venetian paved square and charming spire, St Mary Abchurch has an otherworldly feeling. The sober, rather Dutch-looking exterior gives little clue to the richness inside, partly achieved in Protestant panelling and gilding. In the words of John Betjeman, it is 'a great square room roofed by a dome springing from eight pendentives', within which is a painted firmament by William Snow (1708) to complete the Italianate feel.

The church was damaged in the Blitz, but it hardly shows after the reconstruction by Godfrey Allen (1945–57). The reredos of 1686 is the only one in a City church that is by the actual hand of Grinling Gibbons, and although broken into two thousand pieces by bombing, it was fully reconstructed. His swags and drops descend from a broad pediment with pairs of flaming urns above. The font, tucked in beside the door, has a timber cover linked to the ceiling with a wooden screw that winds round to raise it off its marble base.

Opposite
Classical buildings of the interwar years, such as the one commissioned from Curtis Green by the London Life Association at nos 81–82 King William Street, make a significant contribution to the architectural variety of the City.

NICHOLAS LANE
cafe

The only work in the City by a major Modern architect of the 1930s, Walter Gropius's shopfront is a sensitive response to the brief, even if at odds with its neighbours.

14 NO. 115 CANNON STREET

EC4 • Walter Gropius and Maxwell Fry 1936

This simple shopfront in black Vitrolite coloured glass, currently belonging to a firm of shirtmakers, speaks of the 1930s at its most stylish. Rather surprisingly, it is the work of one of the 20th century's greatest architects, Walter Gropius, the founder of the Bauhaus School in Weimar and Dessau, who sought refuge in London from the Nazis between 1934 and late 1936, when he left to teach at Harvard. During this time he was in partnership with the English architect Maxwell Fry, but this work is usually ascribed to Gropius. The client was the Mortimer Gall Electrical Centre, one of several showrooms promoting electrical appliances in London. In the 1990s the exterior was conserved and missing elements added. The long tubular metal door handles and the glass bricks in the lower shop fascia, helping to throw daylight into the basement, are notable period features.

Morning light casting deep shadows on the old Rothschild's building in St Swithin's Lane. It has been replaced twice since the war, most recently with a new building by Rem Koolhaas and OMA.

15 ST SWITHIN'S LANE

EC4

St Swithin's Lane, a convenient cut-through between Cannon Street and King William Street, holds several pleasures and surprises. No. 113 Cannon Street by E. A. Gruning (1869–70) frames the southern end, with remarkable cast-iron goats' heads close to the pavement beneath the windows. Higher up on the left, a tailor's and basement barber's shop share an entrance, and one can step back thirty years or more, so unchanged are the signs, the shopfronts and the merchandise. The matching café, on the other side of the entrance door to the former Founders' Hall at no. 13, is much the same.

In the cobbled yard behind no. 20, Sandeman House recalls the presence of a well-known wine merchant from 1805 onwards, the user of the 'Capital Patent Crane' attached to a surprising timber shed, now part of a restaurant. Higher up, Rothschild's New Court has been replaced by a tall thin glass building by Rem Koolhaas and OMA.

16 TALLOW CHANDLERS' HALL

Dowgate Hill EC4 • John Caine 1671–3; Joseph & Pearson 1883–4

The 1672 courtyard of the Tallow Chandlers' Hall is concealed from view by Victorian building on the street.

Tallow, an animal fat, was the main material for candles in pre-modern times. The Tallow Chandlers came to this site in 1476. The original hall was destroyed in the Great Fire, but what remains of the rebuilding represents one of the most complete authentic survivals of its kind. As so often with the livery halls, you would not guess this from the street, where the finely coloured coat of arms in the entrance to an 1880s redbrick Gothic warehouse is all there is to signal what lies beyond.

Down the passageway and into the courtyard, the 1672 hall, by the master bricklayer John Caine, stands over a Tuscan colonnade whose arches are infilled with rusticated masonry and carved spandrels above them. It is delightful and rather Dutch in its neatness and restrained richness. The hall above is panelled and carved, with a splendid niche behind the Master's chair.

Tallow Chandlers' Hall contains the customary display of ceremonial silver in a typical panelled interior.

17 PELLIPAR HOUSE

9 Cloak Lane EC4 • Green Lloyd Adams 1987–91

Postmodernism does not get a good press in the architecturally austere early 21st century. This example, by J. Sampson Lloyd of Green Lloyd Adams, an architect whose hand was found all over the City in the 1980s and 1990s, is in a higher class, playing with the classical orders but not breaking the toys in the process. Lloyd was the grandson of W. Curtis Green, one of the best interwar classicists (see nos 81–82 King William Street). He made a transition to Modernism but had a good grounding in historical styles and, when the occasion came to cross them over to suit the tastes of an ornament-hungry public bored by restraint, he knew how to do it.

This elevation is part of the Skinners' Hall complex. Canted window bays have decorative lead panels, like Lloyd's new Founders' Hall in Cloth Fair (1984–6), and between them rise piles of columns, suggesting a set of children's building blocks.

The ground level detail of Pellipar House only hints at the ingenious manipulations of classicism in the upper floors.

18 SKINNERS' HALL

8 Dowgate Hill EC4 • John Oliver 1668; William Jupp 1778–9

The south elevation of Dyers' Hall in 1830. The charming double stair no longer exists.

The Skinners (originally trading in furs) feel comfortable in their domestic palace alongside Cannon Street Station, with its jolly façade by William Jupp. There is a pleasant courtyard inside, down a long passageway, and behind it a complex of buildings altered at various dates. The Court Room has robust cedar panelling from 1670, with pedimented doorcases flanking the fireplace.

The main hall is the showpiece on account of its cycle of murals on the theme of the Company's history and exploits by Sir Frank Brangwyn (1902–9), who succeeded in capturing the swagger of Edwardian commerce and projecting it backwards through time into a history-book imperial past, full of brightly coloured clothes and interesting natives. The actual narrative and symbolism may not have mattered as much to him as the abstract problem of composing a related series of panels. Beautifully lit, they are the best survivors of a mania for mural painting that gripped the City at this time.

19 DYERS' HALL

11–13 Dowgate Hill EC4 • Charles Dyer 1839–41; D. A. Cobbett 1856–7

The Worshipful Company of Dyers goes back to the 15th century, when their skill applied to cloth was one of the most important and valuable ways of adding value to a product. The present hall, built by the aptly named Charles Dyer in 1839–41, is the third on its site, just south of the Skinners' and forming a corner with College Street. Dyer's robust elevation with its Doric pilasters contrasts with the Dowgate Hill building, less than twenty years later, where, in the hands of the little-known D. A. Cobbett, the sense of compositional balance and proportion in classical architecture has been mysteriously washed away.

The Court Room, doubling as a banqueting hall, is the work of several hands, starting with Charles Dyer and finishing in 1990 with the distinguished modern architect H. T. Cadbury-Brown, who contributed (also appropriately in terms of his name) a chocolate-brown colour scheme, with curtains by Eduardo Paolozzi.

20 ST MICHAEL PATERNOSTER ROYAL

College Street EC4 • Sir Christopher Wren 1685–94, 1713–17

The church is named after the rosary (paternoster) makers who occupied a nearby building called 'La Reole'. It stands at a remove from the traffic in Upper Thames Street with a garden between, although a row of houses to keep the enclosure of College Street might have been a kinder solution.

Wren and his team came late to St Michael, in 1685, and the delicate steeple, a miniature building in itself, was even later,

The elevation of Skinners' Hall on Dowgate Hill conceals rich interiors, especially the hall with its murals by Frank Brangwyn.

The Cedar Room of Skinners' Hall, painted by Frank Crowther, 1890.

possibly by Hawksmoor. The interior is a well-lit box with a flat ceiling on a deep coving. It was shaken by bombing in 1944 and only restored in 1966 (by Elidir Davies), when the tower and part of the nave were converted to house the Missions to Seamen, leaving the remaining church area a square. Within this space the surviving furnishings were reassembled, including some from other churches, such as the stone figures of Moses and Aaron, receivers of the Ten Commandments, that flank the original reredos. The stained glass by John Hayward works much better here than at St Mary-le-Bow, having less competition from the architecture.

College Street in 1884, a picturesque composition remarkably recognizable today.

21 COLLEGE STREET/COLLEGE HILL

EC4

Looking down College Street from the corner of Dowgate Hill, the view of St Michael Paternoster Royal is framed by the Innholders' Hall to the left and the Dyers' Hall to the right, making a sudden transition to buildings whose scale is pre-Victorian, even if their dates are mixed. Here one could imagine what more secluded parts of the City were once like, although the noise, dirt and smell of earlier times are missing.

Round the corner to the right, in College Hill, where the most famous Lord Mayor, Dick Whittington, lived in the 15th century, a jumble of buildings includes no. 22, with its spectacular carved stone surrounds to carriage entrances, from before 1676. Their exuberant trophies of fruit, flowers and bones beneath curved pediments are a unique survival of the best-quality post-Fire ostentation.

St James Garlickhithe is not one of Wren's best-known designs, but shows his ability to recombine the basic elements in ways that fitted each site.

22 ST JAMES GARLICKHITHE

Garlick Hill EC4 • Sir Christopher Wren 1676–82

Wren made an exceptional interior at St James, facing the Vintners' Hall across the canyon of Upper Thames Street. It is the tallest of his City churches and has the largest proportion of window area, a response to the buildings then blocking the south side, earning it the name 'Wren's lantern'. Inside, Ionic columns carry aisle ceilings with lunette clerestory windows over them. The plan is similar to St Stephen Walbrook, with the effect of a 'crossing' at the centre of the church, although the ceiling is flat rather than domed. The church survived an unexploded wartime bomb and the 1719 organ by 'Father' Bernhard Schmidt/Smith and Johann Knopple remains in use.

The west tower has one of the 'family' of steeples designed around 1700, including St Stephen Walbrook and the neighbouring St Michael Paternoster Royal, possibly by Hawksmoor, and a variant on the west towers of St Paul's.

Opposite
St Michael Paternoster Royal is a plain box set off by an intricate steeple.

The street façade of the Vintners' Hall is an enjoyably incorrect piece of classical design – columns grouped in odd numbers are one of the greatest sins.

23 VINTNERS' HALL

Upper Thames Street EC4 • Edward Jerman 1671–5; A. H. Kersey 1908–10

From the elevations in Upper Thames Street and Queen Street little can be inferred about the much older structure surviving within the Vintners' Hall, including a 17th-century staircase with highly decorated carved balusters by William Woodroffe, the Court Room and the hall itself, the latter both with woodwork by a joiner called Symes. On these bases and in the connecting spaces are overlaid sculptures and other decorations, some salvaged from other buildings, others inserted over the succeeding centuries.

The livery hall in a watercolour by John Crowther from 1880.

The exterior is mainly by A. H. Kersey, when street widening caused the removal of parts of the earlier building. The Thames House office building (1911–12) by Stanley Hamp forms part of the same block, formerly including Vintry House, a restrained stripped classical design of 1927 by Kersey, Gale & Spooner – sadly destroyed in the 1980s because it contravened the 'St Paul's Heights' regulations imposed subsequently, although its carved portal was allowed to survive. The pompous classical Vintners' Place by Whinney Mackay-Lewis (1990–93) took its place.

Southwark Bridge, repainted in 2010, brightens the Thames with its strong colouring.

24 SOUTHWARK BRIDGE

EC4 • Sir Ernest George with Mott & Hay 1912–21

The present bridge was designed by the architect Sir Ernest George late in his career, in 1914, but not completed until 1921. It has five steel arches and some architectural features where the piers rise above the carriageway and offer sitting places. In the late 1980s, the original green and yellow colour scheme was reinstated and was refreshed in 2010.

Much more interesting was its predecessor, the second in date of the three Thames bridges by the engineer John Rennie, after Waterloo Bridge. Completed in 1819, this bridge was commercially unsuccessful because a toll was charged, and the incline was too steep for horses. Nonetheless it was an engineering marvel, with three spans of cast iron, made by Walkers of Rotherham. The central span of 73 m (240 ft) was the largest ever made. It was demolished because of the gradient problem, but the replacement was not much better, and it has remained the least well used of the City bridges.

25 WATERMARK PLACE

One Angel Lane EC4 • Fletcher Priest 2010

Two new buildings fill the section of riverside between Cannon Street Station and Swan Lane as a background to an enlarged river walk, reached by a newly pedestrianized Angel Lane. To the east is Watermark Place (One Angel Lane), designed by Fletcher Priest to replace the early 1970s Mondial House, which was built for the GPO as a bomb-proof telephone exchange and resembled a giant typewriter. Watermark Place is notable for its timber shade screening applied to one of the buildings, while structural timbers, reminiscent of riverside history, carry horizontal sun-breakers on another. A ground-level restaurant

encourages the public to spend some time here, enjoying the views that are also available to workers in the linked buildings rising behind.

The neighbouring building by David Walker Architects is a sleeker office block, characterized by a gentle application of Deconstructionist geometry, with the undersides of the projecting floorplates coloured daffodil yellow in long triangular strips.

The design strategy at Watermark Place succeeds in making a new and enjoyable public walkway, well placed for catching the sun.

26 LONDON BRIDGE

EC4 • Mott, Hay & Anderson with Lord Holford 1967–72

The London Bridge built in 1176–1209 survived until the 1820s, although shorn of its houses after 1762 when the central arch was enlarged. The obvious man for the replacement, built upstream, was John Rennie, who submitted his design in 1821, the last year of his life. The bridge that was opened in 1831 was carried out by his son, with five elliptical spans – not quite attaining the level carriageway of his Waterloo Bridge ten years before, but still a masterful piece of engineering and architectural embellishment. A land arch spans Tooley Street in Southwark, giving some idea of the quality, and parts of the screen walls can be seen by the Fishmongers' Hall.

Rennie's bridge became too narrow and started to show signs of weakness around 1900. It held together, however, until 1968,

The shallow-arched spans of the 1968 London Bridge reproduce something of the character of John Rennie's earlier design, using reinforced concrete. Adelaide House at the northern bridgehead is a notable 1920s office building with contrasting verticals.

when the present concrete bridge by Mott, Hay & Anderson, with Lord Holford as architectural consultant, was built. The granite facings were sold for re-erection at Lake Havasu City in Arizona, forming part of the state's second biggest tourist attraction.

27 FISHMONGERS' HALL

London Bridge Approach EC4 • Henry Roberts 1831–5

The Fishmongers compete with the Goldsmiths for the grandest neo-classical hall. Appropriately, they are on the river's edge, by London Bridge. The creation of John Rennie's replacement for the medieval bridge meant a new building was needed. The architect was Henry Roberts, a pupil of Robert Smirke, otherwise remembered for his early efforts in working-class housing. The Greek Revival design is chaste and correct, but the interiors are warm in feeling, somewhat like one of the contemporary Pall Mall clubs.

The entrance hall with its fine cast-iron stove leads to an imperial stair, delivering people to the doors of the Banqueting Hall that fills the main body of the building. There walls are divided by scagliola pilasters imitating yellow Siena marble. It is roofed with a most un-Greek elliptical barrel vault, following the curves of Rennie's London Bridge. The Drawing Room and Court Dining Room, facing the river, complete the sequence.

Despite changes all around, the serene Greek classicism of Henry Roberts's Fishmongers' Hall is a high point along the river front.

A view from 1761, looking down the river to St Paul's and old London Bridge, at that time still the only crossing of the Thames from the City to the south bank.

LONDON AND THE RIVER THAMES

The Thames is an unavoidable presence in London, but since the river traffic has for so long been diminished to a few barges towing waste it needs an effort of imagination to recapture its meaning. The change occurred in living memory. In January 1965 at least thirty cranes opposite the Tower of London dipped to honour the passing funeral barge of Sir Winston Churchill. Five years later most of these were idle or had disappeared, along with the warehouses they served. The whole system was designed for smaller ships and labour-intensive bulk cargoes, both suddenly overtaken by containerization.

The area between Tower Bridge and London Bridge is called the Upper Pool. It was the heart of London's trading activities, with a great variety of goods received at quaysides and transferred to warehouses and, in some cases, processing factories in the streets behind them. It was possible to trade higher up river until ships grew in size. Queenhithe, a small tidal bite from the river's edge formed by the extension of the land on each side, dates from 899, although it was not named after Queen Matilda until the 1100s. The last warehouse on the site was demolished in 1996, but at Walbrook Wharf, next to Cannon Street Station, waste is still shipped out in barges and construction materials are brought in.

The Steelyard, on the site of the station, was owned by three Baltic cities and formed an enclosure for German Hanseatic merchants who extended their reach into the English production of woollen cloth, which they then exported. Jealousy of their success caused Elizabeth I to close them down in 1598, and although they returned, their influence declined. Below London Bridge, Billingsgate (the City's first 'hithe', designed by King Alfred in 880) – where the fish market was formally established in 1699 – dealt with a commodity appropriately delivered by water until its closure in 1982. From here down to the Tower were the Legal Quays, a free-for-all landing place with cranes operated by treadwheels (an example is preserved at Harwich) and balances on the quayside. The opportunities for pilfering goods were rife, so regular traders sought to use closed wharves, which blocked off access to the river for centuries.

The Port of London Authority was created in 1908 as a result of fears that London was losing its competitive edge as a port. The Authority was active in building further down river, creating the King George V docks and developing both cargo and passenger services at Tilbury between the wars, accompanied by some of the best buildings of Sir Edwin Cooper, architect of the headquarters building in Trinity Square.

As well as cargo, the Thames historically served for transport, mostly by watermen acting as taxis for hire. This was more easily achieved upriver of old London Bridge, where the tide was modified by the narrow arches and, prior to the embanking, it was easier to get ashore. The same effect helped the river to freeze for weeks at a time, when it acted as a shortcut by road as well as hosting the Frost Fairs with their eating, drinking, sports and entertainments: a 'bacchanalian triumph, or carnival on the water', as the diarist John Evelyn wrote.

In 1934 the foreshore by the Tower of London was granted by royal decree for use as a beach for children to play on, with the aim that even the least privileged could enjoy it. For the purpose, 1,500 barge loads of sand were brought to cover the stones, much of which has remained, although the beach itself closed in 1971 owing to water pollution.

Today the river represents a threat of flooding, especially if sea levels rise as a result of glacial melting and combine with the existing risk of storm surge and a spring tide. The removal of the docks to the Thames estuary meant that the Thames Barrier could be built at Woolwich between 1974 and 1984.

On John Outhett's map of 1821, the docks stand out, with the recently completed East India Dock beginning the development of the Isle of Dogs.

Tower Bridge Beach in 1934. It was closed in 1971 but several points on the Thames foreshore can still be reached at low tide.

Additional Places to Visit

O a Nail

This sculpture by Gavin Turk (b. 1967) was installed in 2011 in the vista from One New Change (p. 286) across to St Paul's. The deftly angled blunt nail is juxtaposed with Jean Nouvel's glass façade.

O b John Milton

At Bow Bells House in Bread Street, one of the trade streets running south off Cheapside, is a blue plaque to John Milton (1608–74) on the site of his birth. On the side of St Mary-le-Bow (pp. 286–8), further along Cheapside, is an older plaque from the Church of All Hallows in Bread Street that recorded Milton's birth on Friday, 9 December 1608 and baptism on 20 December. It was moved here when that church was demolished in 1876.

O c St Swithin's Church Garden

North of Cannon Street, just opposite the station, the alley of Salters Hill Court leads to the tiny modern churchyard of the former St Swithin's, tucked in behind Norman Foster's big Walbrook building. Densely planted, it contains a striking sculpture designed by Nic Stradlyn-John and sculpted by Richard Renshaw in 2001 of Owain Glyndŵr's daughter Catrin, who was buried here, now reset with an English/Welsh text by Menna Elfyn.

O d The London Stone

Surely the oddest monument in the City, the ancient 'London Stone' is buried in a dirty glass case in the lower part of the wall at no. 111 Cannon Street, a bizarre and mysterious relic (see introduction, pp. 279, 282). Who knows what it means? It is most likely to be the tip of a Roman distance marker that stood at the entrance to the Governor's Palace; there are current plans to display it better at the corner of Walbrook and Cannon Street.

O e The City alleys

South off Cornhill, the small opening of Ball Court leads to the City's most authentic 18th- and 19th-century alleyways: the old tavern of Simpson's (in late 17th-century houses occupied by Simpson's from 1757) leads to Castle Court, with the George and Vulture chophouse (established 1600) mentioned in Charles Dickens's *Pickwick Papers* (also accessed from Bengal Place off George Yard, with its quiet stone benches). Other routes in include St Michael's Alley, past the fine Victorian doorway of that church, which houses the Jamaica Wine House, site of London's first coffee house, as a blue plaque relates, 'at the sign of Pasqua Rosee's Head 1652', and St Peter's Alley at no. 53 Cornhill, turning past St Peter's church garden to emerge by the shop of Ede and Ravenscroft in Gracechurch Street. The alleys lead back to

Birchin Lane, or south through George Yard to Lombard Street. (To the west of Birchin Lane are the less interesting Change Alley and Cowpers Court.) At no. 15 Lombard Street, a blue plaque shows the site of the first Lloyd's Coffee House, 1691–1785, now a Sainsbury's.

O f **Cleary Garden**

One of the nicest of the City's quirky and precious open spaces, this terraced site off Huggin Hill and Queen Victoria Street (just opposite no. 30 Cannon Street, p. 92) is named in honour of long-serving City committee chairman Fred Cleary, 'tireless in his wish to increase open space in the City'. There is a miniature vineyard in honour of the area's connections with the City wine trade, and a lawn on the site of a Roman bathhouse.

O g **Whittington Gardens**

At the foot of College Hill (p. 309), outside St Michael Paternoster Royal (pp. 306–9), is a garden by busy Upper Thames Street with two sculptures (1924) by Duilio Cambellotti (1876–1960) that were presented by the Italian President in 2005. In College Hill are blue plaques marking the houses of the famous Lord Mayor Dick Whittington (*c.* 1354–1423), and the Duke of Buckingham (1628–87) in 1672.

O h **Laurence Pountney Hill**

Nos 1 and 2 are, according to Pevsner and Bradley, 'the finest 18th-century houses remaining in the City, if not in London'; built in 1703, they have magnificent doorways. At the bottom of the hill is the restored Rectory House of 1670, which won a City Heritage Award in 2004, with a small churchyard garden opposite. A cut-through to the east leads to Martin Lane with the Olde Wine Shades from the 1660s.

O i **Riverside Walk West**

Join this either at the steps by Millennium Bridge (pp. 87–8), or at Southwark Bridge (with a wall display of London views in Fruiterers Passage under the bridge). There is a detour at the site of the ancient Saxon dock at Queenhithe that sends the walker back to noisy High Timber Street, but it then continues along Three Cranes Walk, dips through dull Steelyard Passage under Cannon Street Station, past Watermark Place (pp. 311–12), the excellent Angel Passage development with its new open space, along Oystergate Walk and then to Fishmongers' Hall Wharf by London Bridge (see also area 8, p. 353).

8 The Tower of London & The Monument

If the core of the City around the Bank of England is, appropriately, dominated by banking, the eastern sector of the City's commercial heart is where London's global insurance business is rooted. Lloyd's of London is the key institution, now housed in a spectacular high-tech landmark designed by Richard Rogers. Lloyd's has been on this site since the 1920s, and the demolition of its former premises, a fine classical building by Sir Edwin Cooper, was controversial. Only the main entrance portal on Leadenhall Street now survives, with, across the street, the frontage of the former Midland Bank designed by another great classicist, Lutyens. The Foster-designed headquarters of the insurance giant Willis has replaced the elegant 1950s extension to Lloyd's on Lime Street, in sight of Foster's 'Gherkin'. To the south, on Fenchurch Street, is Lloyd's Register, with another Rogers building tacked on to the magnificent palazzo by Collcutt. Between Mincing Lane and Mark Lane, the extraordinary Postmodern Gothic pile of Minster Court houses the London Underwriting Centre.

One of the virtues of Rogers's Lloyd's is the relationship it achieves with the adjacent Leadenhall Market. The City has steadily lost some of its markets but Leadenhall thrives. Admittedly it has been invaded by fashion chains and cafés, but the structure of the market has been carefully restored and is well maintained by the City Corporation. The covered arcades of the market link up nicely with adjacent alleys and courts leading through to Gracechurch Street. Lime Street is overshadowed by Lloyd's and the Willis building, but the latter has generated new pedestrian routes and a decent area of public space, incorporating some good sculpture from the 1950s Lloyd's building it replaced. Fenchurch Avenue, alongside the Willis building, has little of note but Fen Court, which leads through to Fenchurch Street, preserves the little churchyard of St Gabriel Fenchurch. (The medieval church was not rebuilt after the Great Fire and its parish was amalgamated with that of St Margaret Pattens, which still stands on Eastcheap.)

Within living memory, the Pool of London, between London Bridge and Tower Bridge, was a hive of activity – Tower Bridge was designed to allow ships access to the wharves and warehouses off Lower Thames Street. By the 1960s, however, the Pool was in decline and wharves and warehouses gradually gave way to undistinguished office development. Almost inevitably Billingsgate, London's historic fish market, was closed and removed to Docklands. The old market faced demolition but was saved after a vigorous campaign by conservationists and sensitively restored by Richard Rogers, with a glassy new office

Opposite
Begun by William the Conqueror, the White Tower was completed some years after his victory at Hastings in 1066 and has recently been restored.

4
6
7
Leadenhall Street
Aldgate High Street
Little Somerset Street
Whittington Avenue
Lime Street
Billiter Street
Leadenhall Market
Lime Street Passage
Fenchurch Avenue
Billiter Square
Aldgate
Carlisle Avenue
Northumberland Alley
Lloyd's Avenue
Jewry Street
India Street
St Clare Street
Haydon Street
Portsoken Street
Fenchurch Street
Fenchurch Place
Fenchurch Street
Gracechurch Street
London Street
New London Street
Crutched Friars
Crosswall
America Square
Cooper's Row
Savage Gardens
Vine Street
Minories
Goodman's Yard
Philpot Lane
Rood Lane
Dunster Court
Plantation Lane
Mincing Lane
Hart Street
Eastcheap
Pepys Street
Seething Lane
Mark Lane
Great Tower Street
Trinity Square
Muscovy Street
Tower Hill
Monument
Pudding Lane
Botolph Lane
St Mary-at-Hill
Idol Lane
St Dunstan's Hill
King William Street
Fish Street Hill
Monument Street
Byward Street
Tower Hill
Shorter Street
Lower Thames Street
London Bridge
Tower Hill
Tower Bridge Approach
Tower Bridge

KEY TO AREA 8

- ● 1 Monument
- ● 2 Adelaide House
- ● 3 St Magnus the Martyr
- ● 4 Custom House
- ● 5 St Mary-at-Hill
- ● 6 Plantation Place
- ● 7 Leadenhall Market
- ● 8 Lloyd's of London
- ● 9 Minster Court
- ● 10 St Olave Hart Street
- ● 11 Fenchurch Street Station
- ● 12 Lloyd's Register of Shipping
- ● 13 Ibex House
- ● 14 Port of London Authority (former)
- ● 15 Mercantile Marine Memorial
- ● 16 All Hallows by the Tower
- ● 17 Tower of London
- ● 18 Tower Bridge

- ○ a Old London Bridge
- ○ b Eastcheap; Philpot Lane
- ○ c Plantation Lane
- ○ d Fen Court
- ○ e Roman basilica
- ○ f St Dunstan-in-the-East Garden
- ○ g Seething Lane Gardens
- ○ h Portsoken Street Garden
- ○ i London Wall; Tower Subway; Tower Place
- ○ j Riverside Walk East

Boundary of the City of London

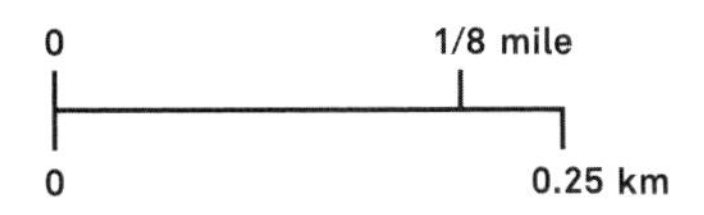

block (not by Rogers) on adjacent land. An earlier campaign to save the Coal Exchange on Lower Thames Street, with its magnificent iron and glass rotunda, was not successful, a City official stating that 'we cannot spend time on the preservation of a Victorian building'. A suggestion that the rotunda might be reconstructed as part of the new Barbican development was not taken up and the Exchange was destroyed in 1962, despite Pevsner's endorsement of it as 'among the twelve irreplaceable buildings of Victorian England'. The site was allegedly required for road widening but remained empty for twelve years, subsequently to be filled by a dull office block – a disastrous and pointless loss.

Lower Thames Street, bookended to the west by the bulk of the 1920s Adelaide House, now has the character of an urban motorway, and even a building as substantial as the Custom House makes little impact against the streams of traffic. The development boom of the 1960s also compromised the setting of the Tower of London. The replacement of the grim, grey concrete 1960s Tower Place development – oddly praised by Pevsner – with a civilized, low-rise development by Foster & Partners has improved the setting of the church of All Hallows and provided an enjoyable public square. Trinity Square is dominated by the former Port of London Authority building, a monumental classical pile by Edwin Cooper now awaiting a new role after Willis vacated it – hotel use has been mooted and seems highly appropriate. Both Great Tower Street and Eastcheap are mixed in character – Eastcheap retains a number of good Victorian buildings, most notably nos 33–35, constructed in 1868 as a vinegar depot to designs by R. L. Roumieu. *The Buildings of England* describes it as 'one of the maddest displays in London of gabled Gothic'. Ian Nairn thought it the sort of building that might form the subject of a nightmare. Talbot Court, just off Eastcheap, is an atmospheric backwater, complete with the Ship pub – nothing remarkable, but typical of so many similar City alleys and courts now swept away.

To the north, Fenchurch Street currently has a large hole in the ground, the site of the unlamented 1960s Kleinwort Benson tower, set to be replaced by the so-called 'Walkie-talkie', a 39-storey office tower of extraordinary form designed by the New York-based architect Rafael Viñoly and featuring a rooftop public garden. Further east, on the north side of the street, Fountain House, completed in 1958, looks unremarkable but was the first application in Britain of the formula, repeated so many times around the world, first seen in New York's Lever House: an office tower set on a horizontal slab. Back on the south side, Arup Associates' massive Plantation Place development replaces Plantation House, a large complex in classical style designed in the 1930s but completed as late as 1954. Fenchurch Street Station is one of the City's commuter hubs, but the destruction of the 1850s train shed for an 'air-rights' office scheme has destroyed its character. The square in front of the station has at least been decently landscaped, in connection with the adjacent office development by John McAslan. Lloyd's Register lies beyond – the

J. B. Bunning's Coal Exchange of 1849 was one of the Victorian landmarks of the City; it had a galleried iron and glass rotunda.

The former vinegar depot at nos 33–35 Eastcheap, completed in 1868 to designs by R. L. Roumieu, is one of the most elaborate (and eccentric) of London's Gothic Revival buildings. The arcaded ground floor has been reinstated since this photograph was taken in 1953.

Opposite
Tower Bridge was designed as a lifting bridge to allow ships access to the Pool of London.

When this photograph was taken in the 1920s Aldgate Pump, an ancient source of fresh water for City dwellers, was still in use, though now connected to the mains water supply rather than the well that had been identified as the source of a 19th-century cholera outbreak.

construction of Lloyd's Avenue to the east was supervised by its architect T. E. Collcutt. Further east again, Aldgate terminates at Aldgate Pump (once claimed as the source of the purest water in London – until it was identified as the source of a cholera outbreak). The plain Victorian warehouse that stood at the junction with Leadenhall Street was replaced in the 1980s by a forceful exercise in Postmodernism by Terry Farrell, a building which does have the virtue of effectively marking a point of entry to the City. Leadenhall Street itself is a mix of rather undistinguished blocks of the 1920s and 1930s with more recent development – the 1630s church of St Katharine Cree is rather overwhelmed by its canyon-like setting.

With the Tower of London – not itself within the City – as an endpoint, this quarter of the City has some of the choicest (and too little known) interiors in the Square Mile – the church of St Magnus the Martyr, the Bevis Marks Synagogue and Watermen's Hall, for example. The Great Fire spared the churches of St Olave and All Hallows, though both suffered badly in the Second World War. Samuel Pepys lived and worked in Seething Lane and was buried in St Olave's; it was from the tower of All Hallows that he surveyed the devastation caused by the Fire. Beyond Aldgate, the City gradually merges into the East End – City polish gives way to the more abrasive ethos of a very different version of London. This sense of transition is part of the attraction of this engaging area.

Opposite
Norman Foster's Tower Place development replaced an unloved 1960s complex and created a new public space for the City, with an open atrium linking the office buildings.

1 MONUMENT

Fish Street Hill, EC3 • Sir Christopher Wren and Robert Hooke, 1671–6

The Monument, a fluted Roman Doric column made of Portland stone, is 61 m (202 ft) high – the distance between it and the site in Pudding Lane where the Great Fire began.

A highly popular tourist attraction – for those fit enough to climb the 311 steps to the narrow balcony on top – the Monument was erected to commemorate the Great Fire of 1666. Despite earlier plans, the Monument ended up in an informal setting, a visual accident in the City's medieval street plan – and it is all the more impressive for that. The provision of 'a Colume or Pillar of Brase or Stone', to be erected close to the site of the house in Pudding Lane, where the Fire started, was contained in the Rebuilding Act of 1667, but the detailed design of the Monument involved both the King and the City. The inscriptions on the base were left to the City fathers – that on the north side, which fictitiously blamed the Fire on 'the treachery and malice of the popish faction' – was erased in 1830. It has been suggested that Hooke – certainly the principal designer of the Monument – intended it to have more than a purely symbolic function. As a leading scientist and member of the Royal Society he may have intended it for use as an observatory, but in any case it was soon superseded by the Royal Observatory at Greenwich. At 61 m (202 ft) the Monument is the tallest freestanding column in the world. It was restored by the City in 2007–9, when the flaming urn at the top was re-gilded for the first time in fifty years.

On the west side of the base there is a showy relief by sculptor C. G. Cibber extolling the vision of Charles II in rebuilding London.

2 ADELAIDE HOUSE

London Bridge Approach EC4 • Sir John Burnet & Tait 1921–5

At 45 m (148 ft), Adelaide House was London's tallest office building on its completion in 1925. Its architect was the Scot Thomas F. Tait, who had become a partner of Sir John Burnet in 1918 and during the 1920s became the effective leader of the practice. His other City projects included the *Daily Telegraph* building on Fleet Street (1928–31) and Unilever House (1930–32, in association with J. Lomax Simpson). Adelaide House, replacing an earlier building of the same name, was a revolutionary building in many respects – air-conditioned, with a mechanized mail distribution system and even a putting green on the roof. Its structural rationalism clearly reflected the influence of contemporary American commercial architecture but the building was clad in masonry featuring ornamental details. These were broadly Art Deco in style but with strong Egyptian influences. (Tait had been architect for the Imperial War Graves Commission in the Middle East and visited Egypt.) Adelaide House represented a clear break with the stodgy classicism of the Edwardian City and has been claimed as the City's first truly modern office building. Its proximity to the church of St Magnus the Martyr was controversial, but Ian Nairn welcomed the 'lucky, accidental contrast' between the two.

The monumental Adelaide House was designed by the Scot Thomas F. Tait and set a new standard for City office buildings on its completion in 1925. It frames the gateway to the City from London Bridge – and in the process overwhelms the adjacent Wren church of St Magnus the Martyr.

The church of St Magnus the Martyr is sandwiched between large commercial buildings and cut off by the traffic of Lower Thames Street.

The interior of St Magnus the Martyr is one of the most memorable in any City church, thanks in no small part to the embellishments added from the 1920s on by the architect Marti Travers that reflect the Anglo-Catholic tradition of St Magnus.

3 ST MAGNUS THE MARTYR

Lower Thames Street EC3 • Sir Christopher Wren 1671–84, 1703–6

St Magnus is one of the most captivating of all the City churches, and only partly on account of Wren's work there. The new church – replacing one destroyed in the Great Fire – was begun in 1668, before Wren took over the rebuilding, which was completed in 1684, with the distinctive cupola added in 1706. The church was extensively altered over the next century and a half – there were major repairs after a fire in 1760 and a programme of 'beautification' took place as late as 1814. But this is a building memorable not so much for its formal architectural qualities as for its unique atmosphere – T. S. Eliot recalled its 'inexplicable splendour of Ionian white and gold' in *The Waste Land* (1922). It escaped serious damage in the Second World War and retains a rich collection of fittings – superb woodwork, including the splendid west gallery and organ case, pulpit with tester, and reredos, and a particularly fine wrought-iron sword rest – as well as some interesting monuments, including one to the biblical translator (and its former rector) Miles Coverdale. The Anglo-Catholic tradition developed in the parish between the wars, and which remains strong today, produced a series of commissions to the architect Martin Travers from the mid-1920s on, all carried out in his favourite neo-Baroque manner and including alterations to the reredos, side altars made up of reused 17th-century woodwork, and shrines. The resulting ensemble, complemented by hanging lamps, votive candlestands and a whiff of incense, has echoes of Flemish Baroque and suggests – very deliberately – that the Reformation never happened and that the church has always been in communion with Rome. The setting of the building, hard up against the towering mass of Adelaide House, is piquant, though the noise and pollution from traffic on Lower Thames Street is less palatable.

4 CUSTOM HOUSE

Lower Thames Street EC3 • David Laing 1812–17; Sir Robert Smirke 1825–8

This is one of London's largest Regency buildings, with a frontage longer than that of the National Gallery, but it suffers from its location on heavily trafficked Lower Thames Street and from the fact that it presents a plain rear elevation to the street. There was a custom house on or near this site from the 14th century onwards – both Wren's building and its 18th-century successor were destroyed by fire. The new Custom House was constructed at a time, after the end of the Napoleonic Wars, when London's docks were booming – the customs revenues of the Port of London amounted to half those collected in the whole of England. The building was designed by David Laing, who had worked for Soane and become the Surveyor to HM Customs in 1810. Laing produced a solid work in an austere neo-classical manner influenced, it has been suggested, by French examples. In 1825 the central portion of Laing's building collapsed – inadequate foundations were blamed – and Robert Smirke, one of the architects attached to the newly created Board of Works, was commissioned to rebuild it. Inside, he designed the striking entrance hall and the Long Room on the first floor, an impressively austere space incorporating much iron in its construction.

This view from 1854 of the Custom House shows it as a monumental presence on the riverside.

5 ST MARY-AT-HILL

Lovat Lane EC3 • Sir Christopher Wren and Robert Hooke
1670–74

A church has stood here since at least the end of the 11th century. The shell of the medieval church, including the tower, survived the Great Fire. Rebuilding appears to have been entrusted by Wren to Robert Hooke. There were a number of subsequent alterations; the tower and west end were rebuilt in 1787–8 and the roof in 1826–7. The centralized plan could be compared with that, on a grander scale, of St Stephen Walbrook. John Betjeman described St Mary-at-Hill as 'the least spoiled and the most gorgeous interior in the City'. Much of the atmosphere that he admired was the result of the rearrangement and refurnishing of the interior carried out in 1848–9 under the architect James Savage, possibly after a fire. W. Gibbs Rogers was the craftsman responsible for splendid new woodwork, closely matching that of the 17th century. The original box pews, often removed by Victorian restorers, were retained in the reordering and by the end of the Second World War St Mary had the only set remaining in the City. The completeness of the ensemble made the church one of the most remarkable of the City churches, but in May 1988 a fire destroyed the roof and seriously damaged the interior. The great majority of the fittings, however, survived and were rescued and put into store, with the prospect that they would be reinstated in due course; several City churches had been carefully repaired after sustaining equivalent damage in the Blitz. Nearly a quarter of a century on, however, only the western gallery and organ have come back, though the roof and plaster ceiling were reconstructed as part of an exemplary restoration of the body of the church begun in 1990. The interior so admired by Betjeman and others appears to have been lost forever; stacking chairs replace box pews. Do the fittings still survive and is there no hope that they can be brought back?

An engraving from the mid-1820s by T. H. Shepherd shows Wren's east end of St Mary-at-Hill. This wall of the church, with the pedimented clock, looks much the same today.

6 PLANTATION PLACE

Fenchurch Street EC3 • Arup Associates 1996–2004

Plantation Place is one of the largest recent office developments in the City. Its site, bounded by Fenchurch Street, Rood Lane, Mincing Lane and Eastcheap/Great Tower Street, was previously occupied by Plantation House, 'that remarkable, incoherent building' (*The Buildings of England*) built in phases between 1935 and 1954 to house commodities markets. The new scheme comprises two buildings – a 15-storey block on Fenchurch Street and a lower, ten-storey block to the south – each of which has a distinct character. The northern block is clad in a double skin of glass, while Plantation Place South has a load-bearing stone façade with a limited area of glazing. Between the two buildings is a new east-west pedestrian route, Plantation Lane, a welcome restatement of the City tradition of lanes and alleys. The Fenchurch Street block has an imposing atrium.

The exterior of Plantation Place features extensive use of glass. The double-glazed skin reduces the energy load of the building. An artwork by Simon Patterson forms one side of Plantation Lane, preserved as a route through the site.

The glassy bulk of Plantation Place provides a neutral backcloth for the Wren church of St Margaret Pattens on Eastcheap.

As part of the scheme, the client commissioned artist Simon Patterson, well known for his 'Great Bear' reworking of the London Tube map, to liaise with Arup Associates on a major piece of public art: *Time and Tide*, a glass screen 41 m (135 ft) long and 6 m (20 ft) tall, forms one side of Plantation Lane, with accompanying text on the ground (see p. 352). This is bold architectural art, properly integrated into the project rather than a pointless add-on.

7 LEADENHALL MARKET

Gracechurch Street EC3 • Sir Horace Jones 1880–81

Horace Jones, as City Architect from 1864 to 1887, was responsible for the three new City markets at Billingsgate, Smithfield and Leadenhall, the latter constructed on a site where market trading extends back to the medieval period. (Part of the Roman forum lies beneath.) Built as a largely wholesale market – it was 'a riot of fish and fowl' when Ian Nairn visited it in the 1960s – Leadenhall has been transformed in recent decades into a specialist retail centre, with pubs (notably the historic Lamb Tavern), coffee bars and fashion outlets as well as food shops, all aimed at affluent City workers. The equivalent, in some respects, to the big market halls found in northern cities, it is less a free-standing building than a series of enclosed streets, covered with glass and iron roofs, which merge seamlessly with the fabric of the City, much in the manner of the covered arcades of Cardiff or Leeds. The principal street elevation of the market is to Gracechurch Street, but the delights of Leadenhall are largely internal, culminating in a great central octagon. Jones was no architectural purist, and he used classical motifs freely to create a building that is both functionally efficient and hugely enjoyable for its decorative details, including lots of City of London dragons. The market was extended to the south-west, in a plainer manner, in the late 1880s. The restoration carried out by the City Corporation in 1990–91 highlighted the qualities of the place, reinstating an appropriate colour scheme and restoring original shopfronts. Richard Rogers's Lloyd's Building, which adjoins the north-eastern corner of the market, complements Jones's work, not least because Rogers looked back with admiration at the iron and glass architecture of the 19th century.

The focal point of the new building designed for Leadenhall Market by Horace Jones is the central octagon, where a number of routes through the site meet.

8 LLOYD'S OF LONDON

Leadenhall Street and Lime Street EC3 • Richard Rogers Partnership 1981–6

A quarter of a century after its completion, Richard Rogers's Lloyd's Building remains the most radical – and certainly one of the most visually arresting – of the City's postwar buildings. Lloyd's is not a company but a market where insurance for anything from an art collection to an oil rig can be negotiated – the building, located in a quarter of the City inhabited by big names in insurance such as Willis and SwissRe, is a place where underwriters and brokers meet to do business. Personal contact, as in any marketplace, remains fundamental to its operations. Lloyd's was founded in the 1680s by Edward Lloyd in a coffee house in Tower Street, later relocating to the Royal Exchange in 1774. In the 1920s Lloyd's moved into its own building, designed by Sir Edwin Cooper, on Leadenhall Street. By the 1950s, the expansion of its business led to the construction of another building, across Lime Street, designed by Terence Heysham and opened in 1958. Cooper's building, a handsome classical structure, was

Opposite
Leadenhall Market is no longer the food market it was until quite recently, but has been recast as a specialist shopping centre with cafés and bars that are much used by City workers.

From 1958 until the opening of the Rogers building in 1986, the 'Room' was housed in a handsome classical building on Lime Street by Terence Heysham, but this has now been demolished and replaced by Foster & Partners' Willis Building.

The Lloyd's Building is clad in stainless steel. Richard Rogers's radical designs placed the services – stairs, lifts, lavatories – around the perimeter of the building, with plant housed in giant boxes on top of the service towers.

demolished to make way for Rogers's – the 1958 building was later sold and the site is now occupied by Foster & Partners' Willis Building.

The brief to Rogers, who won an international architectural competition launched in 1977, was to give Lloyd's a building that would serve its needs well into the next century. Flexibility was vital, since it was in the nature of the insurance business to expand and contract. Rogers's strategy was to provide scope for the 'Room', the focus of Lloyd's, to extend onto a series of upper levels, open to the soaring atrium, linked to the principal ground floor space by escalators. The upper floors of the building have always been let to private tenants, largely linked to the insurance market. From mid-morning onwards on any working day, the interior of the building is a scene of intense animation as the market gets to work – in much the way it has always done (though a lot of business is now done electronically). To provide for internal spaces free of service cores Rogers placed lavatories, stairs, lifts and mechanical services in a series of service towers around the perimeter of the building, which is clad in stainless steel. Elements of the Cooper building were incorporated into its successor, including the wood-panelled library. The eleventh-floor Board Room is, bizarrely, a fine interior by Robert Adam, salvaged in the 1950s from the demolished Bowood House in Wiltshire, and relocated here from the 1958 building.

9 MINSTER COURT

Mincing Lane EC3 • GMW Partnership 1987–91

Designed by the practice responsible for the 1960s Aviva (originally Commercial Union) Tower, Minster Court reflects the move away from the confident Modernism of the 1960s to the eclectic Postmodernist experiments of the 1980s. However,

Opposite
Richard Rogers's Lloyd's Building was completed in 1986 on the site of its 1920s predecessor. The lofty galleried interior is the City's most impressive postwar interior. Animated by banks of escalators, it takes inspiration from Paxton's Crystal Palace and the early 20th-century visions of the Futurists.

MOVING UP IN THE WORLD
ISN'T ALWAYS EASY
WWW.LLOYDS.COM/BRIGHTERFUTURES
MOVING UP IN THE WORLD
ISN'T ALWAYS EASY

GMW's Minster Court on Mincing Lane is a classic example of the Postmodernism fashionable in the 1980s but, instead of the more common classical references, the building's style is distinctly Gothic in character.

Looking upwards in the central atrium of the London Underwriting Centre in Minster Court. With its banks of escalators, it is probably the most impressive atrium in the City after Rogers's Lloyd's.

while most Postmodern architecture is a free paraphrase of classicism, Minster Court is clearly Gothic in inspiration. It consists of three buildings around a central glazed courtyard. The largest of them houses the London Underwriting Centre – the centrepiece of this building is a circular atrium, with a bank of escalators 40 m (131 ft) high, suspended on a huge ring beam (an extraordinary work of engineering designed by Anthony Hunt). All the buildings are clad in a mix of marble and granite, with rippling façades, and topped by distinctive pitched roofs. The giant bronze horses (by sculptor Althea Wynne) at the entrance to the complex have been christened Dollar, Pound and Yen. Widely mocked as vulgar and derivative, this building is certainly an example of a style currently out of fashion, and its relationship to the surrounding streets is less than sensitive. But as a one-off oddity it has real presence – in the context of the universal neo-Modernism of more recent City buildings, its eccentricity is quite welcome.

St Olave Hart Street was rebuilt in 1951–4 after severe damage from wartime bombs. The interior contains important monuments, including one to Samuel Pepys's wife.

10 ST OLAVE HART STREET

EC3 • 15th century; E. B. Glanfield 1951–4

St Olave's is another of the medieval churches that survived the Great Fire only to be badly damaged by Second World War bombing – virtually all the fittings were destroyed. It was painstakingly reconstructed in the early 1950s. One of the most attractive features of St Olave's – dedicated to the patron saint of Norway – is its setting in an almost-rustic churchyard, entered from Seething Lane through a gateway decorated with carved skulls and bones. Most of the fabric dates from the 15th century, though there is a 13th-century crypt beneath the nave. The tower was raised in height in 1732, using brick. The interior has real atmosphere, thanks to the sensitive postwar restoration carried out by the architect E. B. Glanfield, who designed most of the new furnishings. The pulpit is from the long-lost Wren church of St Benet Gracechurch. St Olave's was always noted for its wealth of funerary monuments, some of which were moved here from other closed City churches. The earliest is a brass to Lord Mayor Sir Richard Haddon, who died in 1524, and there are some imposing Elizabethan and Jacobean monuments. The memorial to Samuel Pepys's wife (a parishioner) incorporates a portrait bust that was luckily removed from the church before the bombing. Pepys himself, buried under the nave floor, is commemorated by a Victorian tablet – he is credited with saving the church from destruction in the Fire. The vestry, which is attached to the south-east corner of the church, dates from 1661–2. It survived the war relatively intact and retains a fine plaster ceiling and panelling.

11 FENCHURCH STREET STATION

EC3 • George Berkeley 1853–4; Fitzroy Robinson Partnership 1983–7

'This delightful, hidden old terminus', as Betjeman described it, has changed radically since he wrote about it in the early 1970s, when it had been 'less messed about than any London terminus'. The station was built as the terminus of the London and Blackwall Railway, opening in 1841 and the first railway to penetrate the City. It was rebuilt in 1853–4 by George Berkeley, chief engineer to the London, Tilbury & Southend Railway, which shared the enlarged station. Berkeley's brick façade, with eleven arched windows at upper level beneath a curved pediment and a wooden canopy at street level, remains but the rest was completely rebuilt in the 1980s, with five floors of offices now sitting above the tracks – an example of the 'air-rights' developments that transformed other London stations (including the eastern half of Liverpool Street). The loss of the Victorian train shed is regrettable, although the office development is of some structural interest in its own right, with the new floors contained within a steel A-frame supported on concrete beams. This strategy allows the platform areas to be column-free but, as usual with developments of this type, they are low and gloomy – there is not much pleasure to be gained from the new Fenchurch Street.

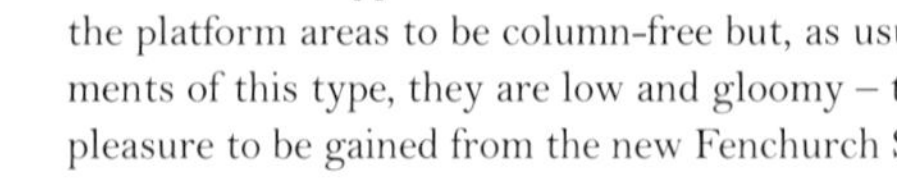

The handsome frontage of Fenchurch Street Station – the first of the City's railway termini – was retained in the 1980s reconstruction that created an 'air-rights' office development over the tracks, a strategy applied to other London stations in recent decades.

12 LLOYD'S REGISTER OF SHIPPING

Fenchurch Street EC3 • T. E. Collcutt 1899–1901; Richard Rogers Partnership 1995–2000

Lloyd's Register – a venerable City institution, quite separate from Lloyd's of London (though with similar 17th-century origins in Edward Lloyd's coffee house) – occupies one of the finest late Victorian buildings in the City, located on the corner of Fenchurch Street and Lloyd's Avenue, which was itself developed to Collcutt's designs. The building is redolent of an age when Britain was the world's greatest maritime power and contains, behind its forcefully Baroque façades (with carved friezes by Sir George Frampton), interiors of great richness, incorporating work by some of the best artists and craftsmen of the period, including tiles by William de Morgan, decorative painting and stained glass by Gerald Moira and Sir Frank Brangwyn, and plasterwork by George Jackson. The committee room, library and chairman's office balance opulence and sobriety in typical City fashion. Richard Rogers was commissioned in the mid-1990s to plan a major extension after plans to move Lloyd's Register out of London were abandoned. The Rogers scheme included a careful restoration of the listed Collcutt building, with the addition of a new conference suite. A new 14-storey building

The Committee Room of T. E. Collcutt's Lloyd's Register is richly decorated and especially notable for its ceiling decorations by Gerald Moira showing the four elements. It is one of a number of outstanding interiors in this lavish late Victorian building.

was slotted in behind retained frontages on Fenchurch Street and Lloyd's Avenue, with access across the former churchyard of St Katharine Coleman. This 18th-century church was sold to Lloyd's Register and demolished in 1925 – its replacement went as part of the Rogers scheme. The Rogers building develops the 'served and servant spaces' strategy of the earlier Lloyd's Building, with service cores boldly expressed as towers, complete with fully glazed lifts, and two dramatic atria providing an internal focus. Double glazing and the addition of motorized louvres to baffle solar gain allowed the building to be fully glazed externally – in fact, it is claimed to be one of the most energy-efficient buildings in the City and is certainly one of the more distinguished recent additions to its building stock.

This aerial view shows how the new building for Lloyd's Register, designed by Richard Rogers, is slotted into a confined site behind Fenchurch Street.

THE LONDON INSURANCE MARKET

Outsiders often assume that the City of London's prime position in the global economy is due to the concentration of banks and other financial institutions within its boundaries. But another area in which the City leads the world is that of insurance, a legacy from the days when London was one of the world's leading ports and the capital of a major maritime trading nation. Lloyd's of London, founded in the late 17th century in a City coffee house, has been the central focus of the London insurance market for centuries. Ships and cargoes were the first commodities to be insured. Fire insurance followed in the wake of the Great Fire – the trauma of this unprecedented disaster led to the establishment of companies (beginning with Nicholas Barbon's Fire Office, founded in 1681) specializing in this area of insurance. They set up their own private fire brigades, and the buildings they insured carried fire marks – a collection of these can be seen in the Museum of London. Life insurance became widely available to a growing middle class during the 19th century. The first motor insurance policies, initially along the lines of those covering horse-drawn vehicles, were issued in 1896. Insurance companies were a major element in the economy of the Victorian City and the headquarters buildings of the Scottish Provident, Royal Insurance, London Life and Commercial Union rivalled in splendour those of the banks.

The quarter of the City east of Gracechurch Street and Bishopsgate, close to Lloyd's, Lloyd's Register and the London Underwriting Centre in Mincing Lane, has developed as the heart of the London insurance sector. The 1960s Commercial Union Tower, now housing Aviva, reflects the wealth of the big insurance companies in the postwar era. Richard Rogers's Lloyd's of London is one of the most spectacular City buildings of the last fifty years. Its next-door neighbour on Lime Street is the headquarters of international insurance giant Willis, a landmark building by Norman Foster, whose Willis Building in Ipswich, completed in 1975, is now Grade I listed. Foster's most famous City building, however, is the 'Gherkin' at no. 30 St Mary Axe, built by the reinsurance company SwissRe, which still has offices there.

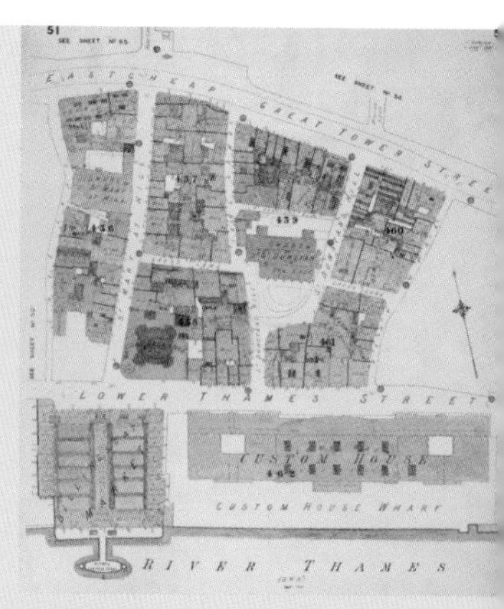

This extract from Goad's 'Insurance Plan of London' (1887) shows the area around Billingsgate Market and Great Tower Street.

Fire insurance became increasingly common in London from the late 17th century onwards. Fire insurance marks on properties showed which company insured them. Those shown here denote the Sun, established in 1710, and the Hand in Hand.

The Willis Building on Lime Street is the London base of one of the world's largest insurance companies and was designed by Norman Foster on a site across the street from Lloyd's.

13 IBEX HOUSE

Minories EC3 • Fuller, Hall & Foulsham 1935–7; Rolfe Judd 1994–5

Art Deco is not a style one associates with the City (though it emerges in Robert Atkinson's foyer for the *Daily Express* in Fleet Street and Fox's umbrella shop on London Wall). But there are certainly strong Deco influences in Ibex House, an excellent example of the Modernistic commercial architecture of the 1930s on the edge of the City: it could be in Los Angeles and certainly enlivens the humdrum expanses of Minories. Faced in glazed faience, Ibex House features long bands of glazing and spectacular centrally placed glazed staircase towers – all within a symmetrical composition which has not met with the approval of Modern movement hardliners. The building was faithfully restored by Rolfe Judd in the 1990s and now houses a number of businesses, along with a health club. Fuller, Hall & Foulsham was a successful commercial practice, working into the 1970s – its projects included the original Beaufort House at Aldgate, demolished in the 1980s.

Ibex House is the largest 1930s commercial complex in the City, Modernistic in style and taking its inspiration more from the USA than from European Art Deco.

The former headquarters of the Port of London Authority is one of a number of monumental London buildings designed by Edwin Cooper. It was vacated by the PLA in 1970, used as offices for nearly forty years and is now set to be converted into a luxury hotel.

14 PORT OF LONDON AUTHORITY (*former*)

Trinity Square EC3 • Sir Edwin Cooper 1912–22

The Port of London Authority was established in 1908, assuming control of London's docks at a time when Britain was still the world's leading maritime power and London was one of the world's greatest ports. The PLA commissioned Edwin Cooper to design a headquarters that reflected its importance – and he did them proud. Cooper's massive tower, set on top of a monumental Corinthian portico, is designed to dominate the surrounding area and be clearly seen from the river. Its completion was delayed by the Great War – the building, however, clad in Portland stone and enriched with quantities of decorative sculpture, oozes Edwardian confidence. The PLA occupied it until 1970 and it was subsequently the London headquarters of insurance giant Willis (now relocated to new offices in Lime Street). Some fine interiors remain, including the board room and a series of committee rooms, all richly wood-panelled. However, the great central rotunda, the fulcrum of Cooper's plan, was infilled with offices in the 1970s. The departure of Willis has opened the way for restoration of the building to its original splendour, for use as a hotel – which seems highly appropriate.

The imposing Corinthian entrance portico of the building rises through three storeys.

The Mercantile Marine Memorial is one of a number of fine memorials to the dead of the First World War designed by Edwin Lutyens – the most famous of them is the Cenotaph in Whitehall. Into both, Lutyens instils dignity and enormous gravity with no hint of triumphalism or sentimentality.

15 MERCANTILE MARINE MEMORIAL

Trinity Square EC3 • Sir Edwin Lutyens 1926–8

Lutyens's first designs for a memorial to the merchant seamen who lost their lives in the First World War were intended for a site on the Embankment, close to the Temple. They were, however, vetoed by the Royal Fine Art Commission, which felt that a site closer to the Port of London was more appropriate. One was found close to the Tower of London and the memorial was unveiled by Queen Mary on 12 December 1928. Lutyens was vexed by the relocation of the memorial but produced new designs that reflect his ability to commemorate the tragedy of war in a dignified way but without any hint of sentimentality or triumphalism. The memorial takes the form of an open temple with plain Doric columns supporting a stone vault. The names of the dead and missing are inscribed on bronze plaques. Adjacent is a memorial to the merchant seamen lost in the Second World War in the form of a sunken garden, designed by Sir Edward Maufe (1952–5), with carved reliefs by Sir Charles Wheeler. Alongside Lutyens's work, Maufe's appears hesitant and somewhat insubstantial.

16 ALL HALLOWS BY THE TOWER

Byward Street EC3 • Anglo-Saxon; Seely & Paget 1957

Also known as All Hallows Barking – it was a daughter church of Barking Abbey in Essex – All Hallows retains the only standing remains of Anglo-Saxon building in the City. A Saxon arch and fragments of walls of pre-Conquest date were discovered after the medieval church was bombed – and largely destroyed – in December 1940, a tragic loss of a significant pre-Fire survivor. The outer walls, 17th-century tower, Victorian porch and undercroft survived and were incorporated into what was virtually a new church designed by Seely & Paget (under Lord Mottistone) and completed in 1957. The ancient origins of the church are

All Hallows by the Tower was almost entirely destroyed by wartime bombs and was rebuilt by the architects Seely & Paget – the fanciful steeple is a distinctive feature.

evident from the Roman pavements and Saxon crosses (again uncovered after the bombing), which can be seen in the undercroft. The postwar reconstruction was bold, with no attempt to replicate what had been lost. A slender spirelet added to the tower is a distinctive feature. The attractive interior is covered by a concrete vault, Gothic in form. The late 17th-century pulpit originates from the destroyed church of St Swithin Cannon Street, which was not rebuilt after war damage (it was also known as St Swithin London Stone, after the ancient distance marker now relocated to no. 111 Cannon Street). Other fittings are a mix of old and new, well arranged to create a rich effect, and there is some decent postwar stained glass. The font cover is a magnificent thing, confidently ascribed to Grinling Gibbons (1682), and stands on a plain postwar font. The monuments include an important late 15th-century tomb chest, carefully restored after the war, commemorating Alderman John Croke, and a collection of late medieval and Tudor brasses unrivalled in the City. The Rev. P. B. ('Tubby') Clayton, incumbent of All Hallows from 1922 to 1962, was the founder of Toc H, an international charitable movement launched to help ex-soldiers after the Great War. His memorial, a recumbent effigy in the church, was completed in 1972. All Hallows is one of the more successful of the postwar City church reconstructions.

Among the contents of All Hallows that survived the wartime Blitz was the remarkable font cover reputedly the work of Grinling Gibbons and certainly an exceptional work of craftsmanship.

17 TOWER OF LONDON

Tower Hill EC3

Fortress, royal palace, mint, menagerie, arsenal, archive, armoury, prison, place of execution: with a history extending back almost a thousand years, the Tower has been all those things in its time. Today it is one of London's biggest tourist attractions, with 2.25 million paying visitors annually. Though located just beyond the boundary of the Square Mile, its history has been closely linked to that of the City over ten centuries.

When William the Conqueror began to construct the Tower, soon after his victory at Hastings in 1066, he intended to overawe the native population and sited the fortress at the south-eastern corner of the City, with the surviving Roman wall enclosing it on two sides. The White Tower, the great keep from which the Tower derives its name, was complete by the end of the 11th century. Even today one can sense the impact this structure must have had when new, towering over the mean timber houses of the City. Neither the fancy turret tops, added in the 1530s, nor the alterations made in subsequent centuries detract from its significance as a symbol of conquest. Never a favoured royal residence, the White Tower was for many centuries primarily a military arsenal. Today it houses spectacular displays of armour – notably that of Henry VIII – and also contains one of the most numinous interiors in London, the chapel of St John, which the Victorians rescued from use as a store for state papers.

The late 15th-century tomb of Alderman John Croke, with its fine fan-vaulted canopy, was repaired after wartime damage to All Hallows and is among the finest medieval funerary monuments in the City.

Between 1190 and the end of the 13th century a succession of monarchs enlarged the Tower as an impregnable fortress contained within two lines of walls, and the royal lodgings, though little used, were expanded and improved. James I was the last monarch to reside in the Tower and then only for a few days. Subsequently abandoned and partly demolished, the royal apartments have now been partly recreated as a convincing evocation of medieval court life. Many of the Tower's best-known residents were kept there against their will – always a state prison, the Tower was most actively used as such in the 16th century, when Anne Boleyn, Thomas More, Lady Jane Grey and Walter Raleigh were among those confined within the walls. For all the popular imagery of the Tower as a place of torture

Opposite
St John's Chapel, within the White Tower, is the most moving space within the Tower of London and one of the most notable Romanesque interiors in Britain.

The external appearance of the Tower owes a good deal to the 're-medievalization' carried out in the 19th century by the architect Anthony Salvin.

and execution, the use of the rack and other such implements was relatively rare, and only seven executions took place within the walls up to the 20th century – the last (by firing squad) was that of a German spy in 1941. The historic place of execution is marked by a modern memorial on Tower Green, outside the Tower's second chapel, St Peter ad Vincula.

The Tower has been a visitor attraction for centuries – the first guidebook was published in 1741. The royal menagerie, a popular draw, was established at least as early as 1214 and survived into the 19th century, when the few animals there were transferred to what became London Zoo in Regent's Park. The Crown Jewels remain the key attraction for many visitors. Their location has changed several times over the centuries, but today they are housed in a specially designed Jewel House in the 19th-century Waterloo Barracks. The Duke of Wellington, victor of Waterloo, was Constable of the Tower when he had the moat (which had surrounded the Tower for six hundred years) drained and filled after it had become little more than a cesspit, 'impregnated with putrid animal and excrementitious matter'. From the 1840s onwards a programme of restoration and 're-medievalization', initiated by the architect Anthony Salvin, removed a number of postmedieval buildings and restored others to their supposedly original condition – much of the Tower's current appearance is a result of this work. Today the Tower is home to a resident community of over a hundred people, including the famous Yeomen Warders (the 'Beefeaters'). Under the management of Historic Royal Palaces, the character of the Tower has been maintained, with facilities such as a decent restaurant that make a day there – and a full day is needed to see everything – a priority for any visitor to London.

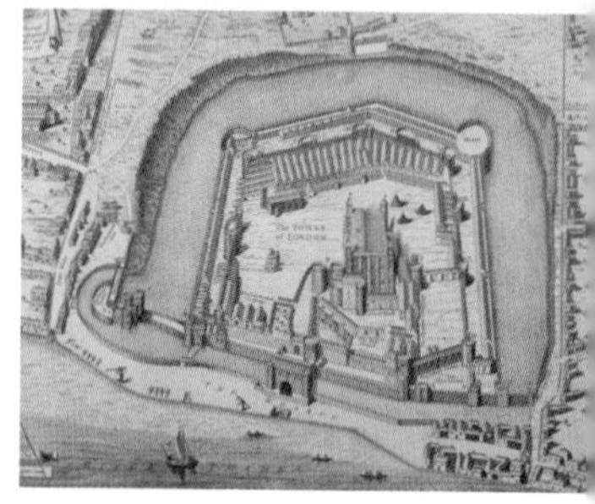

This plan of the Tower in 1597, depicted in an engraving of 1742, shows the moat still in place – it was drained in the 19th century as a danger to health – and details the liberties around the Tower.

Clothed in a Gothic skin, in deference to the nearby Tower, Tower Bridge was a highly sophisticated work of engineering, designed to allow for the regular passage of ships into the Pool of London. Today, the bridge opens only occasionally – to the delight of the countless tourists who pass over it, enjoying fine views of the City and river.

W. L. Wyllie's painting of the opening of Tower Bridge on 30 June 1894 depicts a celebratory scene. There had long been a demand for a river crossing on this stretch of the Thames, linking the City to the wharves and warehouses of Bermondsey.

18 TOWER BRIDGE

EC3 • Horace Jones and John Wolfe Barry 1886–94

Decades of lobbying for a river crossing on the eastern edge of the City preceded the construction of Tower Bridge, finally authorized by Act of Parliament in 1885. The challenge to Horace Jones, the City Architect (who died soon after the start of construction), and his collaborator, the engineer John Wolfe Barry, was to design a bridge that would allow access for shipping to the Pool of London. The solution was a bascule bridge, the central sections of which could be raised to allow the passage of ships. Lifting machinery – powered by hydraulics into the 1970s, when it was converted to electricity – was housed in the towers, which were connected at high level by a pedestrian footbridge, served by passenger lifts, so that City workers could scurry across when the bridge was raised. Today, the raising of the bridge is a rarer occurrence, but a century ago it opened many times on a typical day.

Parliament demanded that the bridge be given a decorative cladding in tune with the nearby Tower; a purely functional structure, which purist critics would have preferred, was out of the question. If the architecture of the bridge has a somewhat Scottish flavour, this can be explained by the involvement of Barry's Scottish assistant, George Stevenson, with the design of the towers. The steelwork underneath the Gothic skin was erected by the Scottish firm also responsible for the Forth Bridge. Tower Bridge long ago became one of the universally recognized, and loved, symbols of London, so that an aesthetic critique seems almost pointless. But the bridge is nothing less than an ingenious fusion of architecture and engineering in the best Victorian tradition.

The Great Fire of London seen from across the Thames in a contemporary engraving.

THE GREAT FIRE OF LONDON

The Great Fire of London began in a bakery on Pudding Lane, just east of London Bridge, in the early hours of Sunday, 2 September 1666. Within the next four days some 13,500 houses, 87 churches and 44 livery halls were destroyed, along with Old St Paul's Cathedral – a catastrophe that left the great majority of the City's inhabitants homeless. The initial spread of the Fire can be blamed on the then Lord Mayor, Sir Thomas Bloodworth, who declined to take action, observing that the conflagration was so minor that 'a woman might piss it out'. By mid-morning, however, the Fire had taken hold and already more than 300 houses and a number of churches had been burned, and the flames also began to engulf London Bridge, which was lined with buildings. Samuel Pepys, a senior official in the Navy Office, rushed off to Whitehall to inform the king of the scale of the disaster. Charles II ordered the Lord Mayor to pull down whole blocks of housing in a bid to halt the spread of the Fire, which was fuelled by strong winds. During the next day, however, it spread to the commercial heart of the City, to Lombard Street and Cheapside, and the Royal Exchange was gutted. Tuesday brought even worse destruction, with St Paul's Cathedral itself engulfed in flames. Thousands of books, stored in the crypt, fed the flames. In the high winds the Fire spread

This gilded figure on the corner of Giltspur Street and Cock Lane marks the point where the Great Fire finally stopped.

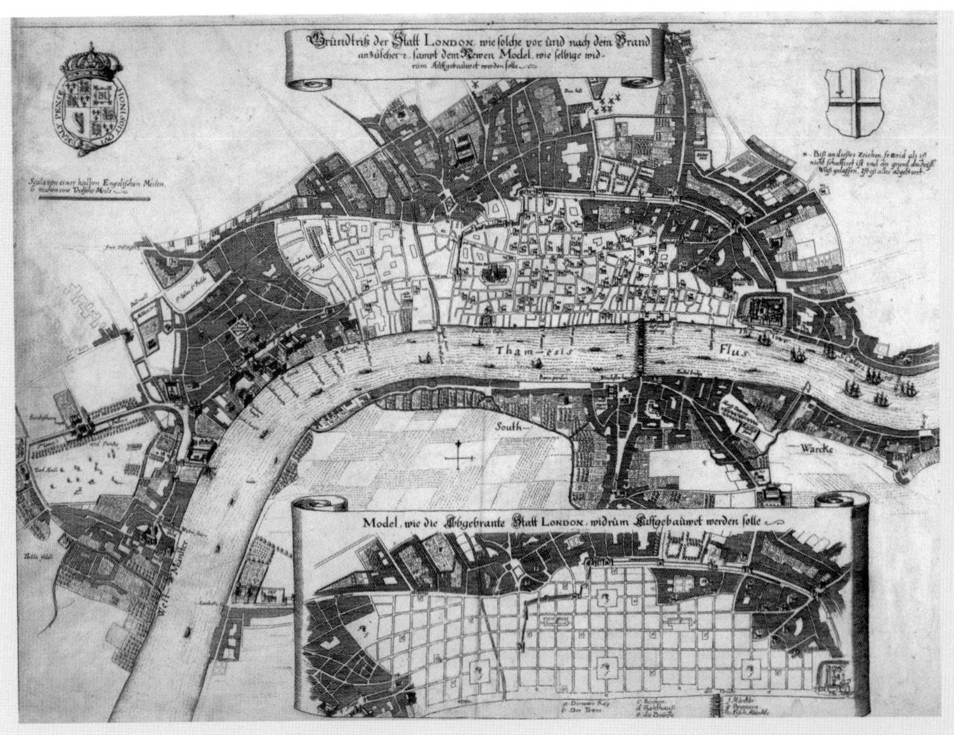

This map, printed in Germany in 1670, provides a graphic record of the extent of the area destroyed by the Great Fire of 1666. The plan at the bottom shows proposals, believed to be the work of the architect and scientist Robert Hooke, for rebuilding the City on a regular grid plan. They were not implemented.

eastwards, stopping short of the Tower – the garrison had blown up hundreds of houses to create a firebreak. By Wednesday 5 September the wind had dropped and the Fire began to abate. Pepys climbed the steeple of All Hallows by the Tower and viewed 'the saddest sight of desolation that I ever saw...Everywhere great fires, oil cellars and brimstone and other things burning'. Huge encampments of desperate refugees were set up in the fields beyond the walls and rumours spread that the Fire was a foreign plot and that an invasion by the French or Dutch was imminent – an innocent Frenchman was hanged for allegedly starting the Fire. The involvement of 'papists' was also suspected and in 1681 an inscription was added to the Monument blaming it on 'the treachery and malice of the Popish faction'. Along with the Monument, completed in 1676, the City has a second monument to the Fire, the Golden Boy at Smithfield, marking the fact that the Fire, begun at Pudding Lane, stopped at Pye Corner. An inscription claims that it was 'Occasion'd by the Sin of Gluttony'. For all the scale of the disaster, rebuilding – on the medieval street plan – took place rapidly, with most of the City's new houses completed by 1672 and Wren and his assistants at work on the new City churches and the new St Paul's.

The gilded urn at the top of the Monument, the work of the sculptor Robert Bird, was the choice of Charles II. Wren had proposed a gilded statue of the King.

Additional Places to Visit

O a Old London Bridge

A fragment of Roman wharf from AD 45, found at Fish Street Hill in 1931, is preserved in the porch of St Magnus the Martyr (pp. 328–9), which was the route down to the old London Bridge, now blocked, though there is a garden on the south side as part of the Riverside Walk (see below).

O b Eastcheap; Philpot Lane

In the shadow of St Margaret Pattens, no. 43 Eastcheap is a very good 18th-century shop with a new front of 1835. Around the corner in Philpot Lane, notice the mice eating cheese on the façade of no. 15, deriving from an incident when a builder accused another of eating his lunch, and fell from the building – but the mice were to blame. Through no. 7 is Brabant Court, which has one interesting house at no. 4. Across the road is the site of the Rafael Viñoly 'Walkie-talkie' (see introduction, p. 322).

O c Plantation Lane

This newly formed pathway runs through the block behind St Margaret Pattens church to the entrance of the faux-Gothic Minster Court (pp. 334–7) in Mincing Lane, behind Plantation Place (pp. 330–31). The finely integrated artwork, conceived by Simon Patterson (b. 1967) and Arup Associates, called *Time and Tide* (2005), includes a fascinating collection of texts and titles and dates relevant to the City inset into the stone pavements in a series of disappearing arcs: an evocative site that could do with more visible interpretation.

O d Fen Court

Off Fenchurch Street, in Fen Court, a quiet passage that was the churchyard of St Gabriel Fenchurch, is a major artwork of 2008 by Michael Visocchi (b. 1977) and the poet Lemn Sissay: *Gilt of Cain* remembers the part played by City sermons in the anti-slavery movement. Seventeen stylized sugar-cane stems stand by a slave auctioneer's pulpit, all inscribed with Sissay's poetry, which combines references to the Stock Exchange with the Old Testament. It was unveiled by Archbishop Desmond Tutu to commemorate the bicentenary in 2007 of the abolition of the transatlantic slave trade.

O e Roman basilica

The hairdressing salon of Nicholson and Griffin at the entrance to Leadenhall Market (p. 333), no. 90 Gracechurch Street, boasts a 'historic site' in the basement: a surviving pillar of the Roman basilica, which was reputedly the largest building north of the Alps in AD 150. It was part of the huge forum that filled this area in the second century.

O f St Dunstan-in-the-East Garden

One of the City's hidden gems, between Idol Lane and St Dunstan's Hill, this superbly atmospheric garden was created in 1967–71 by the City, in the remains of the church after it was bombed in the Blitz. Under the exquisitely arching Wren steeple survive the walls of David Laing's church of 1817–21: a wide range of plants wind around the ruined windows, creating a range of colour at many times of the year.

O g Seething Lane Gardens

By Pepys Street, gardens mark the spot where Samuel Pepys worked in the Navy Office, with a 1983 bust of him by Karin Jonzen (1914–98). Across the road is the beautifully kept garden of St Olave Hart Street (p. 337), the church where Pepys and his wife are buried.

O h Portsoken Street Garden

On the eastern edge of the City, this garden was founded in 1936 for the local community, with playground equipment. The area is within the Tower of London World Heritage Site.

O i London Wall; Tower Subway; Tower Place

Some remains of the Roman wall can be seen north of the Tower of London, on Tower Hill and at Cooper's Row in the courtyard of the former Midland House. A small brick tower on Tower Hill near the Tower of London ticket office is the entrance to the white-tiled second tunnel under the Thames, built in 1869 and used by 20,000 passengers a week before the opening of Tower Bridge. Opposite Tower Place, on the corner of Byward Street and Great Tower Street, is the Hung, Drawn and Quartered pub, with an inscription from Pepys's diary for 1660: 'I went to see Major General Harrison Hung Drawn and Quartered. He was looking as cheerful as any man could in that condition.'

O j Riverside Walk East

From Riverside Walk West at London Bridge (see area 7, p. 317), the walk goes east past St Magnus the Martyr (pp. 328–9), taking in the twin gardens of Grant's Quay and Dark House Walk. Then it passes the old Billingsgate Fish Market and goes along a wooden walkway in front of the Custom House (p. 329) under an avenue of trees, then to Sugar Quay Walk and a new development at Three Quays Walk, emerging into Tower Place by the entrance to the Tower of London, finely renewed in 2004.

Practical Information

Visitors are advised to check details on the relevant websites, and to make contact for information when opening may be limited at short notice.

The City of London Guides run regular tours starting from the City Information Centre (see below), including the Top 10 City Sights on Wednesday and Sunday at 2pm, for which there is a charge.
www.cityoflondontouristguides.com

City churches are most often open Mondays to Fridays, with some staffed by Friends of the City Churches, 11am–3pm.
www.london-city-churches.org.uk

The City of London Festival mounts concerts in churches and livery halls both during the festival and at other times.
www.colf.org

City livery halls are not normally open to the public but have occasional events and exhibitions.

The Open House Weekend across London in September each year enables special openings of buildings.
www.londonopenhouse.org

Bank of England, Bank of England Museum p. 152
Open Monday to Friday, 10am–5pm. Admission free.
www.bankofengland.co.uk/museum

Barbican Centre p. 219
Open Monday to Saturday, 9am–11pm, Sunday and bank holidays, 12 noon–11pm; for architecture tours, venue times and charges see website.
www.barbican.org.uk

Bishopsgate Institute p. 257
Offers a wide variety of talks and courses: reception and box office open Monday to Friday, 9am–8.30pm, Saturday, 10am–5.30pm; Library hours vary.
www.bishopsgate.org.uk

Broadgate p. 245
Events and activities, including a winter skating rink. Admission charged for some events.
www.broadgateinfo.net

Central Criminal Court p. 79
There is no public access to the precincts but the public court galleries are open Monday to Friday, 10am–1pm and 2pm–5pm (approx).
www.hmcourts-service.gov.uk/xhibit/centralcriminalcourt.htm

City of London Information Centre p. 89
Open Monday to Saturday, 9.30am–5.30pm, Sunday, 10am–4pm.
www.visitthecity.co.uk/cic

College of Arms p. 88
The exhibition is open Monday to Friday, 10am–4pm. Admission free.
www.college-of-arms.gov.uk

Dr Johnson's House p. 47
Open Monday to Saturday, 11am–5pm (5.30pm in summer). Entrance fee.
www.drjohnsonshouse.org

Goldsmiths' Hall p. 111
Open twice a year for exhibitions, and tours may be booked at other times. Entrance fee for some exhibitions.
www.thegoldsmiths.co.uk

Gresham College p. 44
A wide variety of free talks and lectures.
www.gresham.ac.uk

Guildhall p. 128
Usually open to the public Monday to Saturday, 10am–5pm (May–September) and 10am–5pm (October–April). It can, however, close when it is being used for events. Admission free.
www.cityoflondon.gov.uk/guildhall
There are guided tours once a month on the days of Court of Common Council meetings, 10.45am–12 noon. Small charge, book in advance.
www.cityoflondontouristguides.com

Guildhall Art Gallery and Roman Amphitheatre p. 128
Open Monday to Saturday, 10am–5pm, Sunday, 12 noon–4pm. Admission free. Entrance fee for some exhibitions.
www.guildhallartgallery.cityoflondon.gov.uk

Guildhall Complex: Clockmakers' Museum, p. 128
Open Monday to Saturday, 9.30am–4.45pm.
Admission free.
www.clockmakers.org

Guildhall School of Music & Drama p. 224
Many lunchtime and evening events.
Admission charged for some events.
www.gsmd.ac.uk

Leadenhall Market p. 333
Usually open 24 hours a day; shops Monday to Friday, times vary.
www.cityoflondon.gov.uk/Leadenhall

London Silver Vaults p. 42
The shops are open Monday to Friday, 9am–5.30pm, Saturday, 9am–1pm.
www.thesilvervaults.com

Mansion House p. 295
Open for tours weekly on Tuesdays at 2pm, except in August and on public holidays, for which there is a charge. Book in advance.
www.cityoflondontouristguides.com

Middle Temple p. 32
Open to the public Monday to Friday, 10am–11.30am and 3pm–4pm. Admission free.
www.middletemple.org.uk

Monument p. 326
Open daily 9.30am–5.30pm (last admission 5pm).
Entrance fee.
www.themonument.info

Museum of London p. 208
Open Monday to Sunday, 10am–6pm.
Admission free.
www.museumoflondon.org.uk

One New Change p. 286
Core opening hours, including the public roof garden, are Monday to Wednesday and Friday, 10am–7pm, Thursday, 10am–8pm, Saturday, 10am–6pm, Sunday, 12 noon–6pm, store hours vary.
www.onenewchange.com

Royal Exchange p. 172
The stores are open Monday to Friday, 10am–6pm, and the bars and restaurants 8am–11pm.
www.theroyalexchange.com

St Bartholomew's Hospital p. 195
Guided tours on Friday at 2pm. Small charge, book in advance.
www.cityoflondontouristguides.com

St Bartholomew's Hospital Museum p. 195
Open Tuesday to Friday, 10am–4pm. Admission free.
www.bartsandthelondon.nhs.uk/st-bartholomew-s-museum

St Bartholomew-the-Great p. 192
Open for services and paid admission for tourists, Monday to Friday, 8.30am–5pm (4pm November–February), Saturday, 10.30–4pm, Sunday, 8.30am–8pm.
www.greatstbarts.com

St Paul's Cathedral p. 94
Usually open to visitors Monday to Saturday, 8.30am–4pm. Entrance fee. Services at other times.
www.stpauls.co.uk

Smithfield Market p. 190
A tour takes place monthly on a Wednesday at 7am. Small charge, book in advance.
www.cityoflondontouristguides.com

Temple Church of St Mary p. 36
Open for services and events and daily openings for paid admission, times vary.
www.templechurch.com

Tower Bridge p. 349
The exhibition is open 10am–6.30pm daily (April–September) and 9.30am–6pm daily (October–March). Entrance fee.
www.towerbridge.org.uk

Tower of London p. 346
Open Tuesday to Saturday, 9am–5.30pm (4.30pm November–February), Sunday to Monday, 10am–5.30pm (4.30pm November–February).
Entrance fee.
www.hrp.org.uk/TowerOfLondon

Wood Street Police Station: City Police Museum p. 119
Open Tuesday and Wednesday, 10am–4pm, Friday, 10am–2pm. Admission free.
www.citypolicemuseum.org.uk

Further Reading

Abramson, Daniel M., *Building the Bank of England: Money, Architecture, So ciety, 1694–1942*, London and New Haven: Yale University Press, 2005

Amery, Colin, Richardson, Margaret and Stamp, Gavin, *Lutyens: The Work of the English Architect Sir Edwin Lutyens (1869–1944)*, London: Hayward Gallery/Arts Council of England, 1981

Barson, Susie and Saint, Andrew, *A Farewell to Fleet Street*, London: English Heritage/Historic Buildings and Monuments Commission for England/ Allison & Busby, 1988

Beattie, Susan, *The New Sculpture*, London and New Haven: Yale University Press, 1983

Betjeman, John (ed.), *Collins Guide to English Parish Churches*, London: Collins, 1958

Betjeman, John, *London's Historic Railway Stations*, London: John Murray, 1972

Bone, James, *The London Perambulator*, London: Jonathan Cape, 1926

Booker, John, *Temples of Mammon: The Architecture of Banking*, Edinburgh: Edinburgh University Press, 1990

Bradley, Simon and Pevsner, Nikolaus, *The Buildings of England, London 1: The City of London*, London: Penguin, 1997; repr. New Haven and London: Yale University Press, 2002

Brown, Jane, *Lutyens and the Edwardians: An English Architect and His Clients*, London: Viking Penguin, 1997

Bumpus, T. Francis, *London Churches Ancient and Modern*, 2 vols, 2nd edn, London: T. Werner Laurie, 1908

Burdett, Richard (ed.), *City Changes: Architecture in the City of London, 1985–1995*, London: Corporation of London/ The Architecture Foundation, 1992

Campbell, James W. P., *Building St Paul's*, London: Thames & Hudson, 2008

Cherry, Gordon and Penny, Leith, *Holford, a Study in Planning and Civic Design*, London: Mansell, 1986

City Architecture Forum and Architects' Journal, *City Architecture: Redesigning the City of London 1991–2011*, London: Emap Inform, 2011

The City of London: A Record of Destruction and Survival, London: Corporation of London/Architectural Press, 1951

Clarke, Basil F. L., *Parish Churches of London*, London: Batsford, 1966

Cobb, Gerald, *London City Churches*, 3rd edn, London: Batsford, 1989

—, *The Old Churches of London*, London: Batsford, 1942

Colvin, Howard, *A Biographical Dictionary of British Architects*, 4th edn, London and New Haven: Yale University Press, 2008

Cookson, Brian, *Crossing the River: The History of London's Bridges from Richmond to the Tower*, Edinburgh: Mainstream, 2006

Davies, Matthew P. and Saunders, Ann, *The History of the Merchant Taylors Company*, Leeds: Maney, 2004

Denison, Edward, *McMorran and Whitby*, London: RIBA Publishing, 2009

Don't Butcher Smithfield: The Threat to Britain's Finest Group of Market Buildings, London: SAVE Britain's Heritage, 2003

Downes, Kerry, *Sir Christopher Wren: The Design of St Paul's Cathedral*, London: Trefoil Publications, 1988

Evinson, Denis, *Catholic Churches of London*, Sheffield: Sheffield Academic Press, 1998

Fox, Celina (ed.), *London: World City 1800–1840*, London and New Haven: Yale University Press/Museum of London, 1992

Frayn, Michael, *Towards the End of the Morning*, London: Collins, 1967

French, Hilary, *Key Urban Housing of the Twentieth Century*, London: Laurence King, 2008

Friedman, Terry, Linstrum, Derek, Read, Benedict, Rooke, Daru and Upton, Helen, *The Alliance of Sculpture and Architecture: Hamo Thornycroft, John Belcher and the Institute of Chartered Accountants Building* (Studies in the History of Sculpture 3), Leeds: Henry Moore Centre for the Study of Sculpture, Leeds City Art Galleries, 1993

Girouard, Mark, *Elizabethan Architecture*, London and New Haven: Yale University Press, 2009

Griffiths, Dennis, *Fleet Street: Five Hundred Years of the Press*, London: British Library, 2006

Hare, Susan M., *Goldsmiths' Hall in the City of London*, 2nd edn, Norwich: Jarrold Publishing, 1996

Harwood, Elain, *Chamberlin, Powell and Bon*, London: RIBA Publishing, 2011

Harwood, Elain and Saint, Andrew, *London*, London: HMSO/ English Heritage, 1991

Heathcote, David, *Barbican: Penthouse over the City*, Chichester: John Wiley, 2004

Hill, Rupert, *Walking London's Statues and Monuments*, London: New Holland, 2010

Houfe, Simon, Powers, Alan and Wilton-Ely, John, *Sir Albert Richardson 1880–1964*, London: RIBA Heinz Gallery, 1999

Howard, Rachel and Nash, Bill: *Secret London, An Unusual Guide*, Versailles: Jonglez, 2009

Hunting, Penelope, *A History of the Drapers Company*, London: The Drapers Company, 1989

Impey, Edward and Parnell, Geoffrey, *The Tower of London: The Official Illustrated History*, rev. edn, London: Merrell/ Historic Royal Palaces, 2006

Jackson, Alan A., *London's Termini*, Newton Abbot: David & Charles, 1969

Jackson, Nicola, *The Story of Paternoster, a New Square for London*, London: Wordsearch, 2003

Jeffrey, Paul, *The City Churches of Sir Christopher Wren*, London: Hambledon Press, 1996

Jeffrey, Sally, *The Mansion House*, London: Phillimore/ Corporation of London, 1993

Keene, Derek, Burns, Arthur and Saint, Andrew (eds), *St Paul's: The Cathedral Church of London, 604–2004*, London and New Haven: Yale University Press, 2004

Kynaston, David, *City of London: The History*, London: Chatto & Windus, 2011

—, *The City of London: Volume 2: Golden Years, 1890–1914*, London: Chatto & Windus, 1995

—, *The City of London: Volume 3: Illusions of Gold, 1914–1945*, London: Chatto & Windus, 1999

Latham, Robert and Matthews, William, *The Diary of Samuel Pepys*, 11 vols, London: Bell (vol. 11 Bell & Hyman), 1970–83

Long, David, *Hidden City: The Secret Alleys, Courts & Yards of London's Square Mile*, Stroud: The History Press, 2011

Mantel, Hilary, *Wolf Hall*, London: Fourth Estate, 2009

Matthews, Peter, *London's Bridges*, Botley: Shire, 2008

Morgan, Dewi, *Phoenix of Fleet Street: 2000 Years of St Bride's*, London: C. Knight, 1973

Nairn, Ian, *Modern Buildings in London*, London: London Transport, 1964

—, *Nairn's London*, Harmondsworth: Penguin, 1968

—, *Nairn's London: Revisited by Peter Gasson*, London: Penguin, 1988

Nokes, David, *Samuel Johnson: A Life*, London: Faber, 2009

Park, David and Griffith-Jones, Robin (eds), *The Temple Church in London*, Woodbridge: Boydell Press, 2010

Pearson, Lynn F., *British Breweries: An Architectural History*, London: Hambledon Press, 1999

Pevsner, Nikolaus, *A History of Building Types*, London: Thames & Hudson, 1976

Piper, David, *The Companion Guide to London*, London: Collins, 1964

Powell, Kenneth, *Lloyd's Building*, London: Phaidon, 1994

—, *New London Architecture*, London: Merrell, 2001

—, *30 St Mary Axe: A Tower for London*, London: Merrell, 2006

—, *21st Century London: The New Architecture*, London: Merrell, 2011

Powell, Kenneth with Strongman, Cathy, *New London Architecture 2*, London: Merrell, 2007

Powers, Alan, 'The Murals of Frank Brangwyn', in Horner, Libby and Naylor, Gillian (eds), *Frank Brangwyn 1867–1956*, Leeds: Leeds Museum and Art Galleries, 2006, pp. 70–97

Price, John, *Postman's Park: G. F. Watts's Memorial to Heroic Self-Sacrifice*, Compton, Surrey: Watts Gallery, 2008

Read, Ben, *Victorian Sculpture*, London and New Haven: Yale University Press, 1982

Saint, Andrew et al., *London Suburbs*, London: Merrell/English Heritage, 1999

Save the City: A Conservation Study of the City of London, London: Joint Committee of Amenity Societies, 1976

Service, Alastair, *London 1900*, London: Granada, 1979

Stamp, Gavin, *The Changing Metropolis: Earliest Photographs of London, 1839–1879*, London: Viking, 1984

Stamp, Gavin and Amery, Colin, *Victorian Buildings of London, 1837–1887: An Illustrated Guide*, London: Architectural Press, 1980

Sumeray, Derek and Sheppard, John, *London Plaques*, Oxford: Shire Publications, 2010

Summerson, John, *Architecture in Britain 1530–1830*, Harmondsworth: Penguin, 1953

—, *Georgian London*, new edn, London: Barrie & Jenkins, 1988

—, *The London Building World of the Eighteen-sixties*, London: Thames & Hudson, 1973

—, 'The Victorian Rebuilding of the City of London 1840–1870', in *The Unromantic Castle and Other Essays*, London: Thames & Hudson, 1990

Symondson, Anthony, *Stephen Dykes Bower*, London: RIBA Publishing, 2011

Thornbury, Walter, *Old and New London*, London: Cassell, Petter, Galpin & Co., 1878

Tinniswood, Adrian, *By Permission of Heaven: The Story of the Great Fire of London*, London: Jonathan Cape, 2003

Tyack, Geoffrey, *Sir James Pennethorne and the Making of Victorian London*, Cambridge: Cambridge University Press, 1992

Ward-Jackson, Philip, *Public Sculpture in the City of London*, Liverpool: Liverpool University Press, 2003

Webb, E. A., *Records of St Bartholomew's Priory and of the Church and Parish of St Bartholomew the Great, Smithfield*, 2 vols, Oxford: Oxford University Press, 1921

Weinreb, Ben, Hibbert, Christopher, Keay, Julia and Keay, John, *The London Encyclopaedia*, 3rd edn, London: Macmillan, 2008

Wolmar, Christian, *The Subterranean Railway*, London: Atlantic Books, 2004

Wren, Stephen, *Parentalia, or Memoirs of the Family of the Wrens*, London: T. Osborn, 1750; repr. Farnborough: Gregg Press International, 1965

Websites

www.visitthecity.co.uk
www.lordmayorshow.org
www.cityoflondon.gov.uk
www.london-city-churches.org.uk
www.museumoflondon.org.uk
http://collage.cityoflondon.gov.uk

Picture Credits

b=below, c=centre, l=left, r=right, t=top

© City of London, Guildhall Art Gallery: Egbert van Heemskerk the Younger, *Bartholomew Fair*, oil on canvas 181t; William Lionel Wyllie, *The Opening of Tower Bridge, 30 June 1894* (detail), 1894–5, oil on canvas, 122 × 213 cm (48 × 83¾ in.) 349r

© City of London, London Metropolitan Archives: *South view of the Tower of London with boats on the River Thames* (detail), *c.* 1800, engraving 12r; 15; S. Gribelin, *View of St Paul's Cathedral* (detail), 1702, engraving 16; *Elevation and Plan of Newgate Prison, Old Bailey*, *c.* 1775, engraving 17; *View of Mansion House with Cornhill*, *c.* 1750, engraving 18t; 18b; 19; Photo Arthur Cross & Fred Tibbs (1942) 20–21; 22; *West view of St-Dunstan-in-the-West, Fleet Street with Temple Bar*, 1812, aquatint 28t; Arthur Croft, *View of Holborn Viaduct from Farringdon Street, looking south*, *c.* 1867, watercolour on paper 28b; Sulman, *Bird's-eye view of Fleet St and Ludgate Hill (to St Paul's and Cheapside)*, *c.* 1890, wood engraving 29; *The Temple Bar Memorial*, 1880,wood engraving 32t; Johannes Kip, *Bird's-eye view of Inner Temple and Middle Temple showing their proximity to the River Thames*, *c.* 1700, engraving 34t; 36t; 43t; John Crowther, *Interior of Gresham College, Barnard's Inn*, 1885, watercolour 44b; John Chessell Buckler, *North-east view of St Andrew Holborn*, 1804, aquatint 45t; 47b; 48b; 50; 51; 52t; 52b; *Daily Telegraph 10-Feeder Printing Machine*, 1860, wood engraving 53t; John Donowell, *Perspective view of the north-west front of St Bride*, 1753, engraving 54; John O'Connor, *View of the Victoria Embankment and the River Thames from Somerset House*, 1873, engraving 57t; *Lud Gate*, 1805, engraving 68t; 68b; Thomas Shotter Boys, *View looking up Ludgate Hill towards St Paul's Cathedral*, 1842, lithograph 69; 70t; Geoffrey Fletcher, Drawing of an Art Nouveau detail on the Black Friar public house 72t; 73b; *Aerial view of Charterhouse*, 1800, engraving 74t; *The Gateway in Charterhouse with a Monk in the Carthusian Habit*, *c.* 1800, engraving 74b; *View of Archway of Blackfriars Monastery in Water Lane, Blackfriars*, 1800, wood engraving 75; 76t; George Shepherd, *View of the Stationers' Hall from the Courtyard*, *c.* 1810, watercolour 78t; 79b; Joseph Smith, *View of the City of London across the River Thames from the south* (detail), 1710, engraving 84t; John Coney, *View of St Nicholas Cole Abbey and Knightrider Street*, 1812, engraving 90l; 90r; 91b; 92b; 96; Thomas Hosmer Shepherd, *View of King Street, looking north from Cheapside to the Guildhall*, *c.* 1840, watercolour 104; 105;106l; Photo Arthur Cross & Fred Tibbs (1942) 106r; 113t; 118r; Henry Edward Tidmarsh, *View of St Mary Aldermanbury's east end*, 1897, watercolour 120r; 125b; *A snug meeting to get up an ultra-loyal address, or a peep at the Tag Rag and Bob-tail; a City ward or precinct meeting, presided over by Thomas Tegg in a loyal address to George IV*, 1821, etching 126; Thomas Hosmer Shepherd, *Front view of Guildhall, looking north, with coach and figures in Guildhall Yard*, 1855, engraving 127t; *Interior View of the Council Chamber in the Guildhall*, *c.*1880, pencil & wash 127b; Henry Edward Tidmarsh, *View of St Lawrence Jewry and Guildhall*, *c.* 1895, watercolour 131r; *St Lawrence Jewry, interior*, 1891, wood engraving 132l; John Crowther, *View of St Olave Jewry, looking from Ironmonger Lane*, 1887, watercolour 135tr; 136b; Augustus Charles Pugin & Thomas Rowlandson, *Interior view of Corn Exchange, Mark Lane* (detail), 1808, aquatint 140; 141t; 141b; John Thomas Smith, *View of Great Winchester Street looking towards London Wall*, 1814, engraving 148; 149t; Photo Arthur Cross & Fred Tibbs (1941) 150; *Plan of the Bank of England, highlighting those areas related to issue, public debt and banking*, *c.* 1840, lithograph 152; 157t; Augustus Charles Pugin & Thomas Rowlandson, *Interior view of the Great Hall at the Bank of England* (detail), 1809, aquatint 157b; John Coney, *Southwest view of St Margaret Lothbury*, *c.* 1815, engraving 159t; 159b; 167b; 168; 172b; 180; Augustus Charles Pugin & Thomas Rowlandson, *Bird's-eye view of Smithfield Market*, 1811, aquatint 181b, *Front view of Thanet House, Aldersgate Street*, *c.* 1750, engraving 182; John Ogilby, *Map of the City of London* (detail), 1676, engraving 184t; 184b; 185; Photo Henry Dixon 186; John Coney, *View of St Bartholomew-the-Less*, 1814, engraving 194t; *Aerial view of St Bartholomew's Hospital*, 1723, engraving 195; Robert Randoll, *Interior view of Christ Church, Newgate Street*, 1896, drawing 199r; Robert Blemmell Schnebbelie, *Bastion of London Wall near Monkwell Street*, 1840, lithograph 202; 204; Robert West, *Northeast view of St Botolph Aldersgate*, *c.* 1740, engraving 208; 212r; Photo Arthur Cross & Fred Tibbs (1942) 217t; 217b; Mary Ann Hedger, *East front of St Alphage London Wall*, *c.* 1830, pen & ink drawing 230t; 238t; 238b; George Arnald, *View of Old Bethlehem Hospital, Moorfields*, 1811, watercolour 239t; 239b; 240b; 242t; 242b; 249t; William Abbott, *Map of the Metropolitan extension of the London, Chatham and Dover Railway showing its connection with the Midland and Great Northern Railways*, 1870, lithograph 255t; *View of Leathersellers' Hall, St Helen's Place, as erected 1820–22*, 1871, lithograph 264l; 271b; Photo James D. Willis (1958) 272; Joseph Skelton, *View of St Katherine Cree*, 1813, engraving 274t; 274b; 282; Charles Rivière, *View of Mansion House and surrounding area* (detail), *c.* 1854, lithograph 283t; John O'Connor, *View of Cannon Street Station and Cannon Street Railway Bridge with boats on the River Thames. Also showing the City of London Brewery Company Building*, 1867, engraving 283b; 284; 285t; 288b; *Interior view of St Mary Aldermary* (detail), 1878, wood engraving 290; *Interior view of the Egyptian Hall, Mansion House, during a banquet* (detail), 1795, engraving 295r; 296; 298; George Shepherd, *North-west view of St Mary Woolnoth*, 1812, watercolour 299t; Robert Randoll, *Interior view of St Mary Woolnoth, looking north east*, 1902, pencil drawing 299b; William Monk, *View of King William Street, looking southeast from London Life Association Office*, 1913, etching 300t; *View of St Mary Abchurch, Abchurch Lane* (detail), *c.* 1760, engraving 300b; 303; 304; Thomas Hosmer Shepherd, *View of the Dyers' Hall, College Street*, 1830, engraving 306; John Crowther, *Interior view of the Cedar Room, Skinners' Hall*, 1890, watercolour 307b; 309t; John Coney, *View of St James Garlickhithe*, 1811, watercolour 309b; John Crowther, *Interior view of the Vintners' Hall, Upper Thames Street* (detail), 1880, watercolour 310b; *Bird's-eye view of London from Somerset Gardens, in the City of Westminster showing the River Thames and the City of London in the centre* (detail), 1760, engraving 314; John Outhett, *Map of the City of Westminster, City of London, River Thames, Lambeth, Southwark and surrounding areas* (detail), 1821, engraving 315t; 315b; B. Sly, *Interior view of the Coal Exchange*, 1849, wood engraving 322t; 322b; 325; Thomas Hosmer Shepherd, *View of the Custom House from the River Thames*, 1854, lithograph 329; Thomas Hosmer Shepherd, *View of St Mary-at-Hill*, *c.* 1825, engraving 330t; 334l; 340t; Joel Gascoyne & William Haiward, *Plan of the Tower of London, Tower Hill and east Smithfield surveyed in 1597* (detail), 1742, engraving 348b; *View of the Great Fire of London seen from across the River Thames*, 1666, engraving 350t

Photo City of London, London Metropolitan Archives. © Country Life 70b

Photo © Cityscape/KPF 2, 263r

© Crossrail 255b

Photo courtesy Terry Farrell & Partners 229

© Fletcher Priest Architects/Tim Soar 312

Henry Frith, Illustration from *The Flying Horse, The Story of the Locomotive and the Railway*, Griffith Farran & Co., 1893 254
Photo courtesy Heron International 224r
Illustrated London News, 5 July 1882 53b
Courtesy The Leathersellers' Company 167t, 264r
© 2011 Chris Lee 220t, 222
Museum of London 11, 209t, 209b, 340bl, 340br, 351t; © John Chase 10, 221; © Amédée Forestier 13; © Frans Franken 14; © Peter Froste 12l; © Henry Grant Collection 171r; © Richard Stroud 332
A Parallel of some of the principal Towers and Steeples built by Sir Christopher Wren, from *London*, vol. 2, edited by Charles Knight, London, 1842, p.12 85b
Photo courtesy Eric Parry Architects 121
Photo © Pipers, London 262
Courtesy The Worshipful Company of Plaisterers 116l, 116r
Photo Matt Stuart. Courtesy the Barbican Centre 223t
© VIEW: Julian Abrams 84b, 109, 113b, 118l, 132r, 135tl, 136t, 215; David Borland 77, 115t, 158t, 158b, 161, 164, 165, 230b, 258, 304–305; James Brittain 60–61; Daniel Clements 97, 194b, 196, 197, 198; Peter Cook 24, 30, 35t, 36b, 37, 38t, 38b, 39, 40, 48t, 188, 335, 336b, By kind permission of The Honourable Society of the Inner Temple 32b, 34b, 35b; Edward Denison, 2011 81t, 119l, 119r; Siobhan Doran 33, 79t, 93t, 199l, 261b, 265, 267t, 267b, 350b; Dennis Gilbert 86l, 86r, 91t, 94b, 95, 212l, 214, 216l, 218, 220b, 224l, 226, 245, 247, 256, 261t, 269, 270, 271t, 330b, 331, 339; Nick Guttridge 108; Fisher Hart 160t, 160b, 169t, 169b, 170l, 170r; Luke Hayes 244, 257b, 259, 328r, 343t, 343b; Tim James Hufton + Crow 243t, 243b; Tim James 86–87, 114b; Quintin Lake 155t, 155b, 187l, 187r, 200, 201l, 201r, 205t, 205b, 210, 211, 231t, 231b; Raf Makda 151, 219, 324; Peter Mackinven 189t, 189b; Von Goetz Monheim/Artur 323; James Morris 38c, 64, 71, 72b, 73t, 78b, 80, 81b, 82t, 82b, 83, 85t, 88t, 88b, 92t, 93b, 120l, 149b, 153, 154t, 154b, 176, 191, 192, 193, 206–207, 266, 273, 293, 294, 318, 328l, 345, 346t, 346b, 347, 348t; Kilian O'Sullivan 144, 172t, 173l, 173r, 252, 253t, 253b; Logan Macdougall Pope 42, 122, 122–123, 134, 137, 138t, 138b, 139, 156, 171l, 246, 248, 249b, 250–251, 275, 305, 344; Paul Raftery 100, 115b, 128, 129, 130, 131l, 135b, 203, 285b, 286t, 286b, 289, 301, 302, 307t, 310t, 311, 312–313, 313; Paul Riddle 31, 43b, 47t, 49, 55, 56, 57b, 58, 125t; Nick Rochowski 162tl, 162tr, 162b, 163, 166, 288t, 334r, 341; Michael Rosenfeld/Artur 349l; Grant Smith 111t, 133, 234, 240t, 241, 260, 268, 272–273, 308, 327, 336t, 337, 338, 338–339, 342; Andy Stagg 23, 41t, 41b, 44t, 45b, 46, 76b, 94t, 110, 111b, 112t, 112b, 124t, 124b, 190, 213, 225, 278, 287, 291, 292t, 292b, 295l, 326t, 326b, 333, 351b; Edmund Sumner 59, 107, 114t, 223b, 257t; Paul Tyagi 117; Nathan Willock 89, 183, 216r, 227, 228
Courtesy Rafael Viñoly Architects 263l
Yale Center for British Art, New Haven. Paul Mellon Collection: Canaletto, *London: Westminster Bridge from the north on Lord Mayor's Day*, 1746–7, oil on canvas, 95.8 × 127.5 cm (37¾ × 50¼ in.) 297

Acknowledgments

The Editor would like to thank:

Chris Duffield, Town Clerk, and Peter Lisley, Assistant Town Clerk, City of London Corporation; David Pearson, Director Libraries, Archives and Guildhall Art Gallery; Barry Ife, Principal, Guildhall School of Music & Drama; Tony Halmos, Director of Public Relations; Sue Ireland, Director of Open Spaces, and her colleague Martin Rodman; Peter Wynne Rees, City Planning Officer; Professor Jack Lohman, Director, Museum of London; many colleagues in the City of London Corporation for their generous assistance, especially Sarah Leigh, Nick Bodger and Elizabeth Amati; and Sue King of the City of London Guides.

The Contributors are grateful to the following people:

Mick Bagnall, The Film Team, City of London; Dr David Bartle, Archivist, the Haberdashers' Company; David Beasley, Librarian, the Goldsmiths' Company; Penelope Fussell, Archivist, the Drapers' Company; Olivia Hogman, Smithfield Market; Colonel H. P. D. Massey, Clerk to the Ironmongers' Company; Richard Middleton, RMA; Alan Radom, Interserve; Terry Stefaniw, Beadle/Hall Manager, Armourers' Hall; Becky Wallower, Administrator, St Vedast; Mark S. Young, Beadle, the Wax Chandlers' Company.

The Publisher appreciates the assistance of the following people in the preparation of this book:

Edward Denison for generously granting us permission to reproduce his photographs of the work of McMorran & Whitby; Sarah Diggins and Ali Ribchester at the Barbican Centre; Dennis Gilbert, Sophia Gibb, Yvonne Peeke-Vout and their colleagues at VIEW; Sarah Leigh and Nick Bodger, Public Relations Office, City of London Corporation; Professor Jack Lohman, Director, Museum of London; Allan Rees, ARKA Cartographics Ltd; Peter Wynne Rees, City Planning Officer, City of London Corporation; Nina Shandloff; Jeremy Smith and Laurence Ward at the London Metropolitan Archives.

Index

Featured buildings and places are in **bold** type and page numbers in *italic* refer to illustrations.